IMAGES
of America

HYATTSVILLE

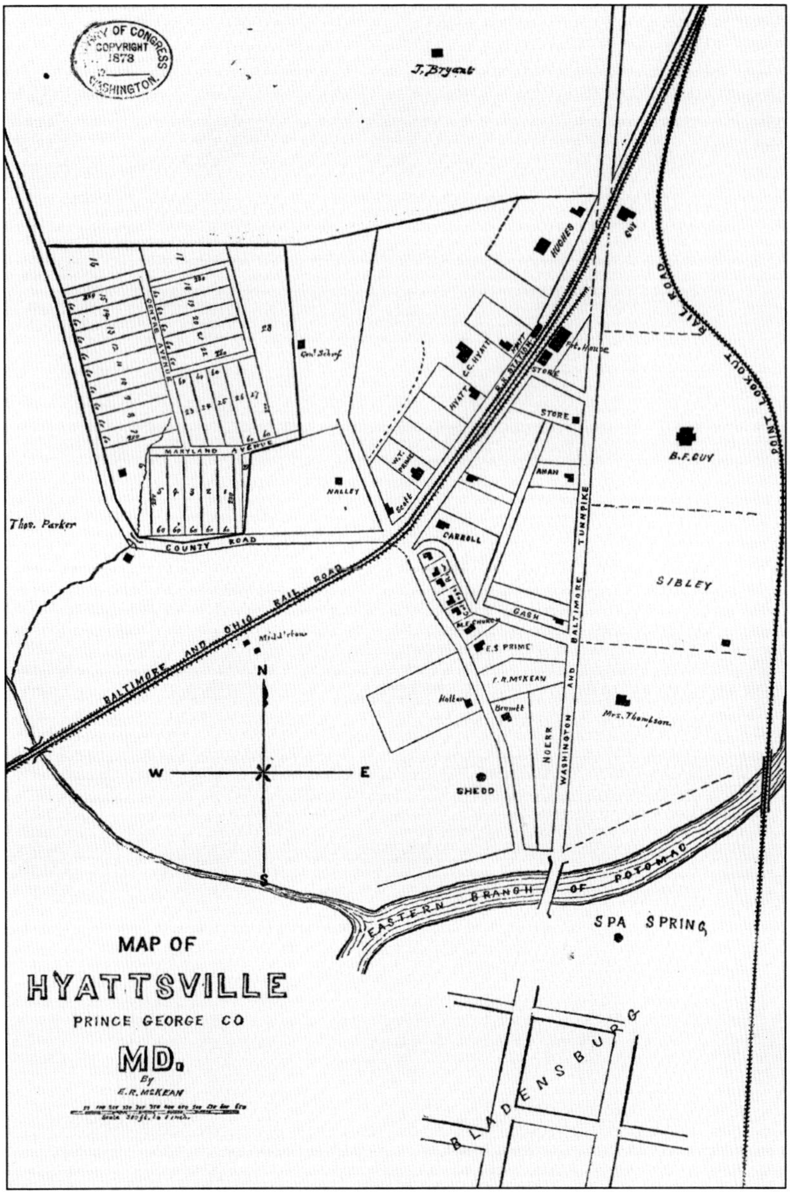

This 1873 map, drawn by attorney Edwin McKean, shows Hyattsville in its infancy—13 years before incorporation. Prince George's County's rural countryside already was undergoing changes: the Washington and Baltimore Turnpike bringing 40,000 passengers annually by 1830; the first telegraph line in 1844; and the Baltimore and Ohio Railroad making seven round-trips daily between Washington, D.C., and Baltimore by 1868. Christopher Clarke Hyatt wisely built his store at this intersection. (Hyattsville Preservation Association.)

On the Cover: The ninth annual Easter Egg Hunt was held April 10, 1944, in Magruder Park. Activities included a pie-eating contest, royal court, and kid-calling contest. Emcee David Ginsberg waves his arms overhead as Alice Degges, with hands to mouth, begins her winning shout—calling son Alfred home from war in the South Pacific. Degges won four consecutive years during World War II, and Alfred came home safely. (Prince George's County Historical Society.)

IMAGES
of America

HYATTSVILLE

Andra Damron on behalf of
the Hyattsville Preservation Association

ARCADIA
PUBLISHING

Copyright © 2008 by Andra Damron on behalf of the Hyattsville Preservation Association
ISBN 978-0-7385-5443-3

Published by Arcadia Publishing
Charleston, South Carolina

Printed in the United States of America

Library of Congress Catalog Card Number: 2008924917

For all general information contact Arcadia Publishing at:
Telephone 843-853-2070
Fax 843-853-0044
E-mail sales@arcadiapublishing.com
For customer service and orders:
Toll-Free 1-888-313-2665

Visit us on the Internet at www.arcadiapublishing.com

To the family historians keeping their portion of Hyattsville history alive,
who graciously opened their collections to me.

Contents

ACKNOWLEDGMENTS

This publication was born from Hyattsville Preservation Association's digital photograph and oral history preservation program. This is meant to be a starting point for Hyattsville history collection rather than a final one. A debt of gratitude is owed to all who follow.

The importance of this project's success was acknowledged by the City of Hyattsville, Mayor Bill Gardiner, and the Hyattsville Community Development Corporation (Executive Director Stuart Eisenberg) and happened through their support.

The majority of photographs came from the Prince George's County Historical Society (PGCHS). Without the knowledge and support of their dedicated staff, this book would not be possible—Susan Pearl, Sarah Bourne, Diane Stultz, and Dusty Rhoads. Most of the Hyattsville material was a lifelong collection donated posthumously by Francis Geary's family.

Miriam Howe was my champion, lending hundreds of hours cataloging 1,000 photographs and giving wise advice.

Doug Dudrow and John Small were the first donators, inspiring the outcome of the book. Eli Pousson, University of Maryland, shared his research, enriching the history.

The book is filled with the expertise and help of so many to whom I am grateful: Lauren Bobier, Arcadia Publishing; Doug Barber, Ellarose Preston, and Lauren Smith, City of Hyattsville; Bridgett Warren, Prince George's County Memorial Library System (PGCMLS) and the Hyattsville Branch staff; Dick Evans and staff, Historical Society of Washington, D.C. (HSWDC); Jan Evans and Scott Nelson, Heurich House Museum; Marcey Katcher, Kent Laborde, and Dave Manning, National Oceanic and Atmospheric Administration; Tiffany Davis and Cathy Allen; College Park Aviation Museum; John Stearne, National Guard Archives; Sarah Wilson, Robert Crown Law Library, Stanford; James Eason, University of California, Berkeley; Jane Barrett, Road and Track; Barbara Coyle and Tom Ponton, DeMatha Catholic High School; Howard Berger, Maryland National Capital Park and Planning Commission; Sarah Hambleton, Schlesinger Library, Radcliffe; Stephanie Stullich; Helen McLeish; Frances Walker; Patrick Dailey; Elaine Lizzio, James Rogers; Violetta Jones; Romaine Lucas; Kathy Albertson; Mildred Ford; Bill Tierney; Naomi and Tom Behrens; Nina Faye; Connie Gasch; Mary and John Sibley; Dorris Sommer; Betty Moureau; Marion Dorne, Ann Barrett; Marialis and Marge Zmuda; Elizabeth Goldberg and Chris Holleman; Herb Hille; Sharon Sweeting; Meg Spurlin; Dennis Campbell; George Denny; Jeff Joeckel; Bill Wright; Jane and James Yagley; Dolores Acquista and Mark Matulef; Bob Harper; and Jean Damron.

Introduction

The land that became Hyattsville was settled originally by the Nanticoke and Susquehannock Indian tribes. With European exploration, the area's animal resources, primarily beaver, were a strong attraction to the region. Hunters could transport their hides along the area waterways and Native American trails. There was a great demand in Europe for the pelts and traded Native American goods. European settlers made two large land purchases in the area in the early 1700s, known as Black Ask and New Dumfreeze. On John Beale's Black Ask parcel, a small riverfront community formed, commonly known as Beale Town. Unhappy with their community's location and economic development, the residents petitioned the Colonial legislature in 1742 to move south, and with that, Beale Town ceased to exist. It seems only one family lived on New Dumfreeze. It would take other factors for development to begin.

In 1783, the first American stagecoach route passed through this area, and two years later, a postal delivery route followed. As the native species' population dwindled from excessive hunting, the area became popular for tobacco production. By 1812, Maryland authorized construction of the Washington and Baltimore Turnpike, connecting the two cities through the Hyattsville area.

By 1828, the Baltimore and Ohio Railroad was chartered—its Washington Line connecting Washington, D.C., and Baltimore—and running near the turnpike. Tracks were completed by 1835. Christopher Clarke Hyatt purchased his first parcel of land in the area on March 19, 1845. Its ideal location near the stagecoach line, mail route, turnpike, and the railroad with new telegraph lines made the land perfect for settlement. Hyatt opened a store and began mail delivery. By 1859, the post office and local cartographers called the area "Hyattsville." The end of the Civil War and slavery forced many of the tobacco plantations to cease production. The sale of this cheap land coincided with a booming federal government expanded by the war and a rise in property prices in Washington, D.C. Hyattsville's location on the railroad made it an ideal location for summer homes and a suburb. Neighboring Bladensburg's Spa Springs, a resort, created a draw with its "healing" waters. Hyattsville was known by Presidents Ulysses Grant, Grover Cleveland, and Teddy Roosevelt, who visited their friends for riding and hunting at the local farms of Hitching Post Hill and Edgewood.

Louis Wine, George Johnson, and developers Benjamin F. Guy, Thomas Parker, and Jeremiah Bartholow joined Hyatt in subdividing and selling lots on a large scale. Hyattsville's population doubled. The Act of Incorporation for the City of Hyattsville was signed April 7, 1886. By 1890, Hyattsville was one of only two communities with a population greater than 1,000 in Prince George's County. Early street names reflected the importance of those individuals, like Wine and Johnson, who contributed to Hyattsville's early success. During this period, Hyattsville's population was expanding steadily. A small immigrant and African American population made Hyattsville their home from its earliest days. Churches, schools, athletic groups, and civic organizations formed in reflection of the growing population. Most of the B&O Railroad traffic at this time was commuters to Washington, D.C. In 1892, Hyattsville gained international fame when it became the first American city to institute the single-tax system, taxing only land and not personal property. Local attorney and supporter of the system Jackson H. Ralston advocated his case to the Maryland Court of Appeals, where the system was found to violate Maryland tax law. The city also boasted the first newspaper, phone system, and utilities in the area. By 1899, the electric streetcar connected the community to Washington, D.C., businesses, boosting Hyattsville's population ever higher.

After the dawn of the 20th century, Hyattsville's population boomed and other national issues faced the community. The Carter brothers designed and hand built an automobile here. A reception was hosted for woman suffragists petitioning the U.S. Senate on July 31, 1913. Maryland National Guard Infantry Company F, based in Hyattsville, was called to service in World War I and found themselves involved in key battles, later supporting the founding of the American Legion. Local inventor Dr. J. Harris Rogers was celebrated internationally for his underwater and underground wireless system credited with winning the war. Maryland's first female justice of the peace was appointed to serve the 16th District during Prohibition. Some 6,000 vehicles a day traveled through town in 1925 when Hyattsville's main road, Maryland Avenue, was federally designated Route 1, part of the main road from Maine to Florida. Automobile dealerships, garages, and service stations began to line the corridor.

Hyattsville's prominence in Prince George's County was affirmed with the establishment of headquarters for the regional Washington Suburban Sanitary Commission and the County Government Services Building, which located here in the 1930s. The St. John DeMatha Monastery was opened in 1931. The monastery was used to train young men for priesthood in the Trinitarian Order. The order officially opened a school, which quickly evolved into a secondary school. DeMatha Catholic High School for boys is known nationally for its academics and athletics. DeMatha coach Morgan Wootten was inducted into the National Basketball Hall of Fame for the most wins by any high school coach.

By the mid-1950s, Hyattsville began to look much as it does today. An area-wide street name change in 1941 erased the nod to early developers. With the closing of the streetcar line and the opening of regional bus service, the older shops in Hyattsville struggled. Prince George's Plaza shopping mall and the new Northwestern High School were built on the outskirts of the community away from the historic core. Early efforts to preserve Hyattsville's historic buildings began in the late 1970s. Homeowners banded together to form the Hyattsville Preservation Association and documented the Hyattsville Historic District, which was listed in the National Register of Historic Places in 1982. Highlighting Hyattsville's history with an annual historic house tour for the past 29 years has preserved the community as it is seen today.

Hyattsville, at first glance, may be seen as a typical Washington, D.C., suburb, with growth spurred by the railroad, streetcar, and automobile. Upon further examination, it is clear that its residents of yesterday and today make it a unique place to live with their commitment to community involvement.

One

Early Development and the Railroad

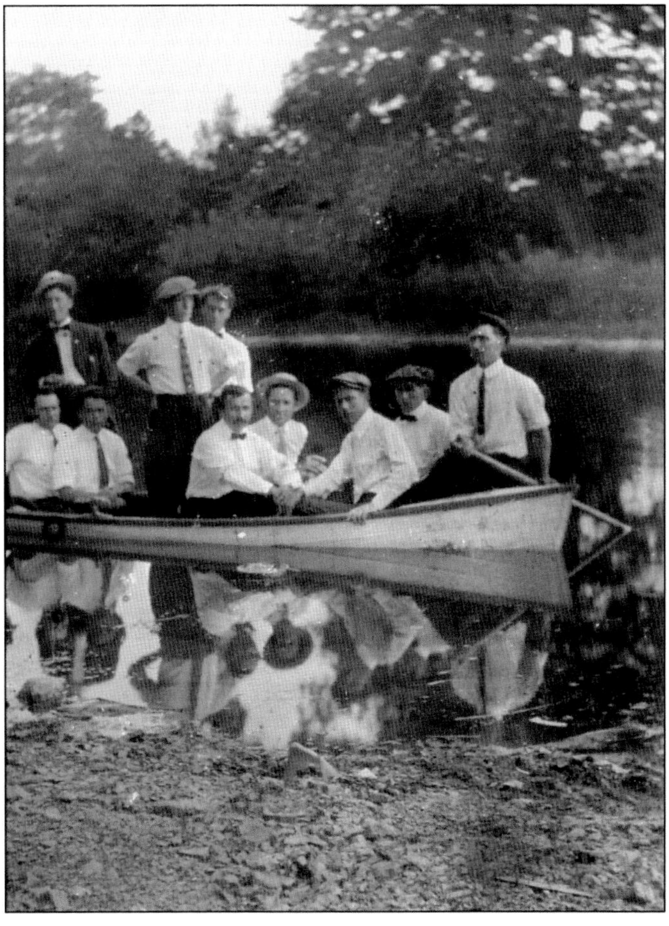

The Anacostia River branches played an important role in early residents' lives. With goods arriving by steamboat and water-powered gristmills, focus on the river was prominent. It was a natural place for recreation, as these early canoers demonstrated. (Doug Dudrow.)

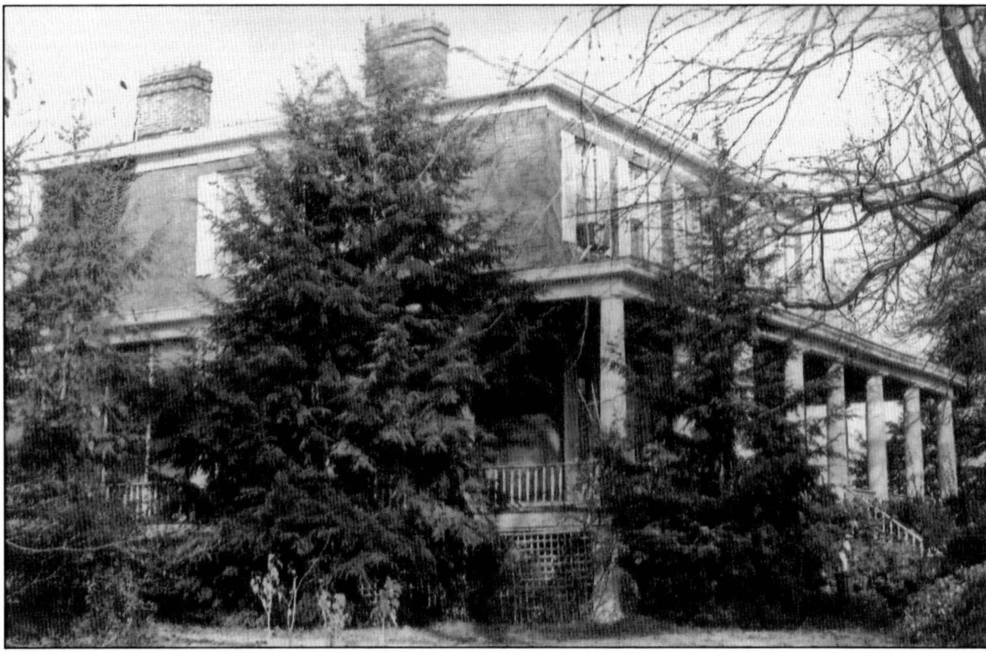

Ash Hill, still extant, was built around 1840 by Washingtonian Robert Clark on 427.5 acres. In 1875, Gen. Edward Fitzgerald Beale of Western exploration fame bought the property and entertained Pres. Grover Cleveland and Buffalo Bill Cody here. Beale's close friend Pres. Ulysses Grant wrote during an 1877 trip, "I will feel more at home . . . no place more than in visiting your farm with you." (Maryland Historical Trust.)

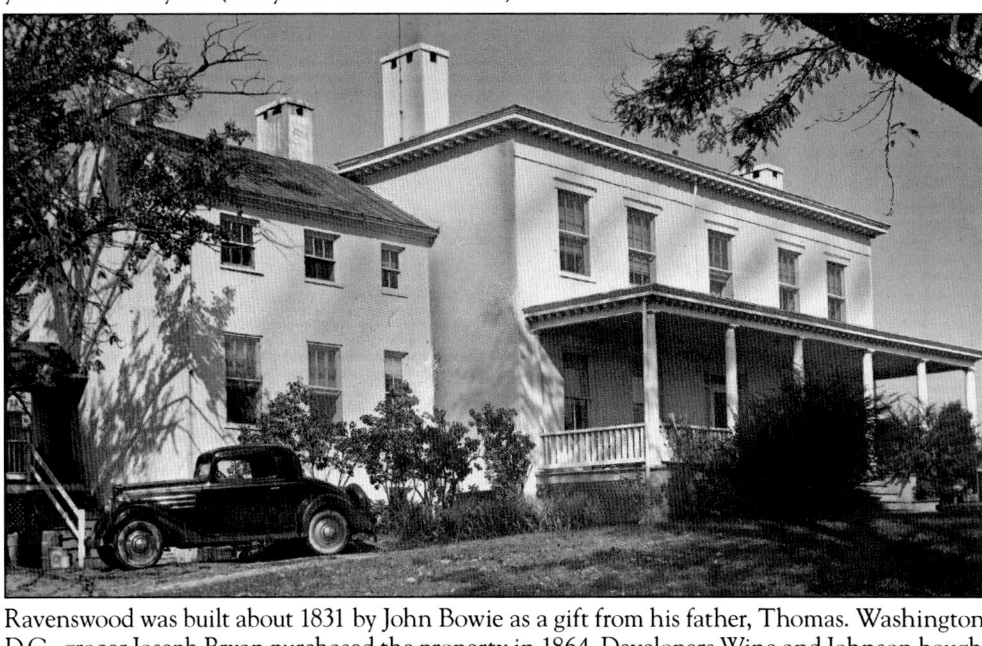

Ravenswood was built about 1831 by John Bowie as a gift from his father, Thomas. Washington, D.C., grocer Joseph Bryan purchased the property in 1864. Developers Wine and Johnson bought the estate in 1882, making it part of their second subdivision and Wine's family home. Michael Tierney purchased it in 1894. The house was razed in the 1950s for the expansion of St. Jerome's School. (HSWDC.)

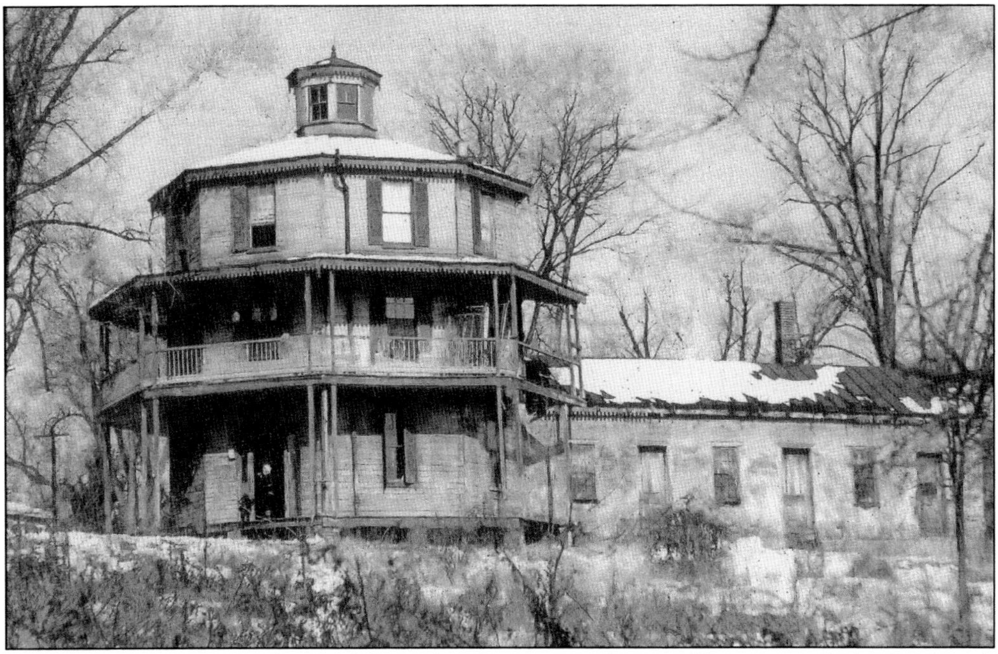

The Octagon House stood east of the railroad on Locust Avenue (Forty-second Place). Though it was built by Bladensburg druggist Henry T. Scott around 1853, its construction was attributed to a Mr. Swain. The spacious entry hall contained the stairs and opened on the main floor into only two rooms, the upper levels having two large rooms and one small one. An addition, the "trailer," was added to accommodate larger families. (James Rogers.)

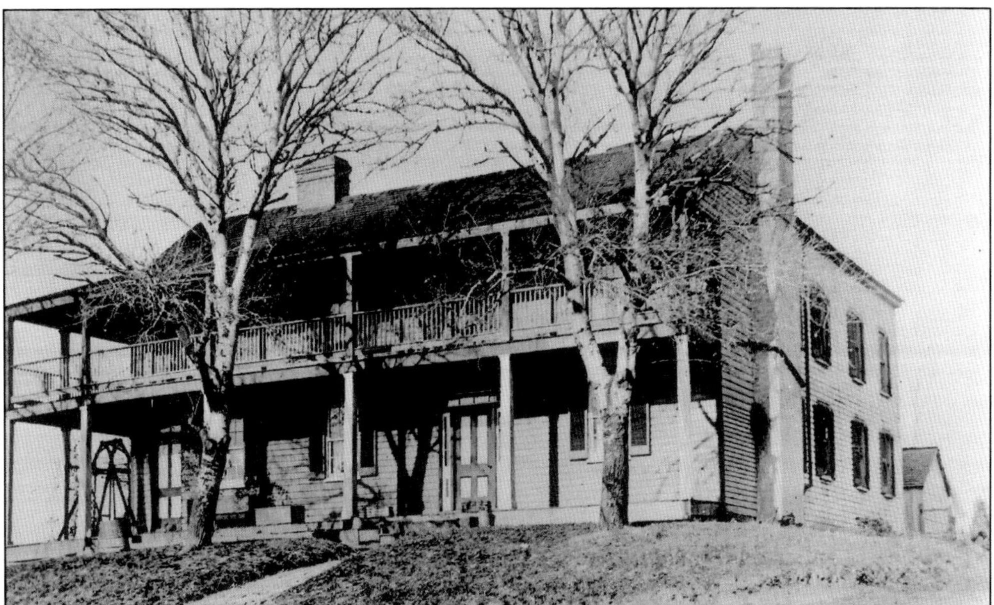

This house, built about 1850 by Gen. H. Cross, stood behind Hyatt's house. Gen. Albin Schoepf purchased the property in 1861. The estate remained in the family, passing to W. K. Schoepf, president of the Washington, Berwyn, and Laurel Electric Railroad. The house burned before 1936. (PGCHS.)

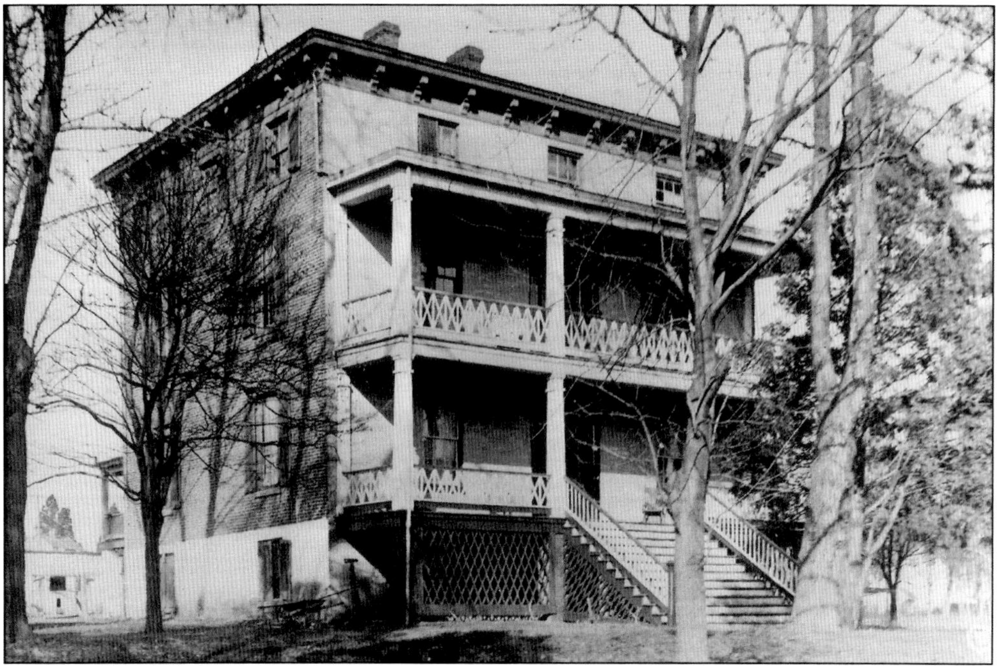

The Hyatt home was located across the turnpike from his store. In 1873, twenty acres of the estate were platted as Hyatt's Addition and subdivided into 28 unimproved lots of 60 by 280 feet. The home was declared uninhabitable by the city in 1947. (PGCHS.)

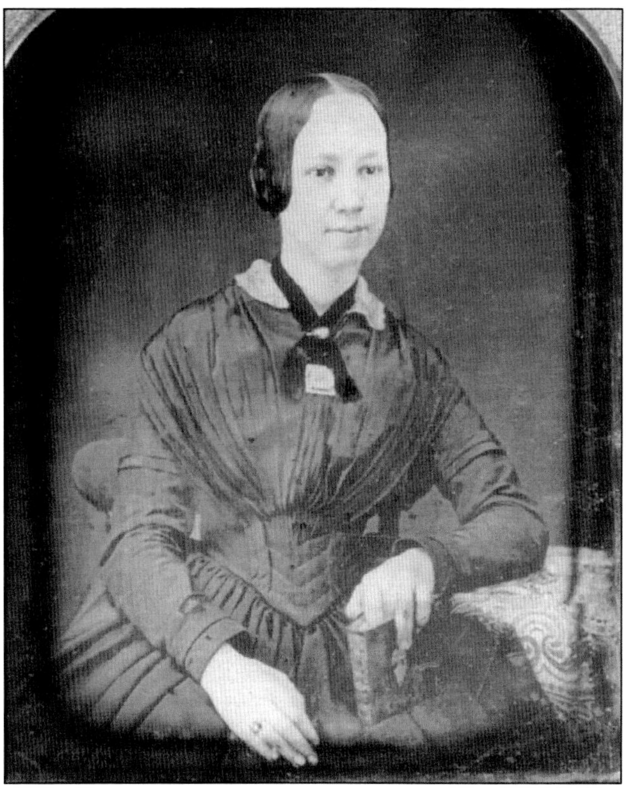

Hyatt's second wife, Frances R. Perkins, married him on October 21, 1846. Their order added four children—Frank, Hattie, Charles, and Albert—to his previous three—Culver, Catherine, and J. H. (Patrick Dailey.)

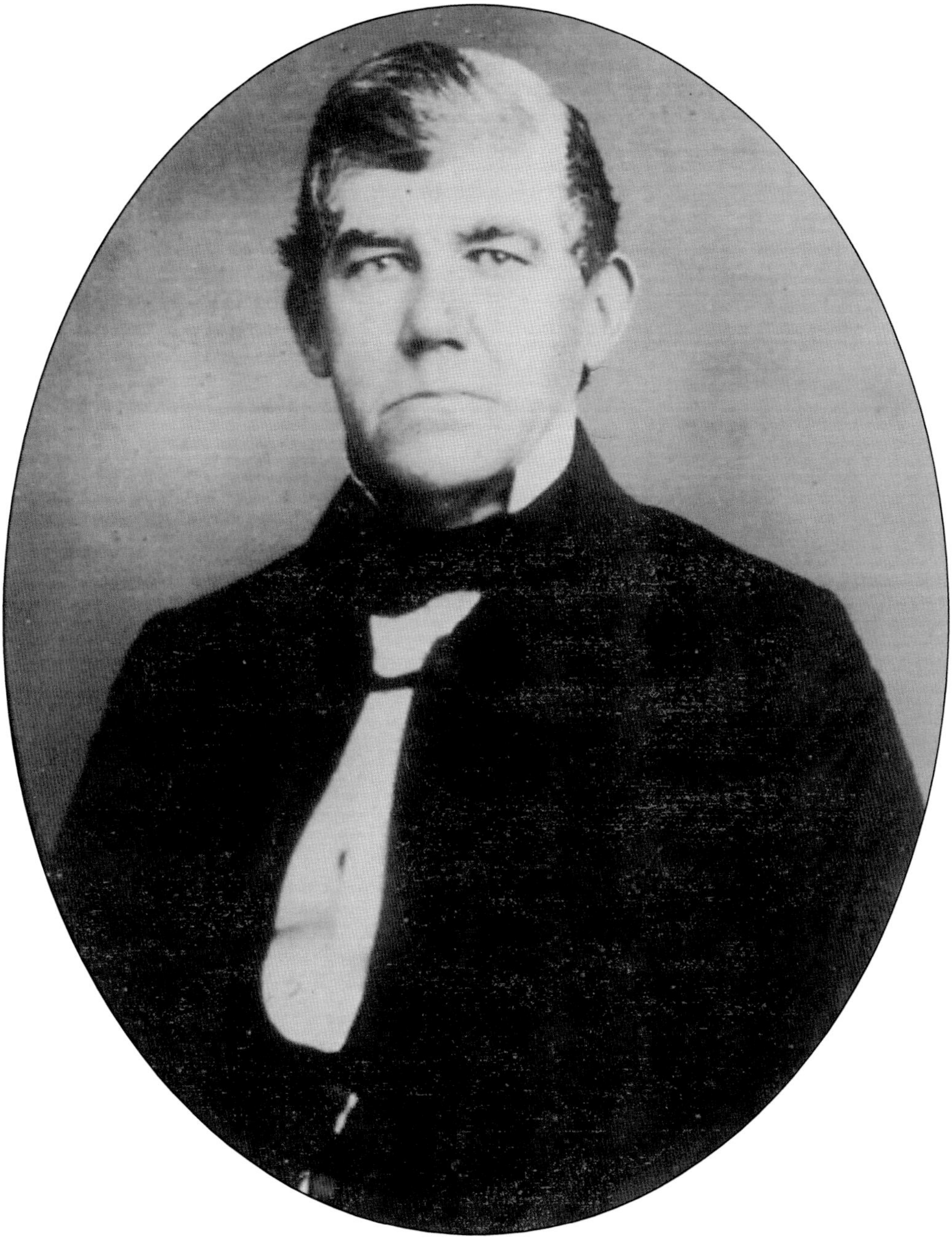

Christopher Clarke Hyatt was born in Hyattstown, Maryland, on September 29, 1799. After losing his father at a young age, Hyatt worked as a merchant's clerk in Baltimore. As a young man, he opened a Bladensburg store dealing in merchandise and tobacco. Hyatt purchased his local property to get away from the gambling and drinking around the Bladensburg stagecoach stop. Hyatt died on July 22, 1884, and was described as a self-made man, shrewd in business and temperate in his personal life. (Patrick Dailey.)

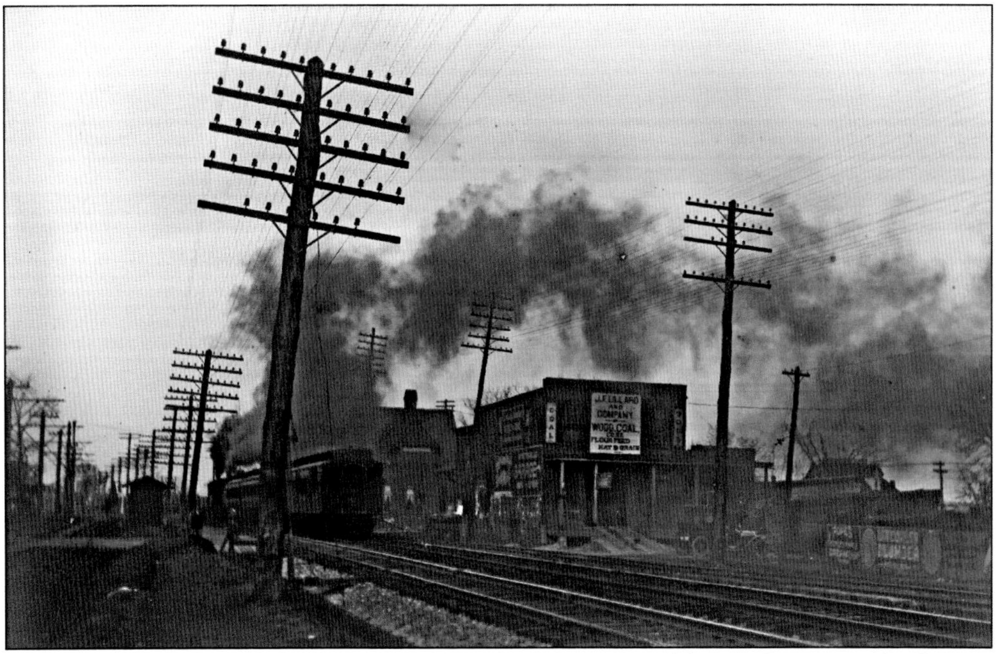

Hyatt purchased his first of three land parcels at the intersection of the Washington and Baltimore Turnpike and the Baltimore and Ohio Railroad on March 19, 1845. He located his general store, pictured here in 1912, from which mail was delivered. By January 1859, when the federal government appointed Hyatt the area's first postmaster, Hyattsville appeared on regional maps and mailing addresses. (HSWDC.)

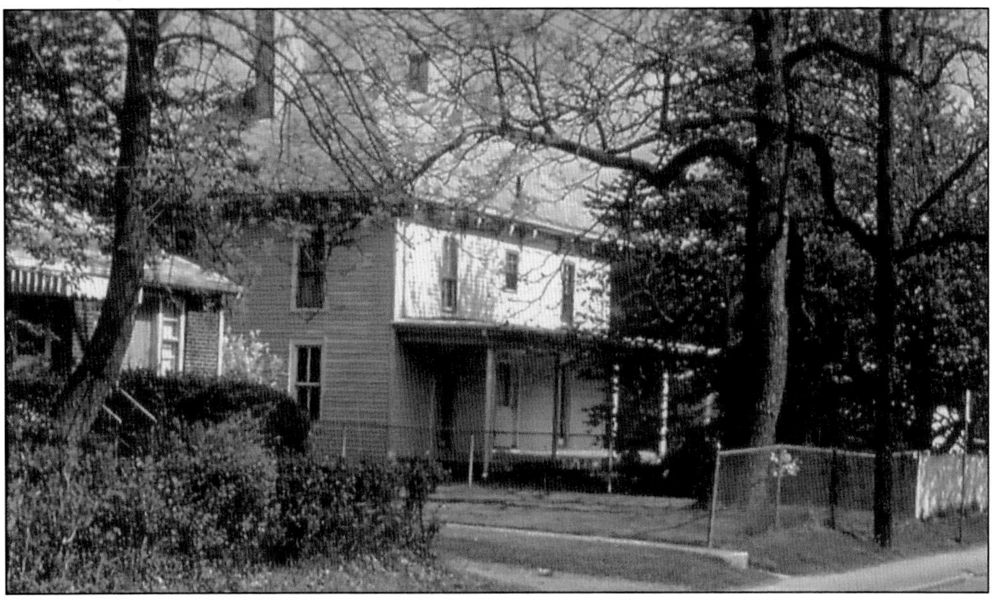

When Hyatt platted his addition in 1873, this house, now 4901 Fortieth Place, already stood at this location, facing the County Road. Hyatt is believed to have built the house shortly after the Civil War. He sold the property with improvements to Rev. John McElhinney of Fairfax in 1877. The house is one of the oldest and few remaining extant properties predating the city's incorporation. (HPA.)

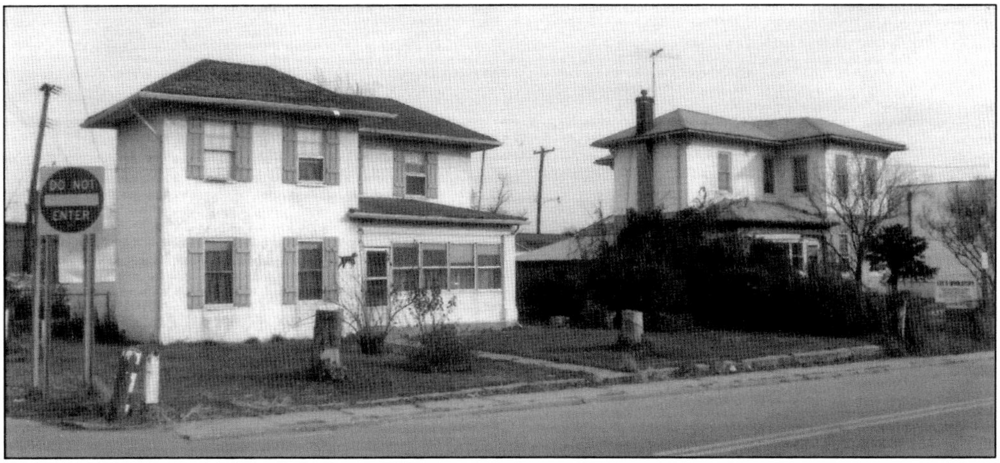

Local businessmen Benjamin Franklin Guy, Thomas Parker, and Jeremiah Bartholow bought 10 acres in 1866 just south of Hyatt's store. In one year, the property was subdivided and improved with five identical Italianate cottages assessed at $8,000 and known as Cottage Square. It was common for these homes to be rented to Washington, D.C., families. The homes at 4639 and 4641 Forty-second Place, though altered, are the only two remaining. (PGCHS.)

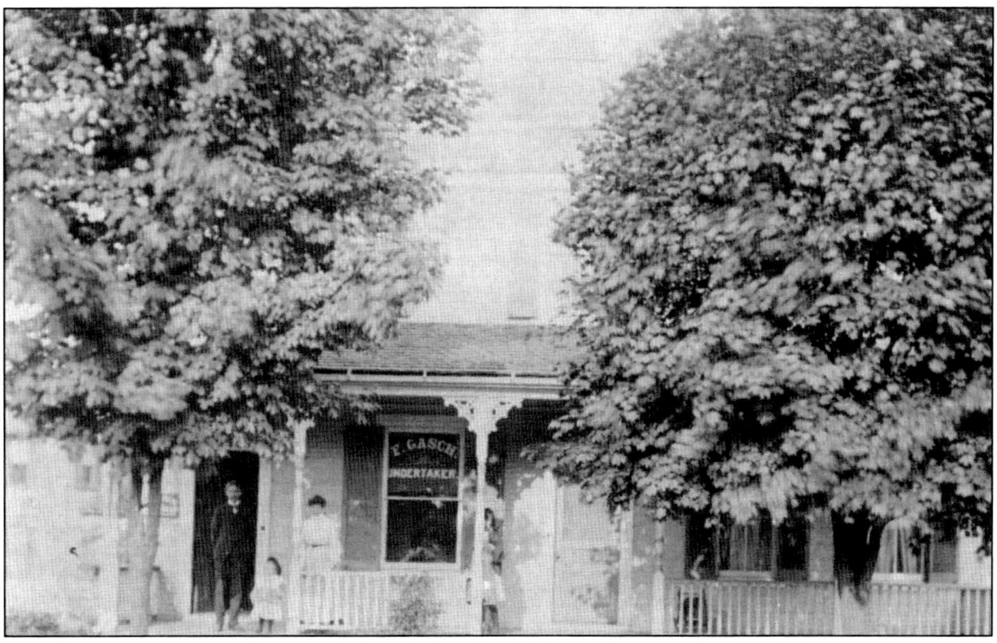

Ernst Franz Bernhard ("Francis") Gasch (1830–1914) was born in Doeblen, Germany, where he was apprenticed to a cabinetmaker. After immigrating to America in July 1850, Gasch worked in Washington. After his 1854 marriage to Katherine Sophia Schron, Gasch purchased a Bladensburg home. Building coffins for area residents led Gasch into the undertaking business by 1859. Sons Edward and Ernest attended mortuary school and continued the family business. (PGCHS.)

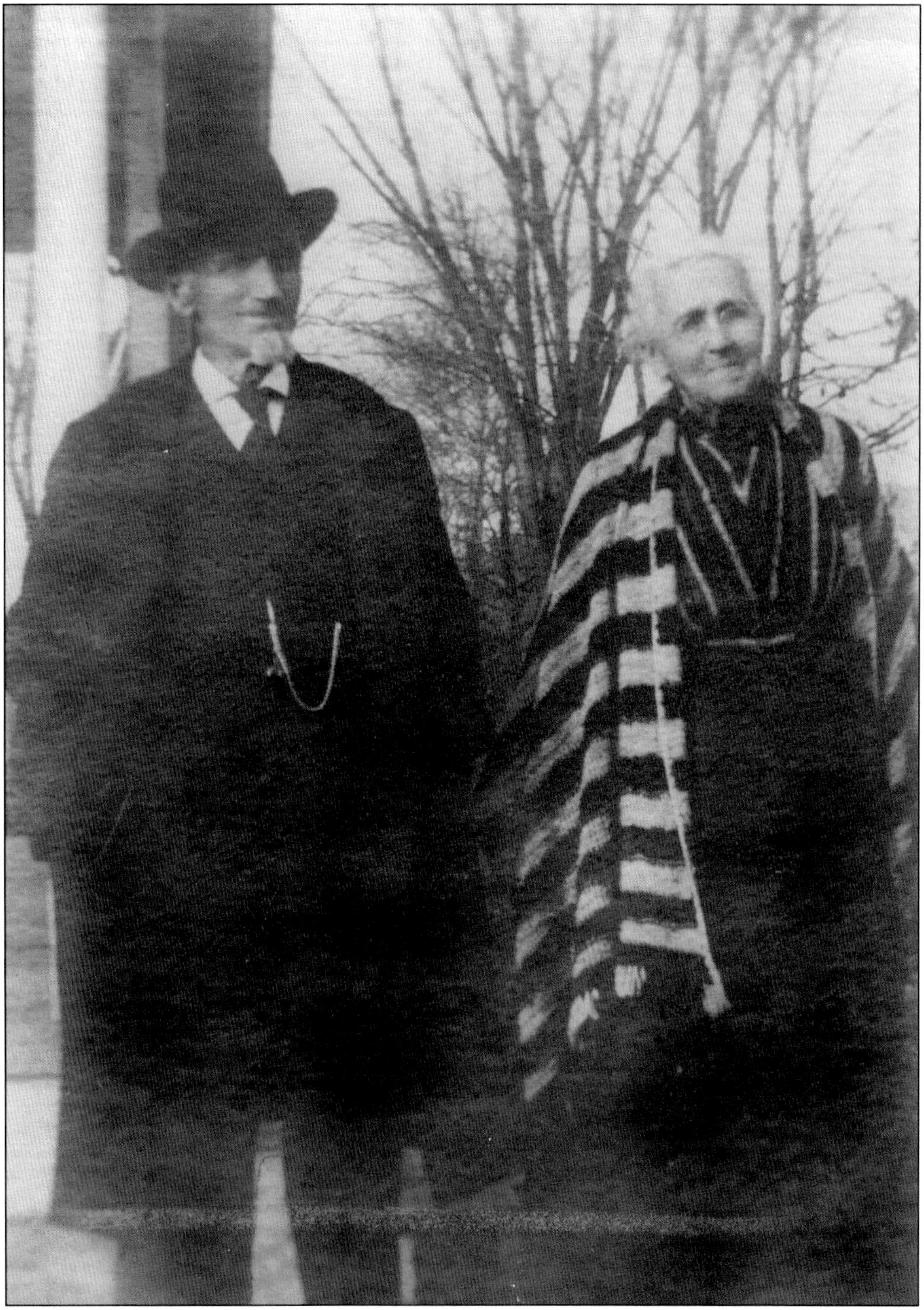

German immigrants Joseph Andrew (born 1830) and Katherine Aman moved to town from College Park in 1873. Joseph worked as a railroad employee, his Baltimore Avenue home located conveniently near the station. He served on the first town commission in 1886 and again from 1892 to 1898. The 1910 federal census listed Aman as superintendent of roads for Hyattsville. (PGCHS.)

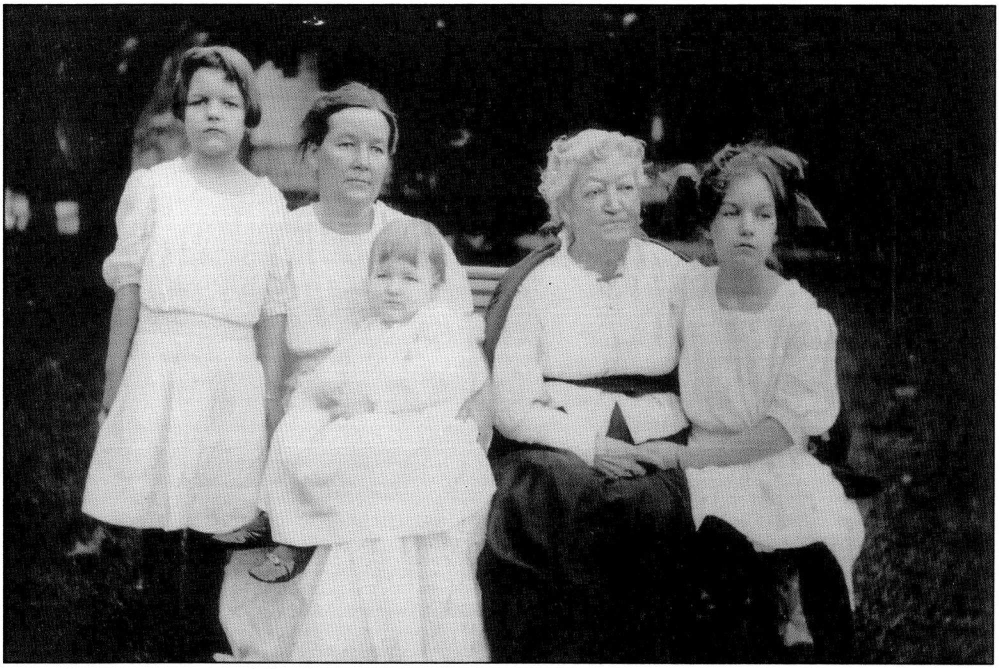

Mary Bowen was one of the first members of the Methodist Episcopal Church South. She encouraged her children to actively participate in church activities. In her yard are, from left to right, Mary Louise Rose McClay, Anna Lewis Bowen Rose, Margaret Bowen Rose (on lap), Mary, and Helen Trent Rose White. (Helen McLeish.)

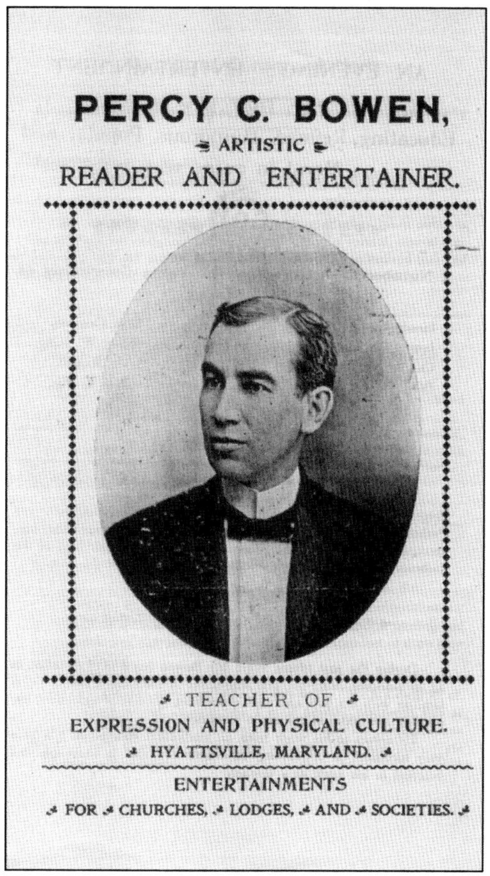

Percy Bowen was born in Washington, D.C., in 1861. His talents led him to literary entertainment as an artistic reader and monologist. Percy studied elocution for 15 years at schools like Kings School of Oratory and Dramatic Culture in Pittsburgh. His programs were billed as "educated, refined, humorous, popular, and moral in every way," including selections from Longfellow, Dickens, and Poe. (Helen McLeish.)

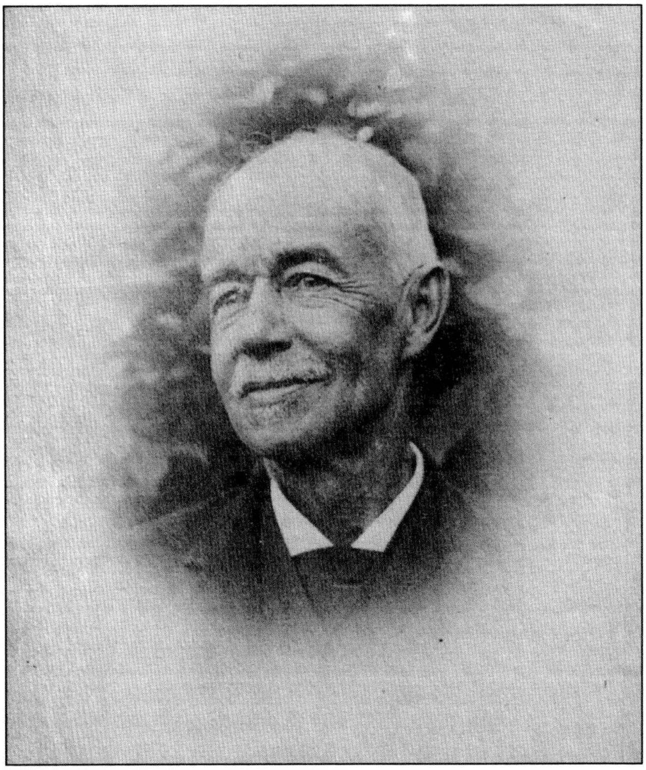

Harrison Bowen (1835–1893) moved from Washington, D.C., in 1867 where he maintained a printing business. Originally renting a Cottage Square home, Bowen moved his wife, Mary Julia Prettyman (1833–1912), to their new home the following year. The Bowens' three children—Anna Lewis, Alice May, and Percy Coleman—were raised there. (Helen McLeish.)

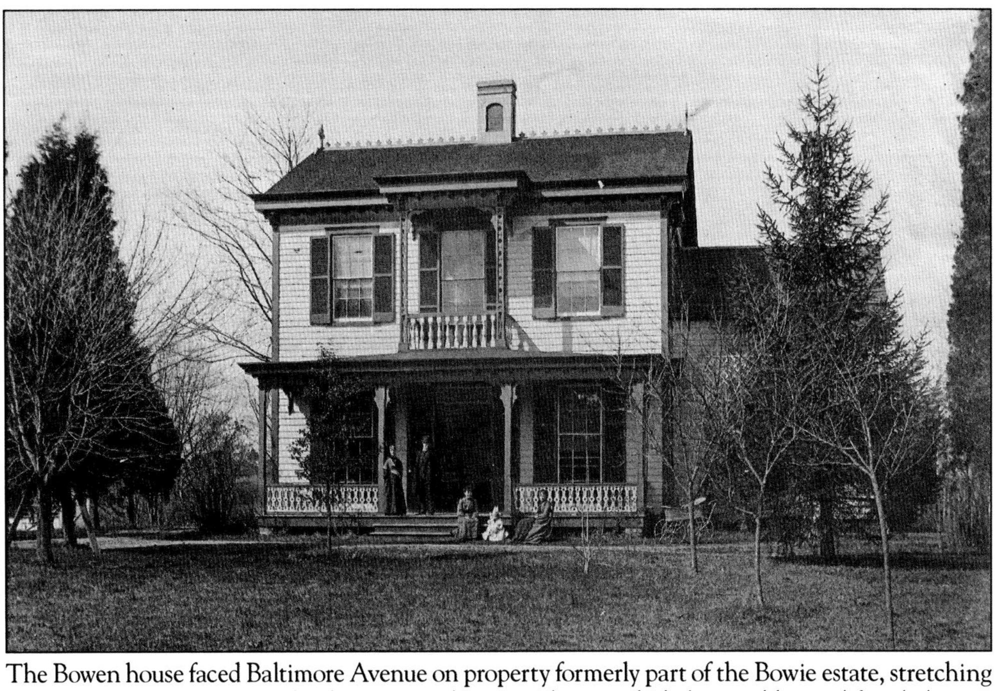

The Bowen house faced Baltimore Avenue on property formerly part of the Bowie estate, stretching from the turnpike to Forty-third Avenue. The estate later included two additional family homes to its north. The home passed from Mary, to Anna, and then to Margaret. At Margaret's death, the property was sold to Lustine's, and the home was demolished in 1978. (Helen McLeish.)

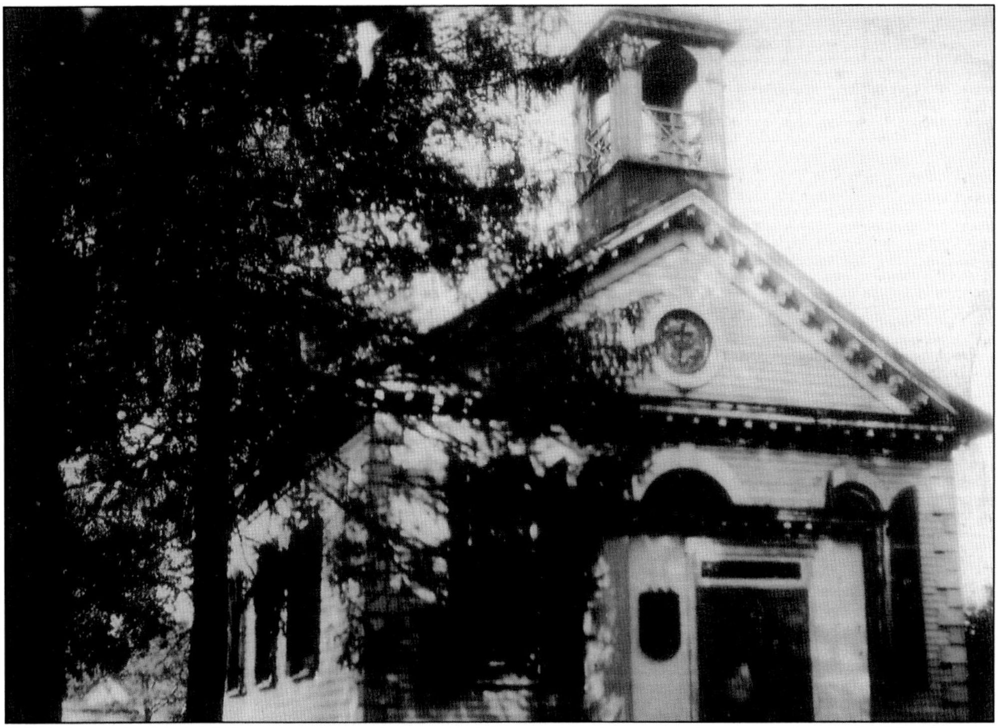

The First United Methodist Church documents worship at Shadrick and Sarah Turner's home near Greenbelt in 1776 as their founding. Officially recognized as the Bladensburg Methodist Episcopal Church in 1793, a church was erected by 40 worshippers near the Peace Cross. In 1869, pro-slavery sentiments split the church, with those favoring slavery opening the Methodist Episcopal Church South, pictured here, at the west end of Cottage Square. The building was used until 1923. (Doug Dudrow.)

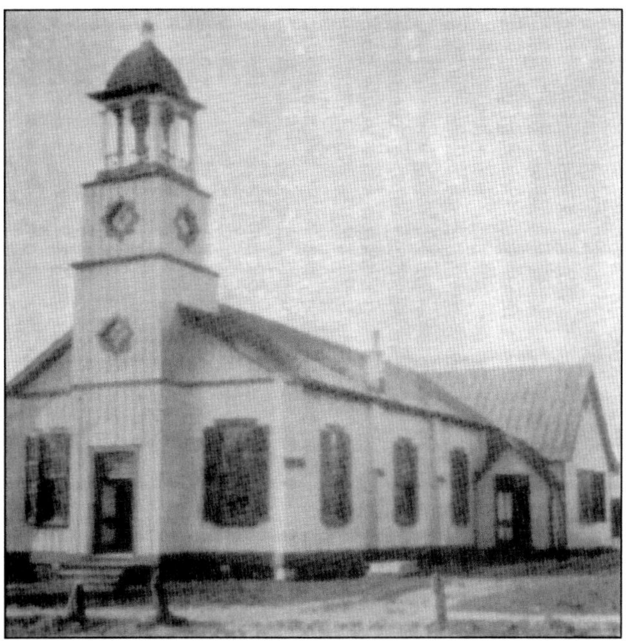

Prince George's County Presbyterians trace their origins to 1704 in Upper Marlboro. The Hyattsville congregation started in 1874, with only six members from Bladensburg building a church on Baltimore Avenue just south of Crittenden Street. The Methodist Episcopal Church South offered space until its sanctuary was completed the following year. The church's bell notified volunteers of fires. Services were held here until 1915. (City of Hyattsville.)

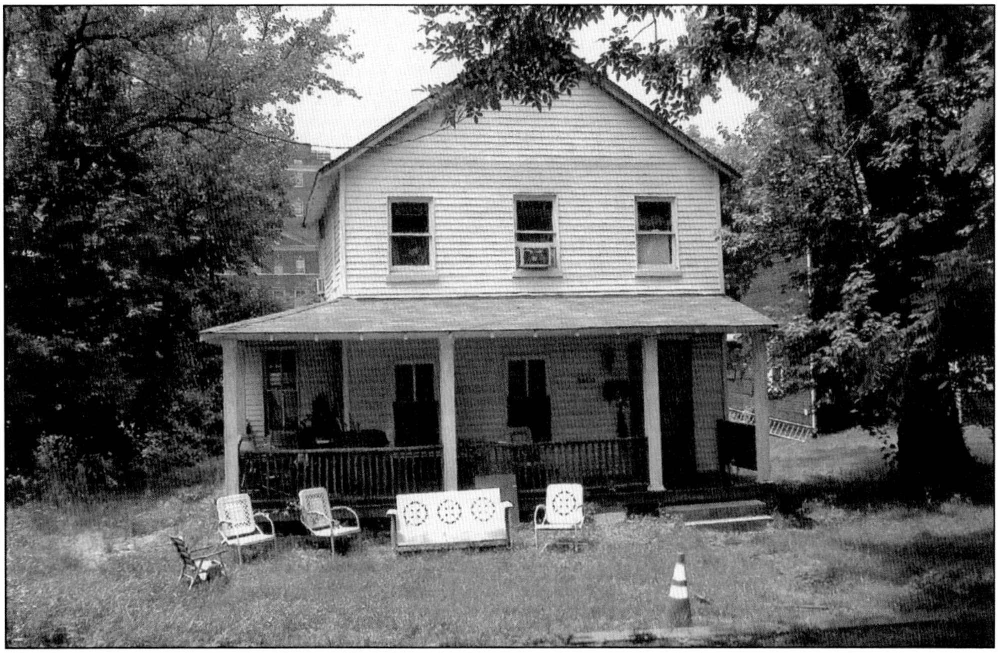

Those at 5600 (above) and 5602 (below) Rhode Island Avenue are the only remaining homes on what was Railroad Avenue. The street, named for its proximity to the tracks, was home to many working-class families. William (born 1830) and Frances Redd moved their family to town a few years after the Civil War. As African Americans, their children attended school in Bladensburg or North Brentwood. They attended St. Jerome's. A marriage with the neighbors, the Sharps, linked the families, who lived side-by-side for a century. (Both Violetta Jones and Romaine Lucas.)

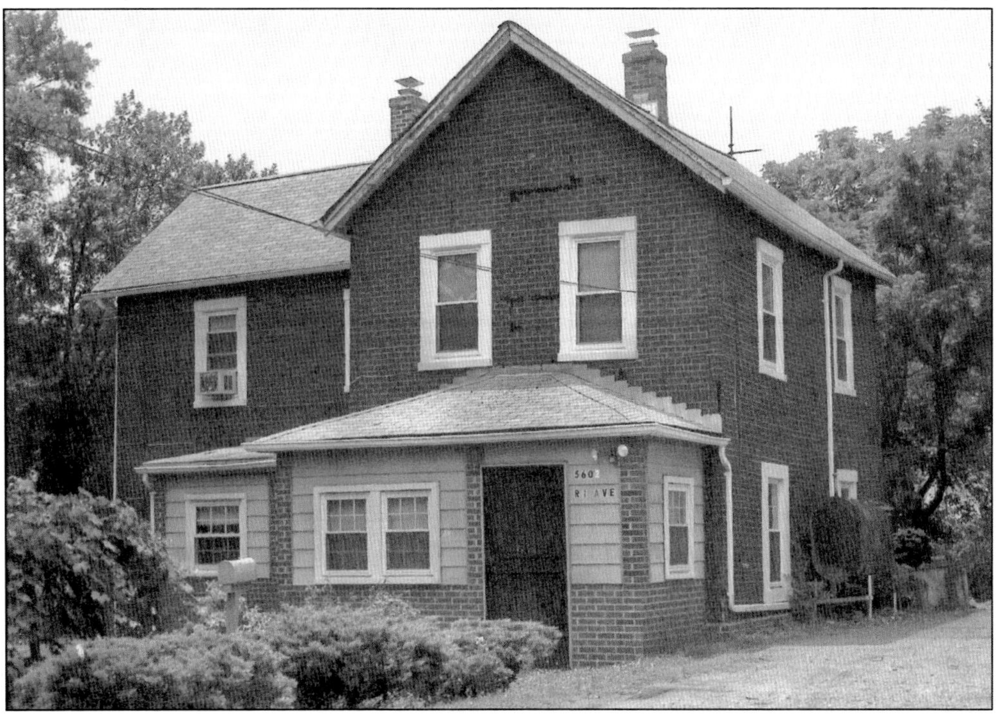

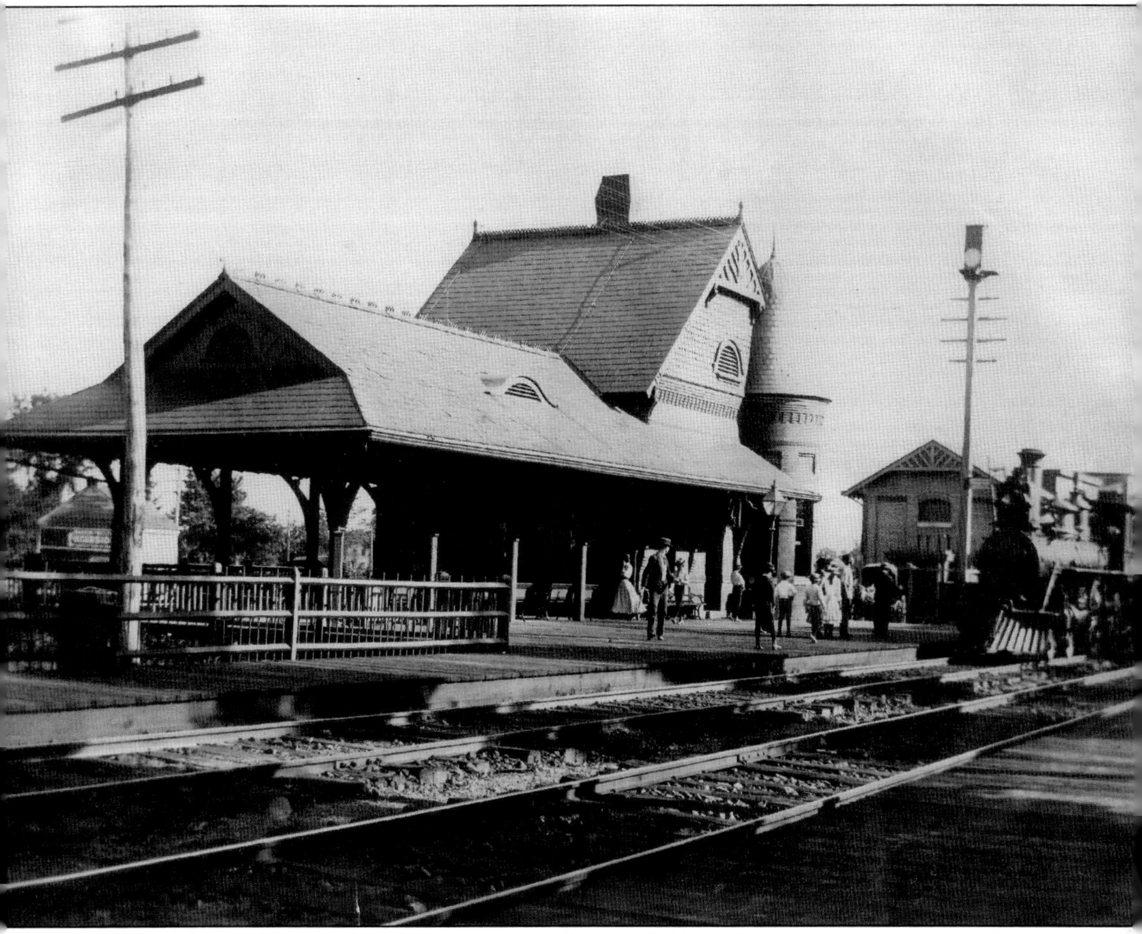

The Baltimore and Ohio Railroad depot opened August 1884 and was constructed during the railroad's greatest period of expansion by architect E. Francis Baldwin. Considered quintessential Baldwin design, it was one of his largest at 25 by 30 feet with an attached frame waiting area of 35 by 49 feet. A small matching brick freight building was constructed to the south in 1885. Now demolished, the depot was located at the intersection of the tracks and the turnpike. (Francis Walker.)

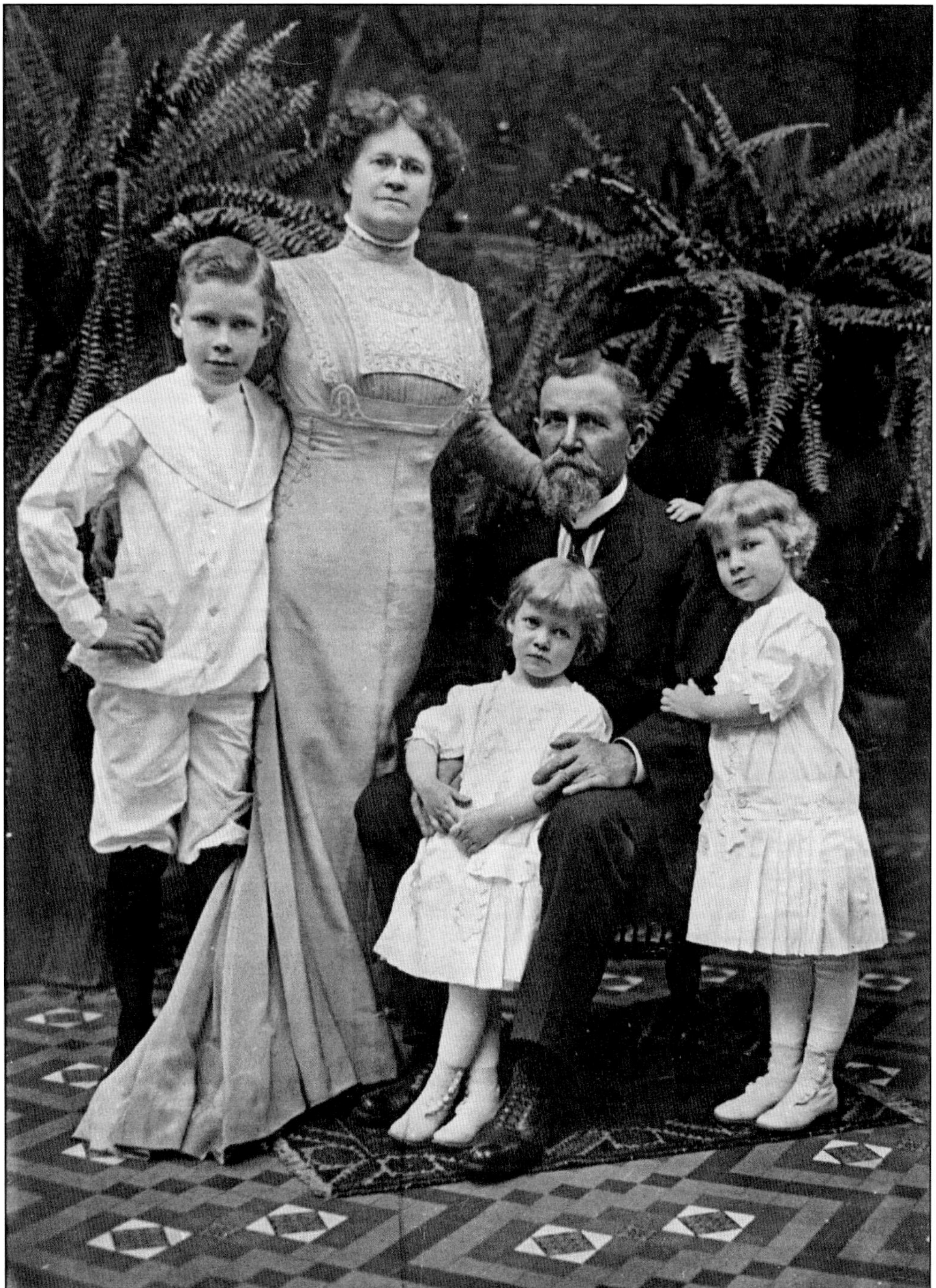

Heurich poses with his third wife, Amelia, and their children Christian Jr., Anita, and Karla in their still-extant Dupont Circle home. Heurich was born in Haina, Germany, and was apprenticed as a butcher and brewer. He immigrated to Baltimore in 1866 with dreams of owning a brewery. Heurich donated beer and milk to the German Orphans Asylum, always promoting civic responsibility to his fellow immigrants. (HSWDC.)

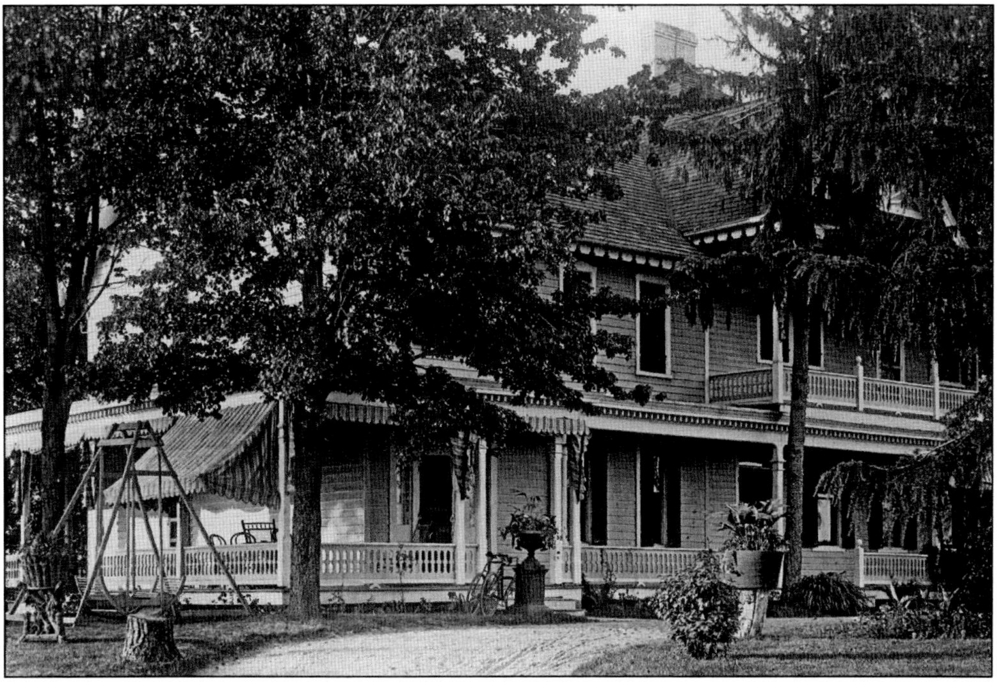

Christian Heurich (1842–1945) was already a successful brewer in Washington, D.C., when he purchased his 376-acre farm in 1884 on the present-day site of Prince George's Plaza. Heurich built this summerhouse, known as Bellevue Farm, here in the 1920s and planned a fully operational dairy with Holstein cows. (HSWDC.)

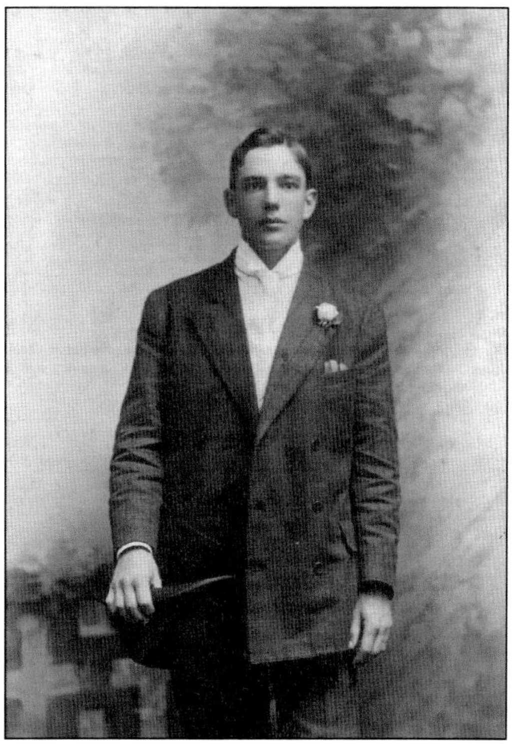

Charles and India Ager purchased acreage west of Hyattsville around 1890. They operated the only farm between what is now Riggs and Ager Roads with a two-and-a-half-story clapboard house and a large red barn. Ager ran a dairy aided by sons Charles, Norman, and Raymond (pictured). The dairy functioned for more than 40 years. (Kathy Albertson.)

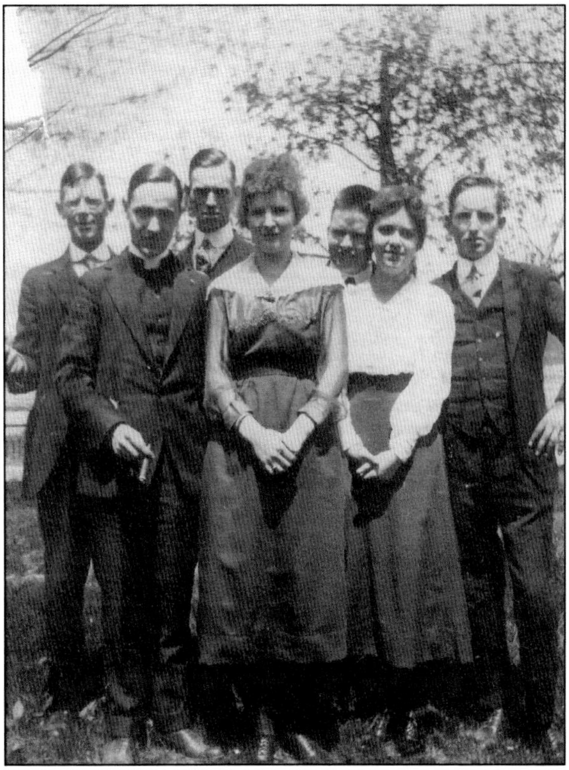

George and Margaret Lanhardt, first-generation Americans of German descent, purchased acreage off the old County Road southwest of town before 1900. The Lanhardts farmed produce sold locally with assistance from resident laborers and their children. From left to right, their children and neighbors Charles, Harry, Edward, Thelma Ager, George, Eleanor, and Rev. Chris McAllister pose here about 1925. Hyattsville annexed the tract in 1953 with 60 homes. (Kathy Albertson.)

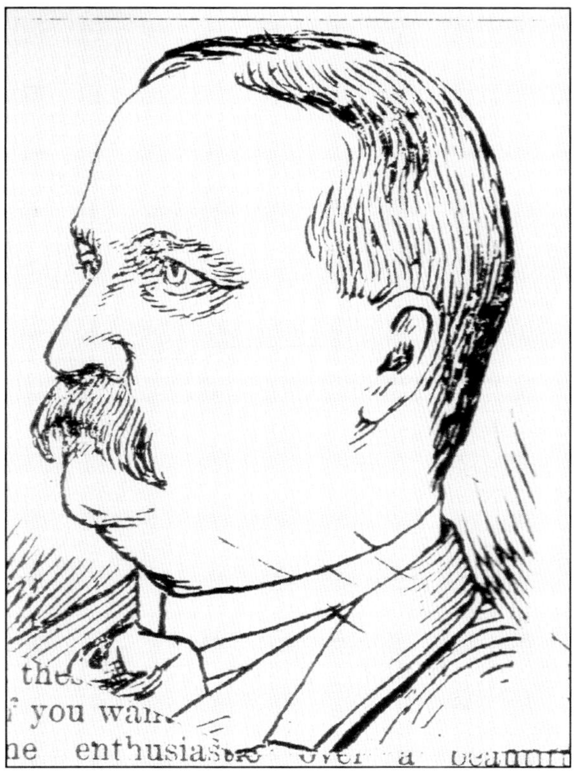

Washington, D.C., developers George Johnson and Louis Wine (pictured) and their wives purchased 196 acres north of Hyatt's property in 1882. Platted as 100 lots 50 by 150 feet, the subdivision contained two parks and eponymous streets. A second addition to the east followed the next year. Wine moved his family to the Ravenswood estate, making land donations to St. Jerome's and the Masons. In 1893, a third subdivision was added. (HPA.)

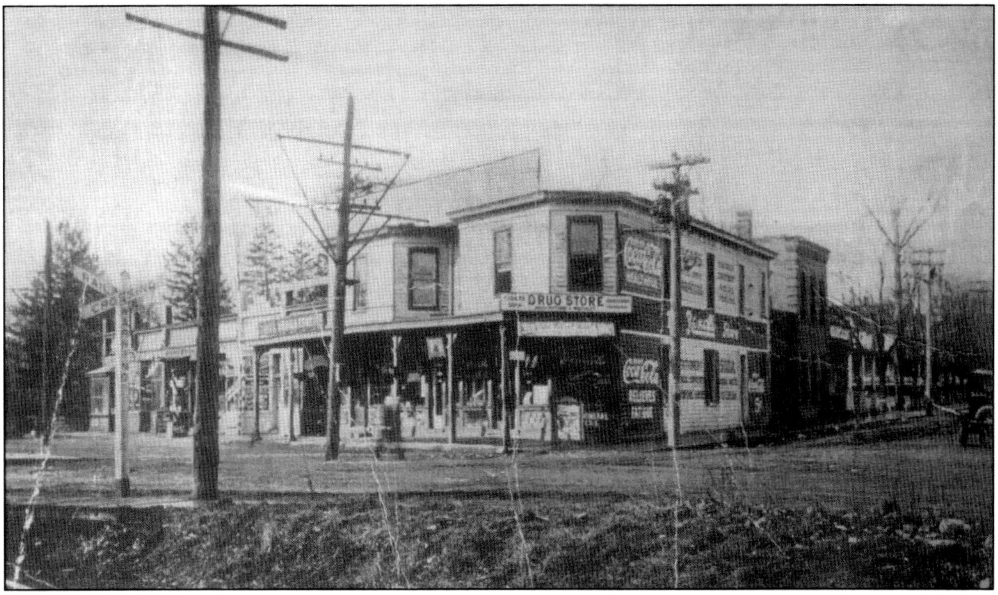

Wells' Drugstore was built at Baltimore Avenue and Decatur Street (above) by owner Dr. Alfred H. Wells. The store was the best-known landmark in early Hyattsville. Its upper meeting hall housed the public school and other fraternal organizations before they found permanent buildings. The drugstore had the first telephone exchange and later housed the first switchboard. This advertisement (below) showed the many other things Wells offered his customers. (Above, PGCHS; below, HPA.)

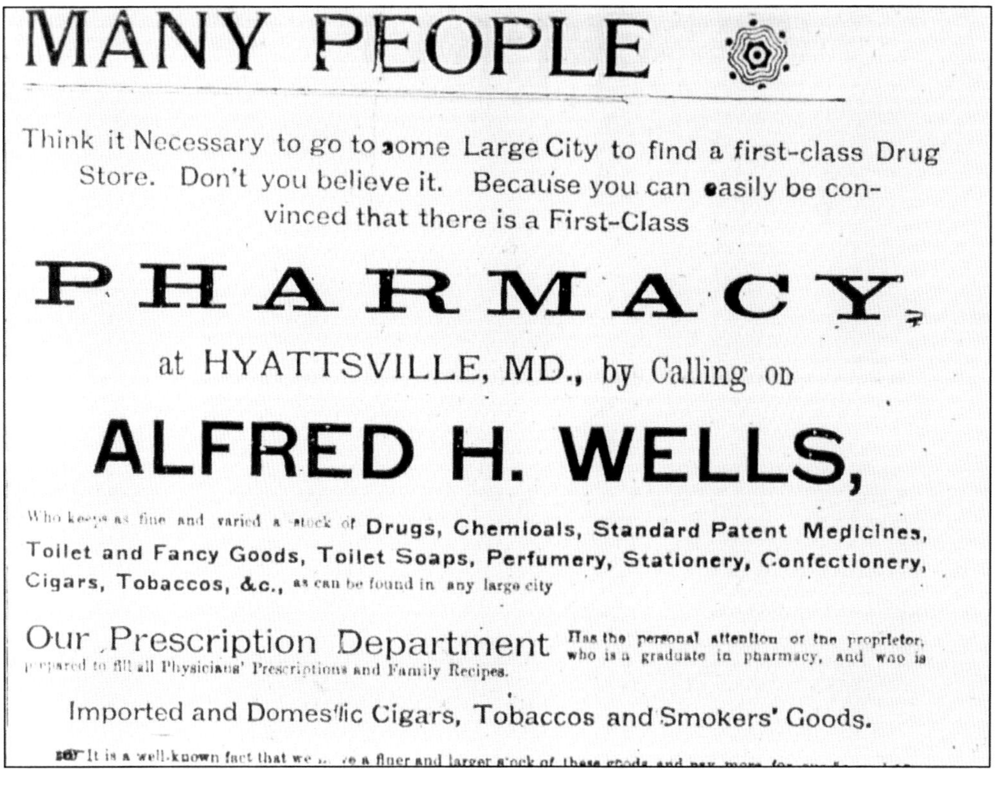

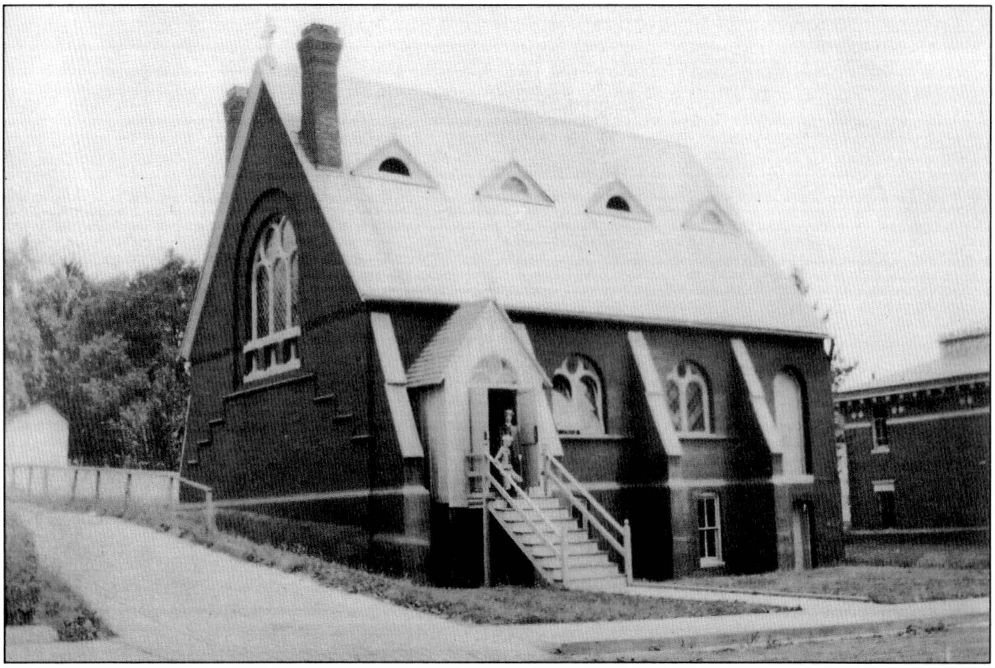

Pinkney Memorial Episcopal Church was built in memoriam to Bishop William Pinkney of St. Matthew's Parish (established 1811). In 1884, a $12,000 goal was set and a Baltimore Avenue and Spencer (Gallatin) Street site was purchased in 1888. Rev. Theodore Reed of Bladensburg then opened a Sunday school in an empty meat market by the railroad. Inaugural services were held in the new church March 2, 1890. (Kathy Albertson.)

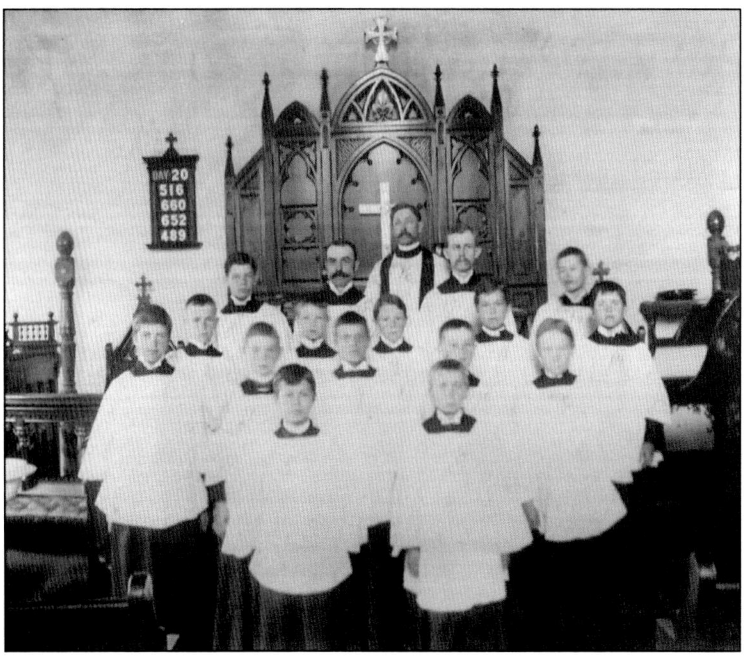

The Pinkney Memorial Boys Choir organized April 1896 and gave their first performance at a confirmation service by Bishop Satterlee the following month. Church organist Adelaide Lepper accompanied the group. This May 20, 1897, photograph shows Rev. Charles Mayo (back row), directors James Burnside and Louis Holden (left to right, fourth row), and the boys in front of the reredos. (PGCHS.)

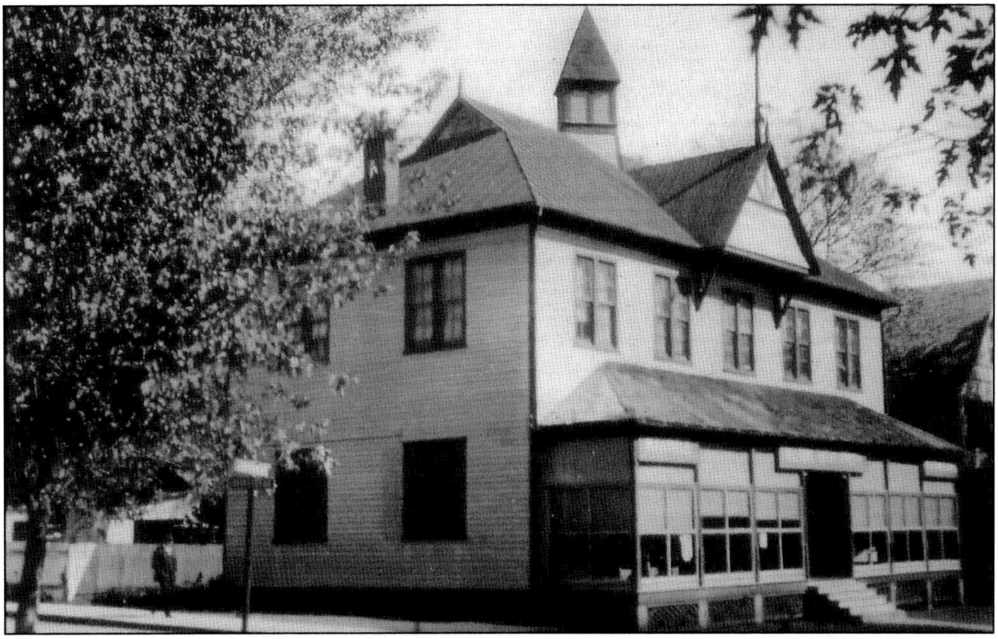

The first segregated public school opened in 1886 above Wells' Drugstore, costing the county $100 monthly. Inadequate space led Henry Drury, James Burnside, and Jackson Ralston to petition the board of education for a schoolhouse. The corner of Ravenswood (Forty-third Avenue) and Johnson (Farragut) Avenue was chosen for this two-story frame building. A contract was let to local builder George Walker in 1890, costing the county $2,000 and Hyattsville $200. (Doug Dudrow.)

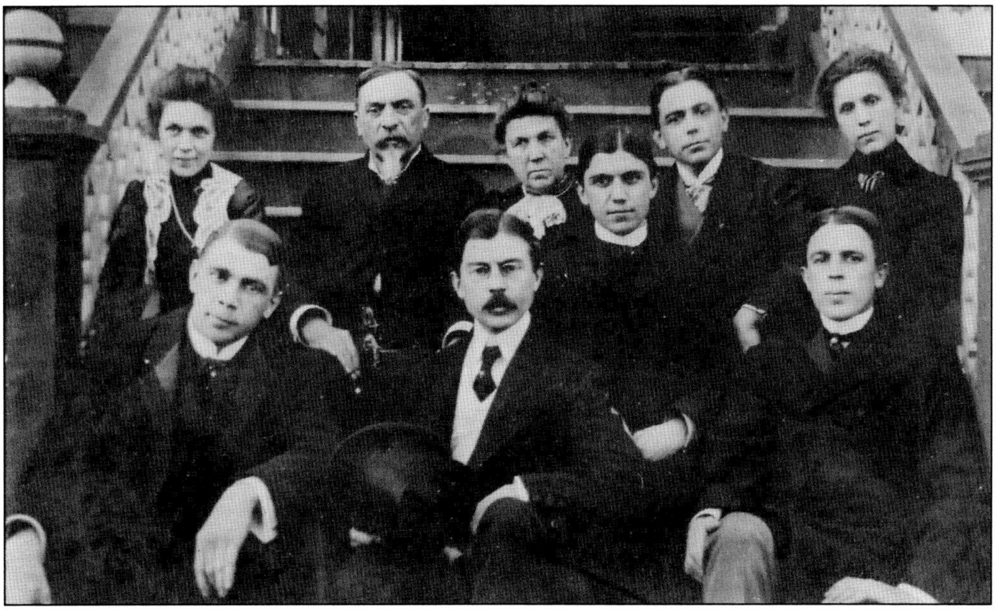

Dr. Charles A. Wells (1840–1924) was nicknamed "Father of Prince George's County" for delivering so many area children. Wells (second from left, back row) moved here from Bladensburg and married Lucretia Hyatt, niece of Christopher. He was elected a town commissioner for three years, mayor (1902–1906), and later state senator. Wells served the Hyattsville Building Association both as director and president, a post he also held at the First National Bank. (City of Hyattsville.)

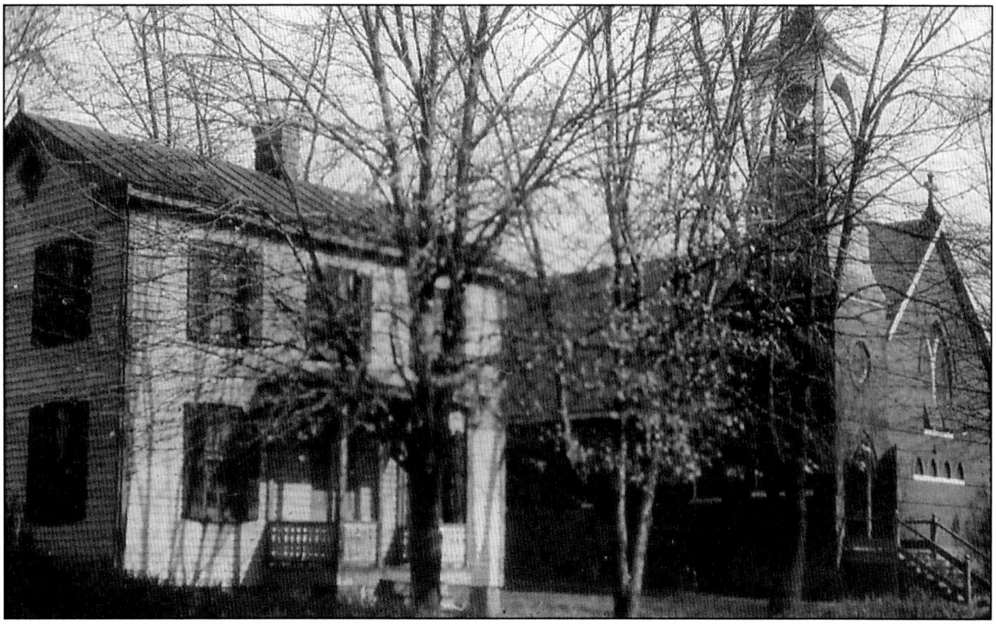

St. Jerome's Parish began in 1884 as a mission of St. Mary's in Laurel, Maryland, when a priest came by horseback to a vacant store for mass. Developers Louis Wine and George Johnson donated the church property at the corner of Gallatin (Spencer) Street and Forty-third Avenue (Olive Street), and in 1886, Cardinal James Gibbons laid the cornerstone. The rectory (left) and church were used until 1924. (Doug Dudrow.)

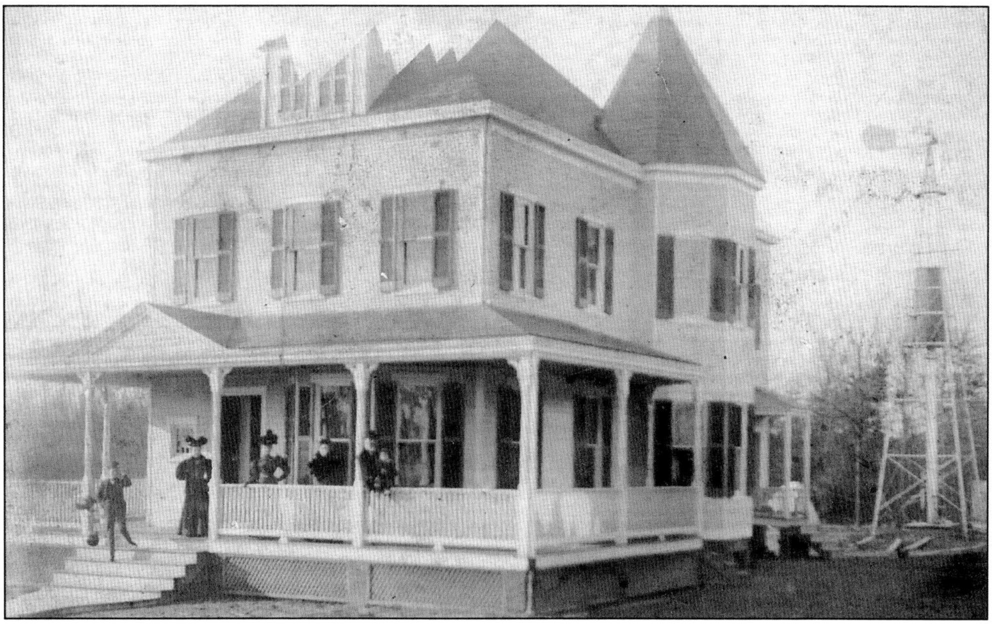

Many early homes had wells to provide water. Some homes, like the Vandorens' at 24 Ralston Avenue (4100 Gallatin Street), used windmills to pump the water. The water was held in a cistern until needed in the house, where a small hand pump next to the kitchen sink was used to draw the water. Homes without windmills had a bucket that was hand filled and placed in the kitchen where it could be ladled as needed. (PGCHS.)

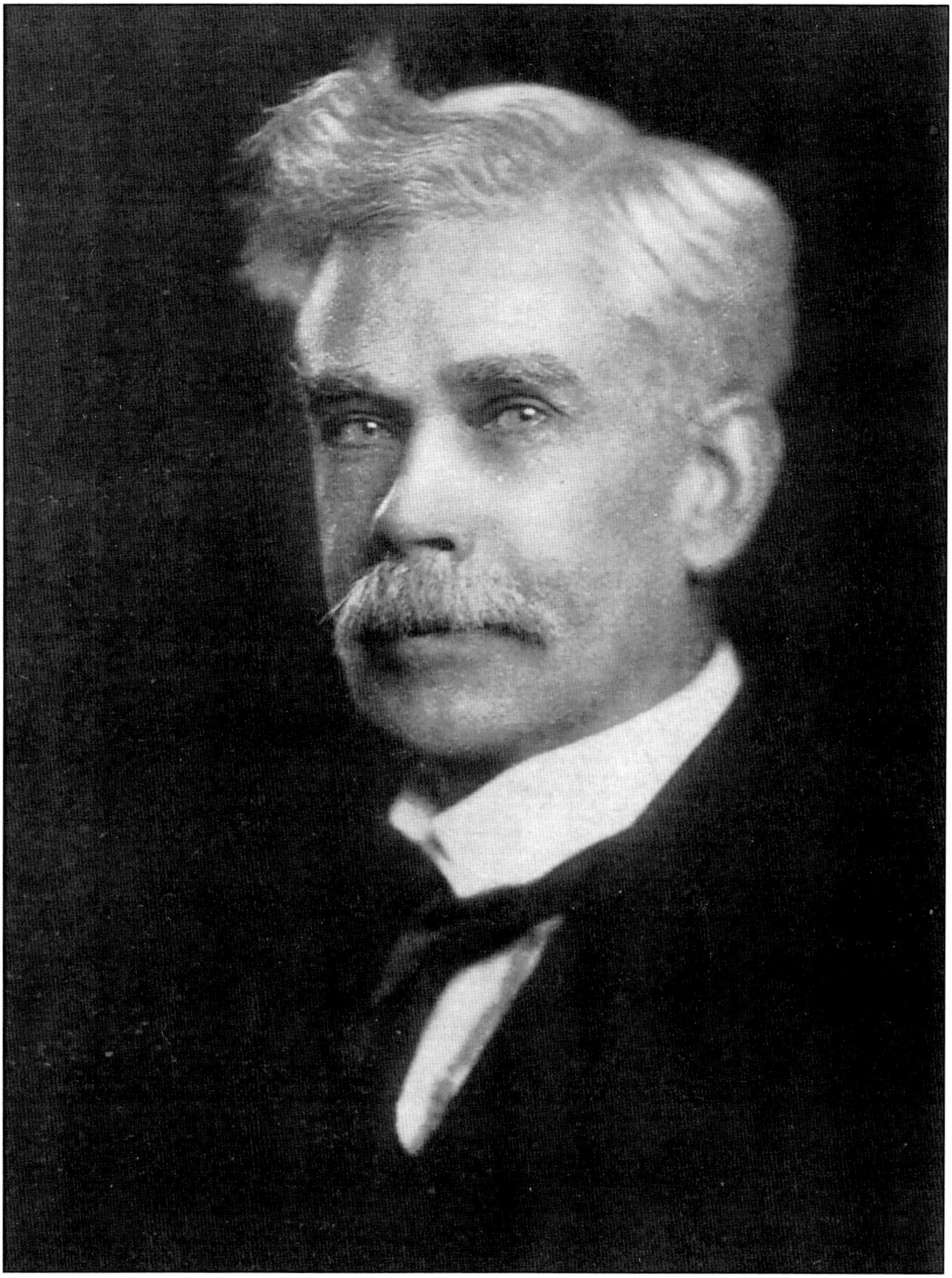

Jackson Harvey Ralston (1857–1945) was an internationally prominent attorney honored by a Stanford Law School prize. Ralston moved to his Hyattsville home, Wing Rest, after his mother, Harriet, purchased and built on the adjoining property in 1882; they are now 4200 and 4206 Decatur Street. Ralston wrote the city's charter and served five years as town commissioner. In 1892, Ralston urged the city to adopt the first single-tax system in the country. Challenged and argued to the Maryland Court of Appeals, where it was found unconstitutional, this case provided standing for modern tax law. (University of California, Berkeley, Bancroft Collection.)

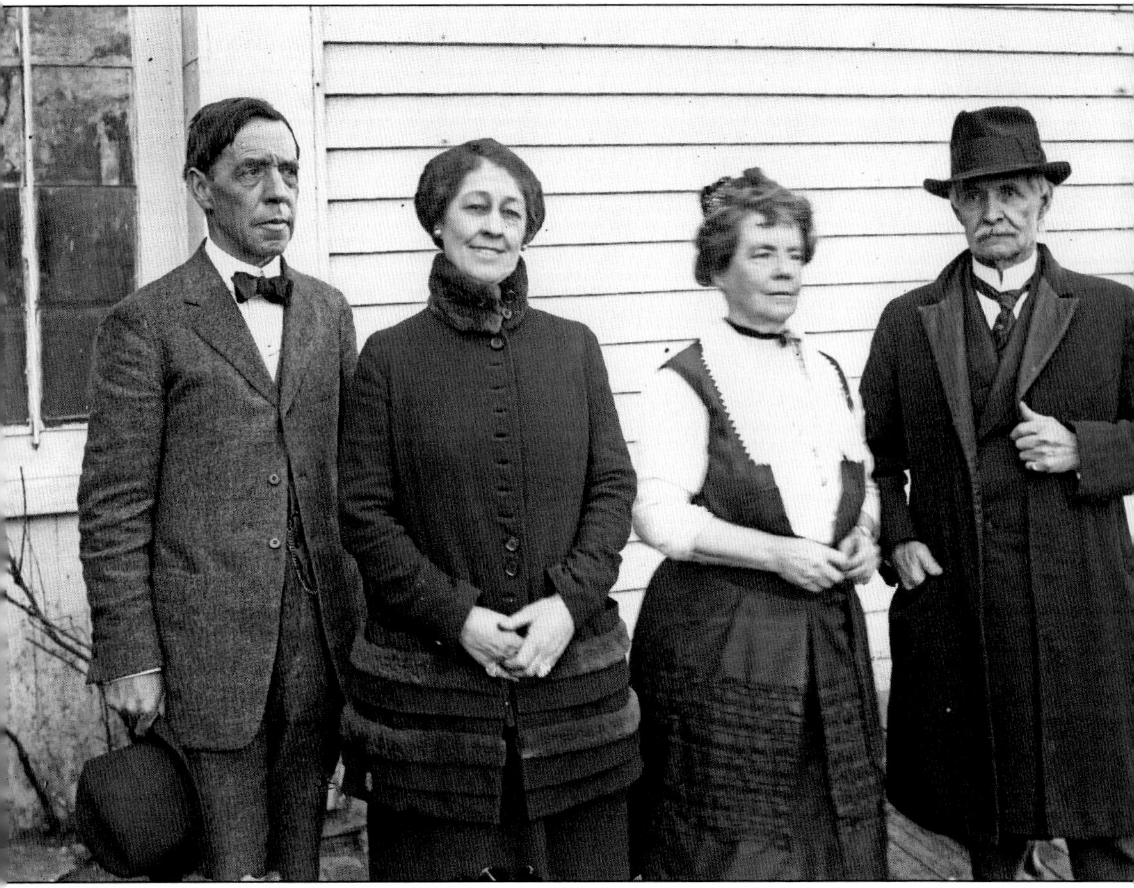

The Rogerses moved to town in 1895 and were significant characters in the community's nascency. From left to right, James C. (1864–1941), wife Blanche Mattingly, sister Anna Mae (1861–1936), and brother Dr. James Harris stand in front of their home, Firwood. James, a prominent regional attorney, served as the city's incorporation counsel and wrote its charter. Mae was renowned for her voice, singing for presidents and often appearing on the stage. (HSWDC.)

William Sheppard Rogers built and lived at 4104 Gallatin Street. With James and Harris, the Rogers brothers were responsible for real estate developments throughout the area, including Cottage City, Edmonston, Mount Rainier, Riverdale, Rogers Heights, and parts of Hyattsville. (James Rogers.)

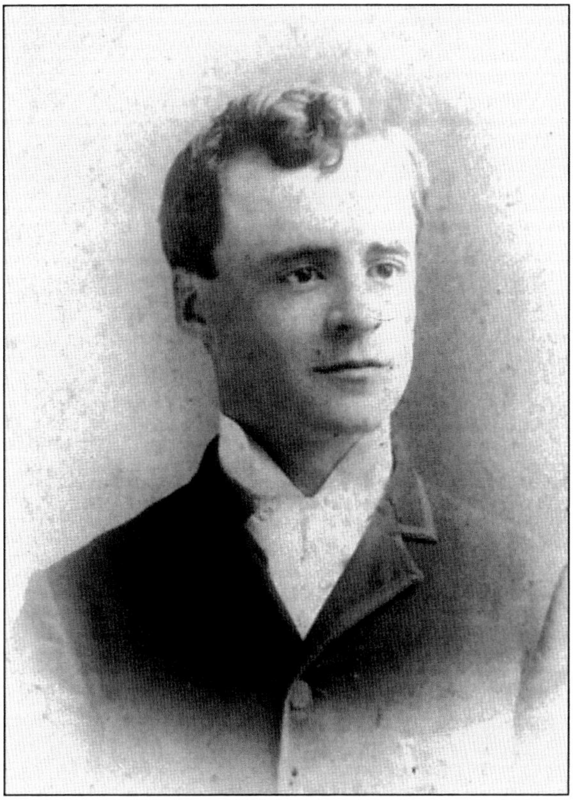

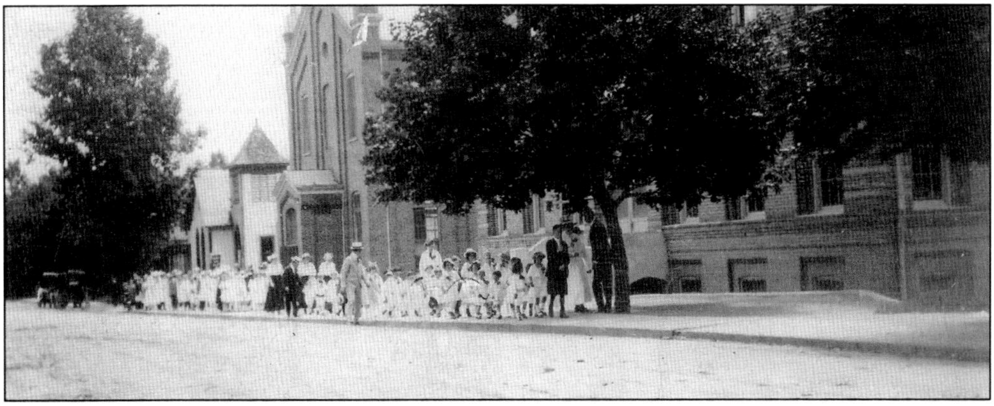

Mount Hermon Lodge No. 179 of Free and Accepted Masons organized on May 26, 1882, with 11 members at Bladensburg's school. The lodge cornerstone was laid on May 2, 1893, with the same gavel used for the U.S. Capital. Ruth Chapter No. 7 Order of the Eastern Star, now the second-oldest active chapter in the state, was constituted on April 21, 1897, with the first worthy matron, Blanche Noel. (Kathy Albertson.)

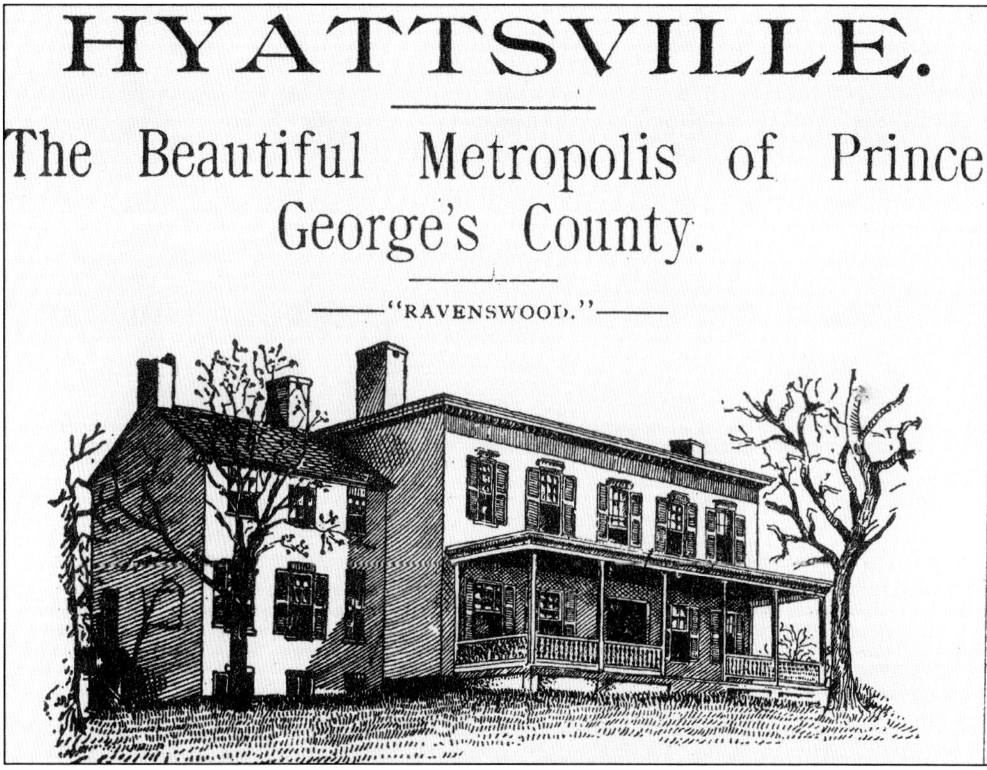

The Suburban Citizen reported on February 6, 1892, "From the first its progress has been slow, but steady, until now as the metropolis of Prince George's [C]ounty. Hyattsville is a beautiful village of nearly sixteen hundred inhabitants. Its surroundings are all of the most delightful character, and as a business or residential location it cannot be surpassed, nesting as it does on and around a beautiful chain of Maryland hills." (HPA.)

Experience Teaches Wisdom

BENJAMIN F. CHINN, Prop.

(*Established* 1893)

Has served you faithfully for over thirty years

SHAVING and HAIRDRESSING PARLOR

Special Attention Given to Ladies' and Children's Work

Up-to-Date Massage and Shampooing

Razors Honed, Set and Concaved

Phone 789

At Car Stop — Hyattsville, Md.

Benjamin Franklin Chinn opened the town's only barbershop in 1893 on Johnson (Farragut) Avenue just west of the Pike. Chinn advertised as a "tonsorial specialist," but shoe shine was available also. His sons Arthur, Emmett, and Benjamin worked with him. By this 1927 advertisement, Chinn had broadened services. Chinn's personal history adds interest with a changing birth date about 1868, a divorce by 1910, and self-identification as mulatto. (City of Hyattsville.)

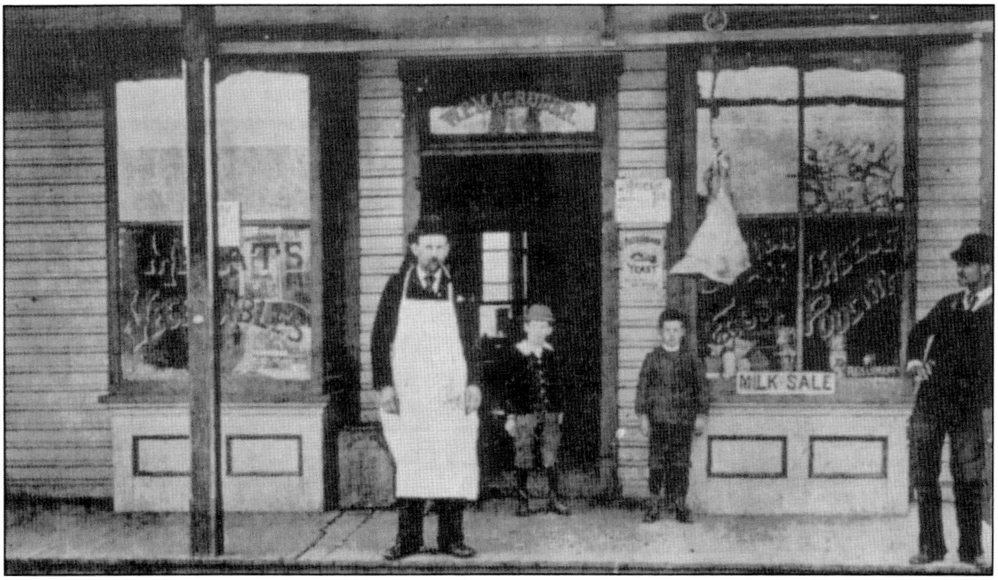

Magruder's store and Chinn's store were located near each other. Magruder (in apron) stands with, from left to right, William Hasson, Raymond Jackson, and Chinn. (City of Hyattsville.)

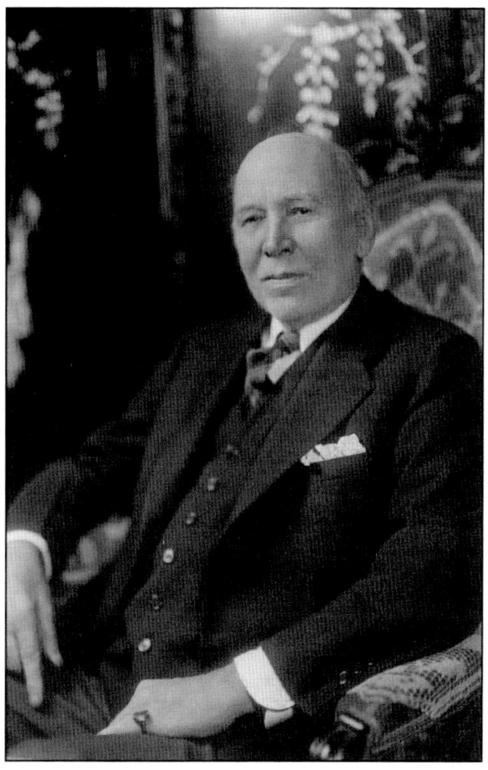

William Pinkney "Pink" (1858–1939) and Sarah Magruder moved to town in 1882, opening a lumberyard and, later, a hardware company. Magruder was a Mason, mayor (1909–1911), and on the board of several local financial institutions. His investment in area real estate made him one of the largest county landholders by his death. Property donations to the city during his life included the park and public library. (City of Hyattsville.)

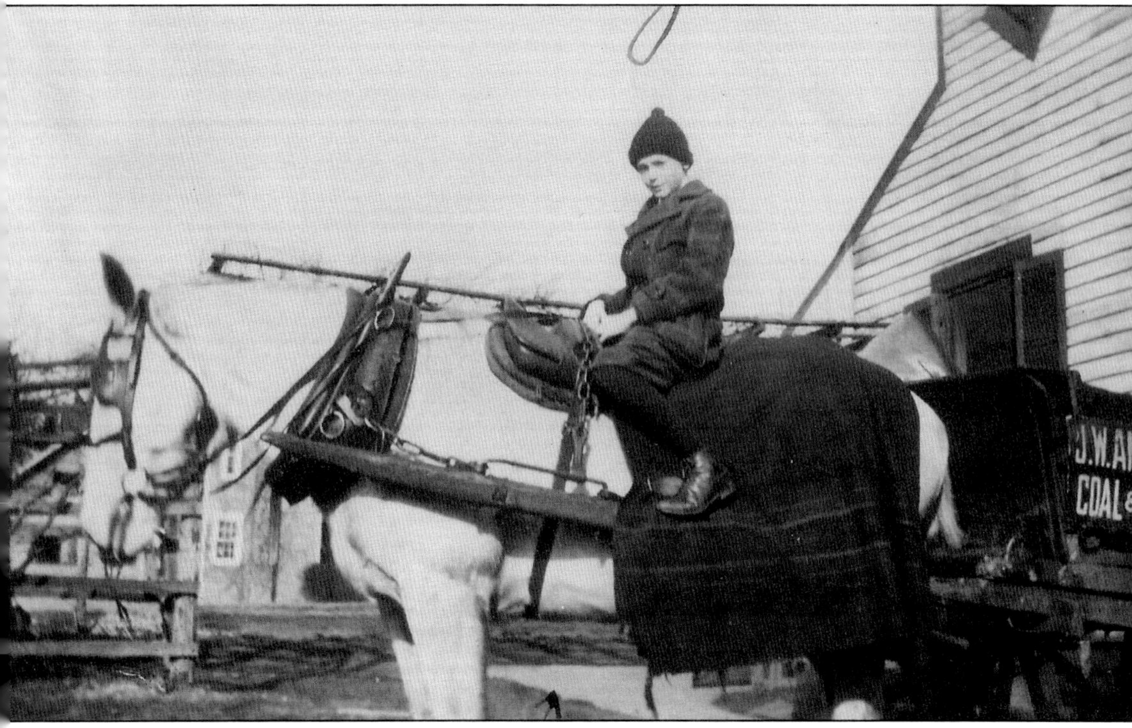

George "Boots" Aman delivered goods by wagon for his father's business, the J. W. Aman Coal and Wood Company. Joseph W. Aman (born 1865) came to town as a child with his parents, Joseph Andrew and Katherine Aman. Joseph W. opened his business on Railroad (Rhode Island) Avenue about 1890, providing building materials for many area houses. Contemporary reports claimed he was socially, religiously, politically, and financially associated with the best interests of the community. (PGCHS.)

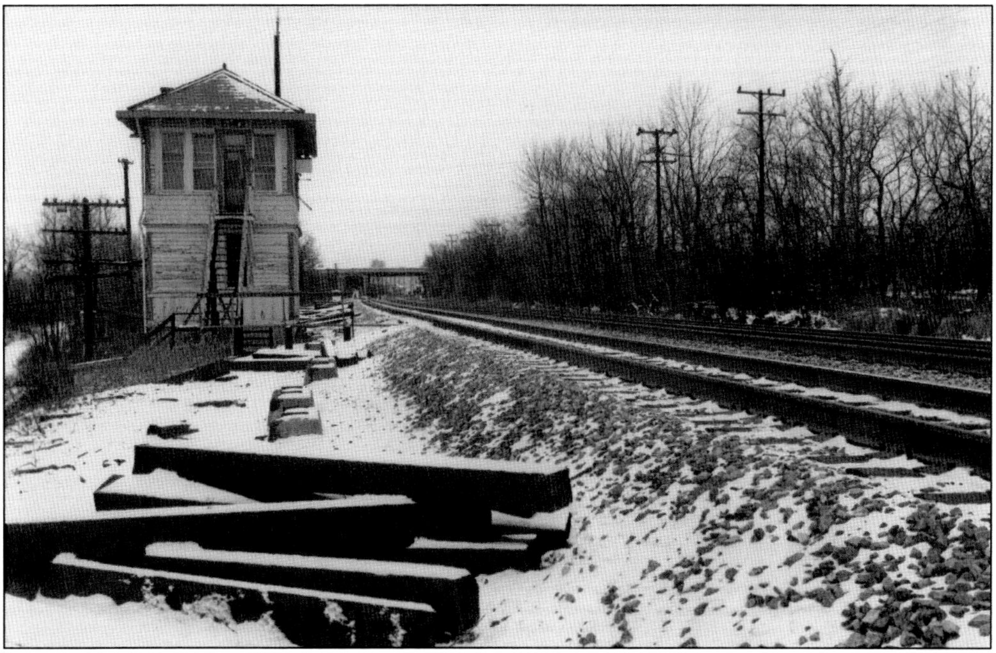

The B&O switching tower stood 1,000 feet north of the Washington and Point Lookout Branch at the Alexandria Junction. The tower opened March 1894 with oil-lamp semaphore signals and an eight-lever machine to operate the switching of rails for southbound trains. The operator's office and interlocking machine occupied the first floor, and the second housed operator and interlocking levers. The tower burned in 1993 after its decommission. (City of Hyattsville.)

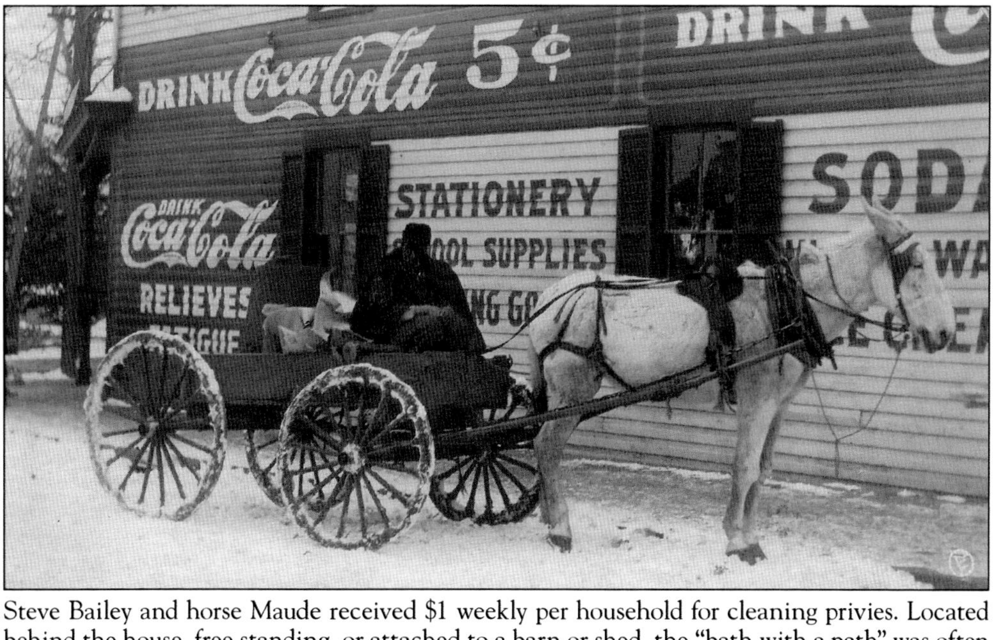

Steve Bailey and horse Maude received $1 weekly per household for cleaning privies. Located behind the house, free standing, or attached to a barn or shed, the "bath with a path" was often covered by honeysuckle or roses. Many homes did not have indoor plumbing until the 1940s. An 1895 resident described the close proximity of homes' wells and cesspools and the constant outbreak of typhoid fever. (PGCHS.)

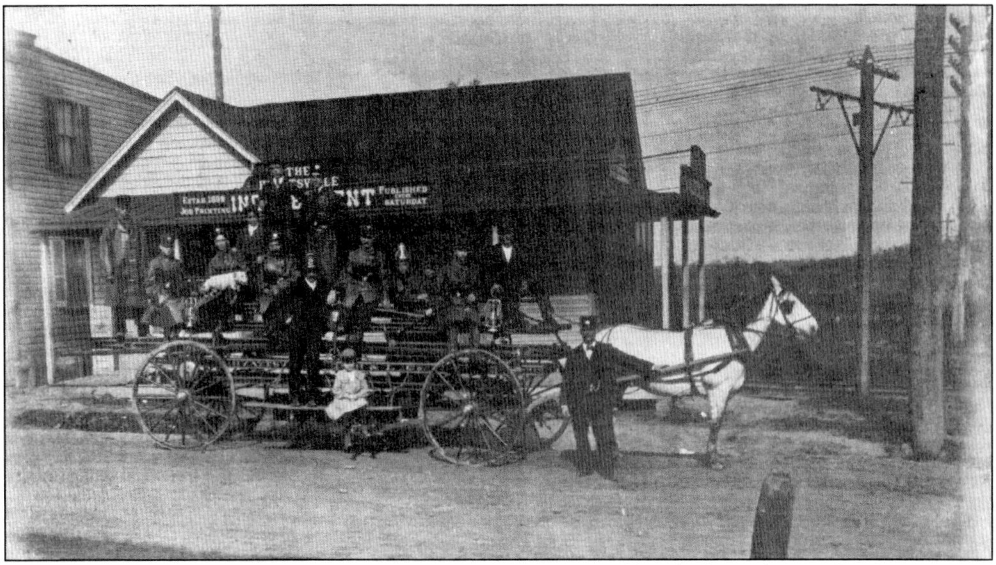

The Presbyterian church bell was sounded to notify Hyattsville of a fire. The Michael V. Tierney Volunteer Fire Department was the community's first organized firefighting unit. On October 17, 1895, Clarence Wilson was appointed the first fire marshal and Tierney the first president. Wilson approached local businessman J. W. Aman to donate a portion of his Johnson (Farragut) Avenue coal yard for equipment storage. (City of Hyattsville.)

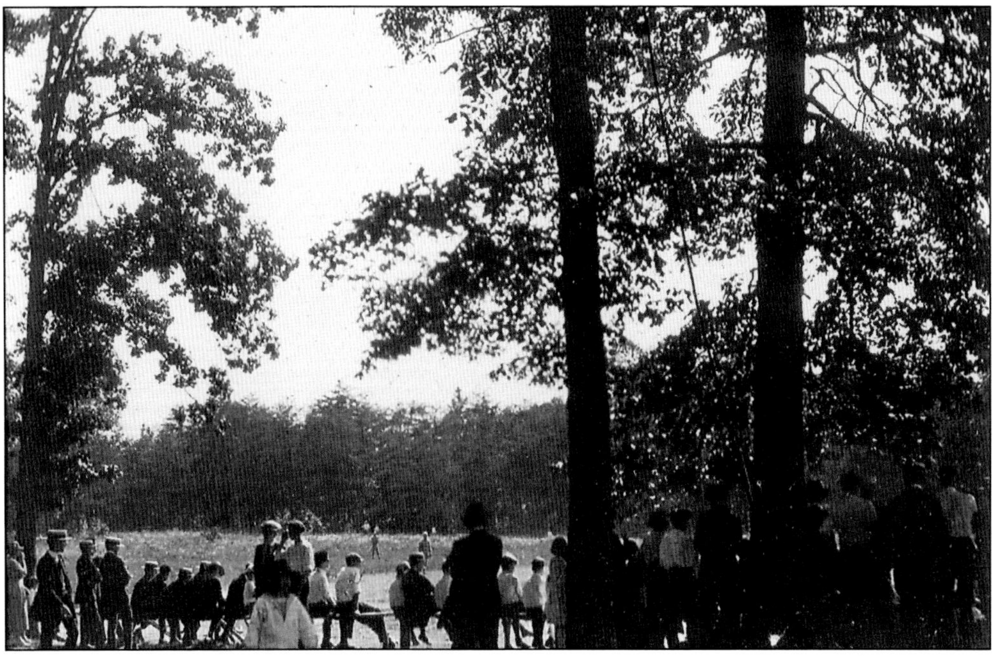

Wine's Woods was located north of Hamilton Street and west of Forty-second Avenue. A grandstand and playing field were built for Hyattsville's favorite pastime. Baseball in Hyattsville predates the city's incorporation. The *Prince Georgian* reported a game in town as early as 1874 between a Washington, D.C., and a Hyattsville team. Early team rosters included important community names like Hyatt, Guy, and Gasch. (Doug Dudrow.)

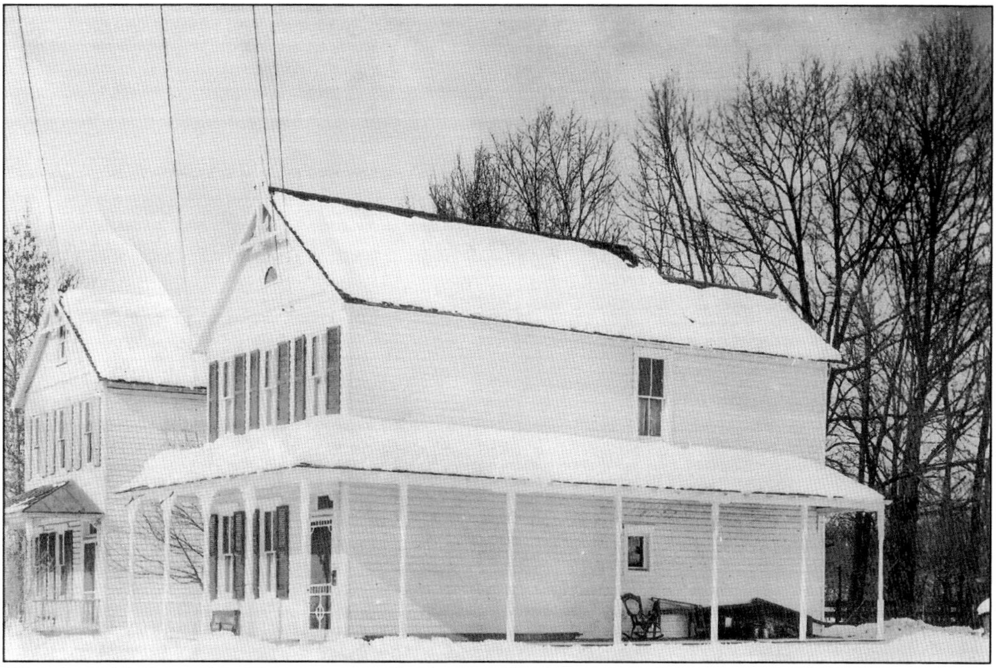

Wine's and Johnson's additions were the largest developments, but many local landowners were subdividing their own, smaller properties contemporaneously. Benjamin Holladay, who had lived in the area since the early 1870s, platted Holladay Company's addition to Hyattsville in 1897 west of Hyatt's addition. The home at 18 Melrose Avenue (4002 Crittenden Street) was one of the earliest houses built in the new neighborhood. (Elaine Lizzio.)

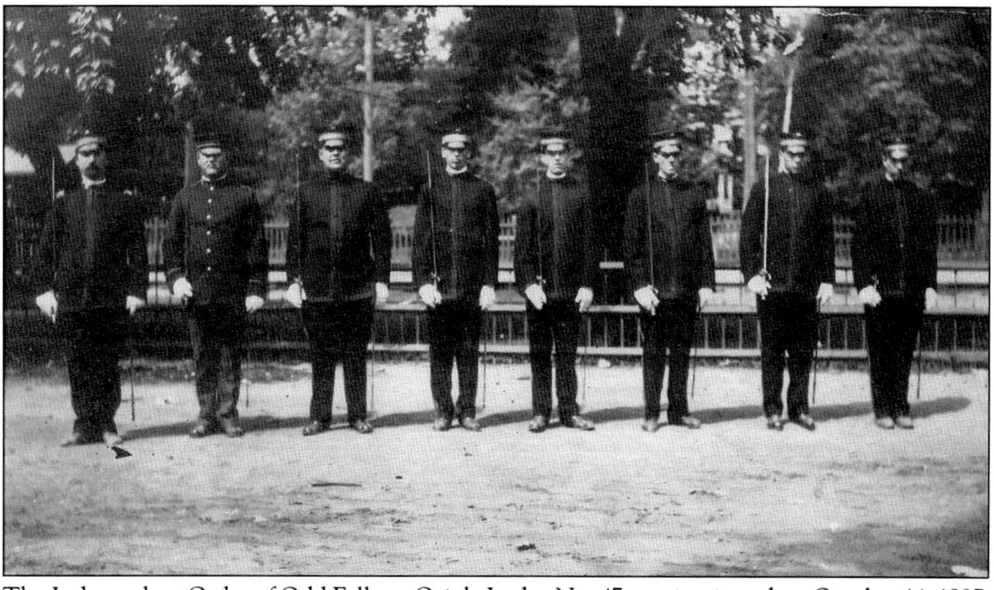

The Independent Order of Odd Fellows Oriole Lodge No. 47 was instituted on October 14, 1897, with 11 members and five candidates. Charter meetings were held in Magruder's Hall (formerly Hyatt's store). Ladies auxiliary Esther Rebekah Lodge No. 20 formed on December 16, 1909, with 119 joining. Here members participate in the Municipal Building cornerstone-laying ceremonies on September 2, 1912. Construction of the still-extant IOOF Lodge began in 1921. (PGCHS.)

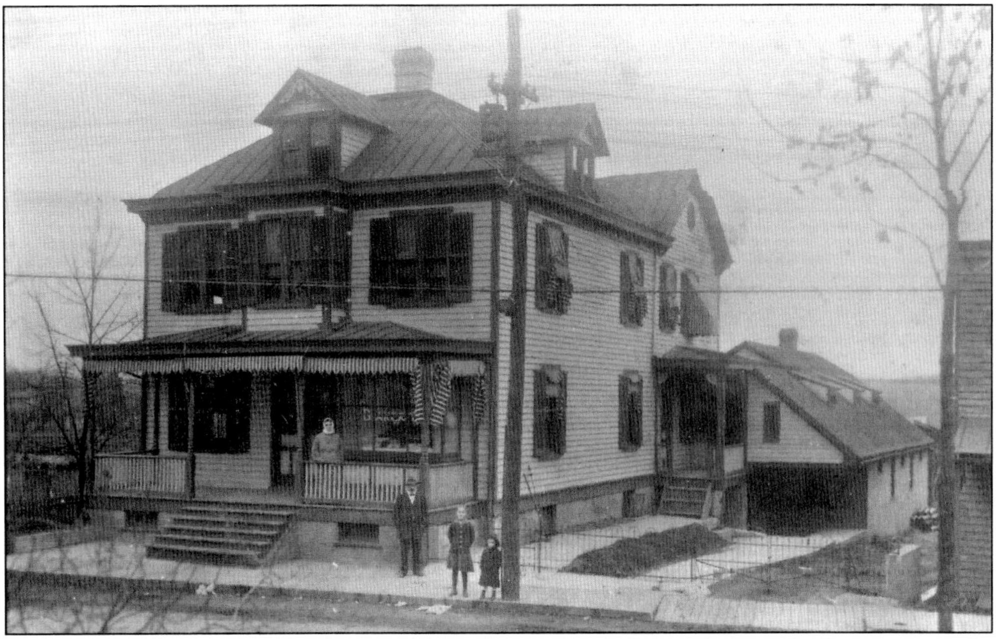

Sonnenberg Bakery, at 98 Maryland (Baltimore) Avenue, was located where the Route 1 overpass is today. German immigrants Gus and Martha Sonnenberg employed the whole family to run the only full-service bakery in town. Purchasing an already existing home, the Sonnenbergs remodeled the basement into the bakery and the ground floor front into a display and sales area. The rest of the house was living space. Martha and daughter Elsie ran sales while son Harry ran deliveries. (PGCHS.)

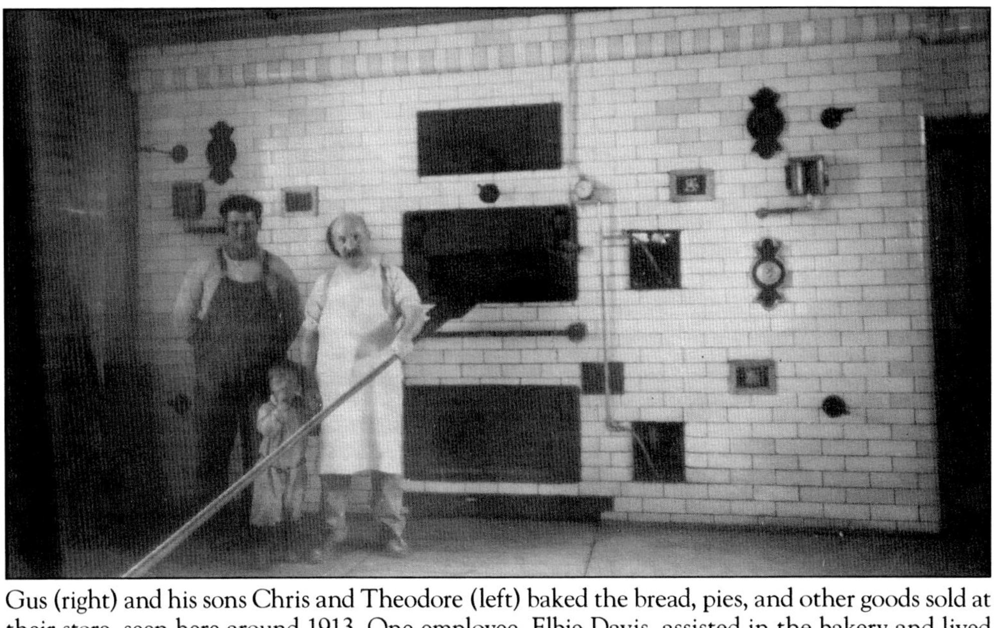

Gus (right) and his sons Chris and Theodore (left) baked the bread, pies, and other goods sold at their store, seen here around 1913. One employee, Elbie Davis, assisted in the bakery and lived with the family after Gus's death about 1918. The bakery operated from about 1900 to the mid-1920s, when railroad overpass construction forced demolition of the home. The Sonnenbergs moved to Riverdale and resumed operations. (PGCHS.)

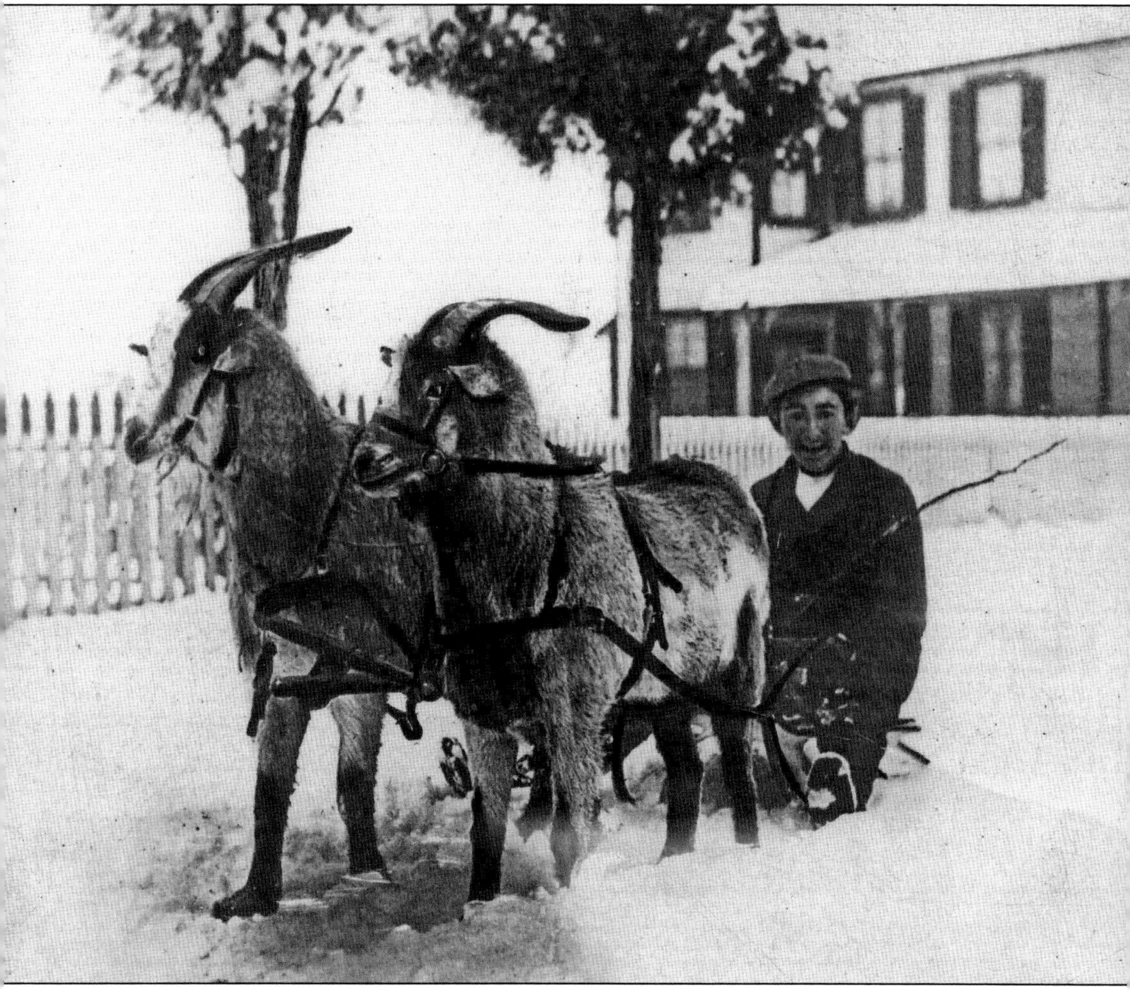

Hyattsville's 1899 residents experienced a historic weather event, setting records not broken for a century. Subzero temperatures started on February 5, lasting more than two weeks with a 36-inch total snow accumulation. Paired with 48-mile-per-hour winds, blizzard conditions blocked transportation of coal and food resulting in rationing. The Midwest and East Coast were affected, with ice floes reported in New Orleans on the Mississippi River. (HSWDC.)

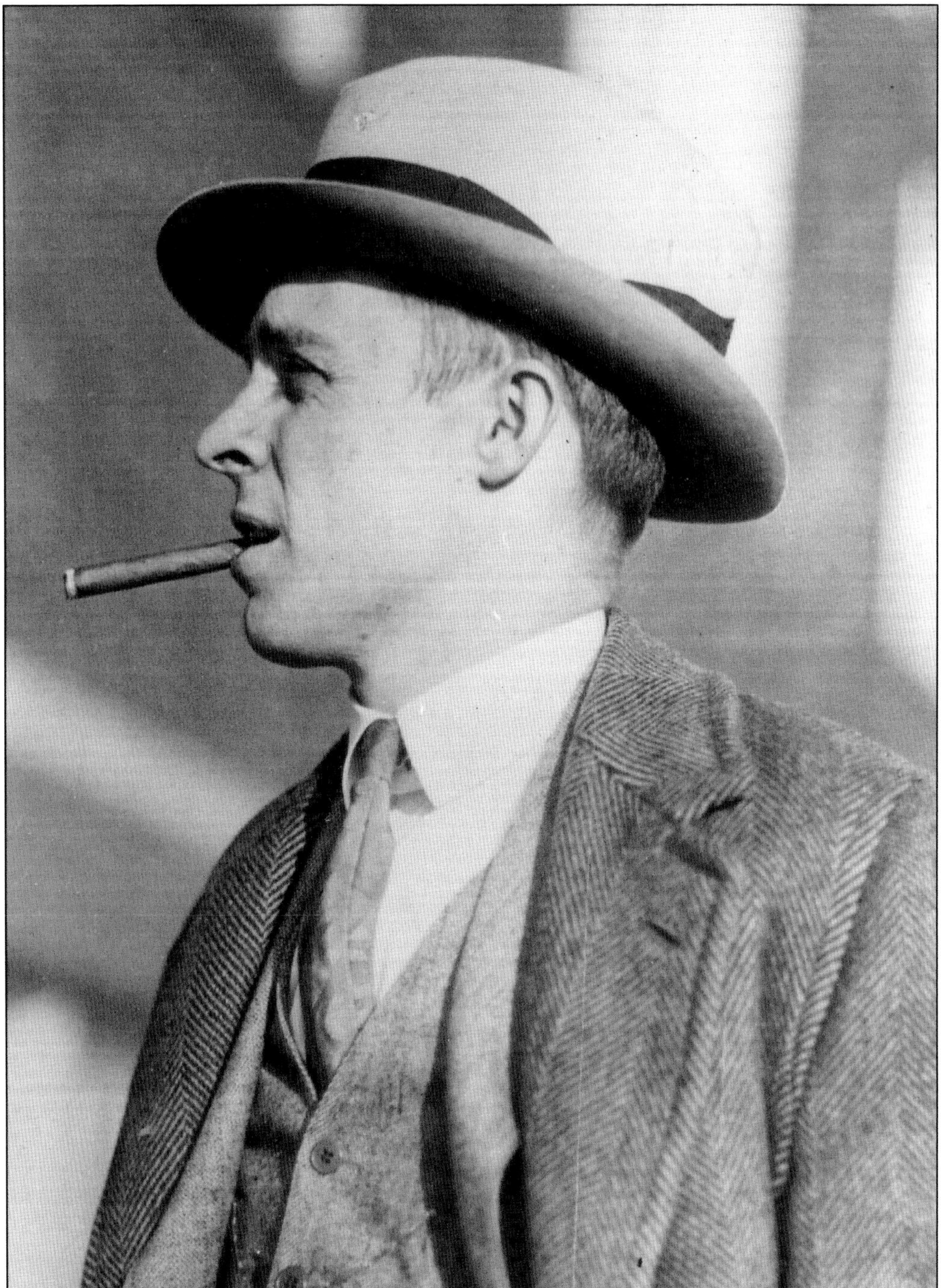

Hyattsville had its own newspaper, the *Hyattsville Herald*, by the early 1890s, one of the earliest suburbs to do so. The *Hyattsville Independent*, founded in 1899, became the local paper under publishers Edward Fuller (pictured) and J. S. McFarland. The Saturday weekly featured local and regional politics, city news, and area social events. Fuller's son Edward A. became editor-in-chief after his father's 1935 death. (PGCHS.)

Two

STREETCAR SUBURB

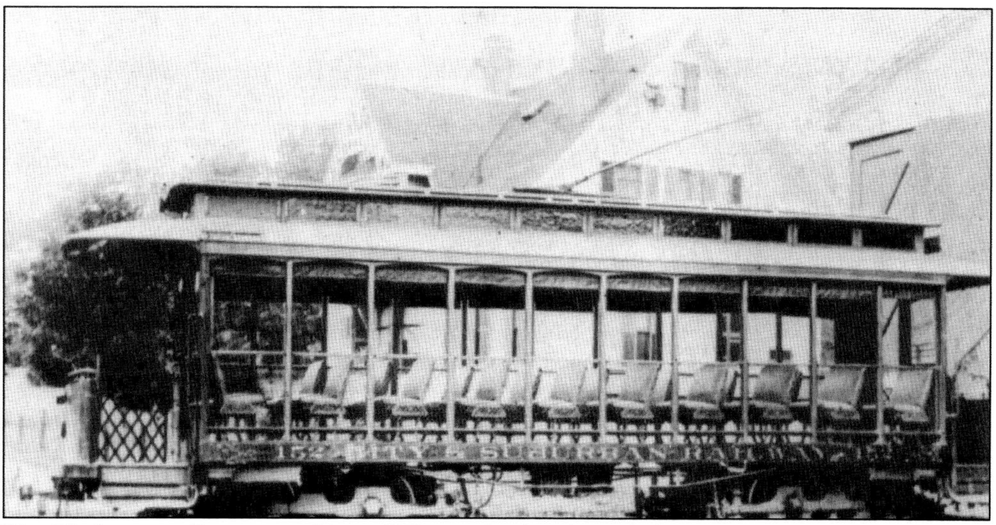

The Washington, Berwyn, and Laurel Electric Railroad traveled through town by 1893, bringing passengers from its Fourth Street and Rhode Island Avenue, Northeast, origination. Wells' Drugstore was the first to sell commutation tickets. This independent line was absorbed by the Washington Railway and Electric Company in 1899. Riders could depart every two minutes during rush hour, traveling along the B&O tracks as far as the Treasury Department. (HPA.)

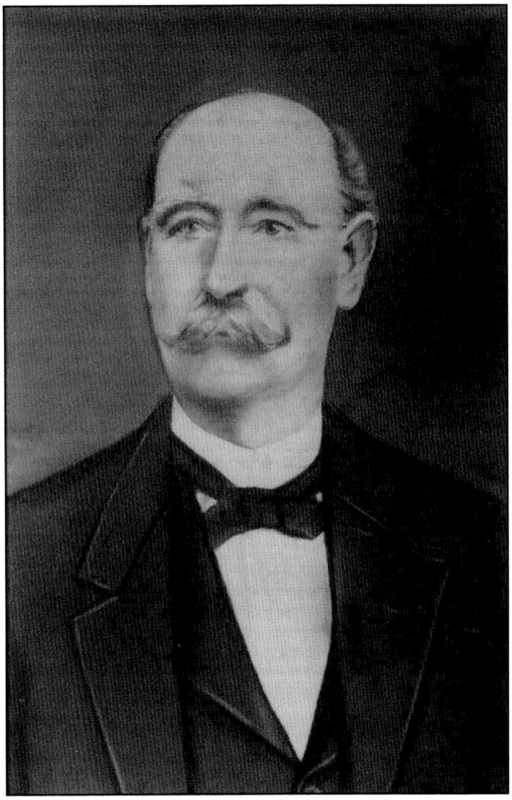

Michael V. Tierney (1853–1906) was Hyattsville's first mayor, elected in 1900. Tierney moved with his wife, Ellen Widdicombe, from Washington, D.C., in 1893, purchasing the Ravenswood estate. He continued service in the District of Columbia National Guard, was commissioned as major, and served as chief ordinance officer. Tierney maintained D.C. law offices, prosecuting the federal government for pension claims. Locally he was instrumental in gaining waterworks and a new schoolhouse. (City of Hyattsville.)

William T. Casey opened his blacksmith and wheelwright shop near the Anacostia branch at the start of the 20th century. It was credited as the only business of its kind servicing the area. Originally a brick warehouse was located here, receiving goods from boats that would dock at the nearby wharf. Casey and his family lived on Maryland (Baltimore) Avenue just south of Sibley (Buchanan) Avenue. (PGCHS.)

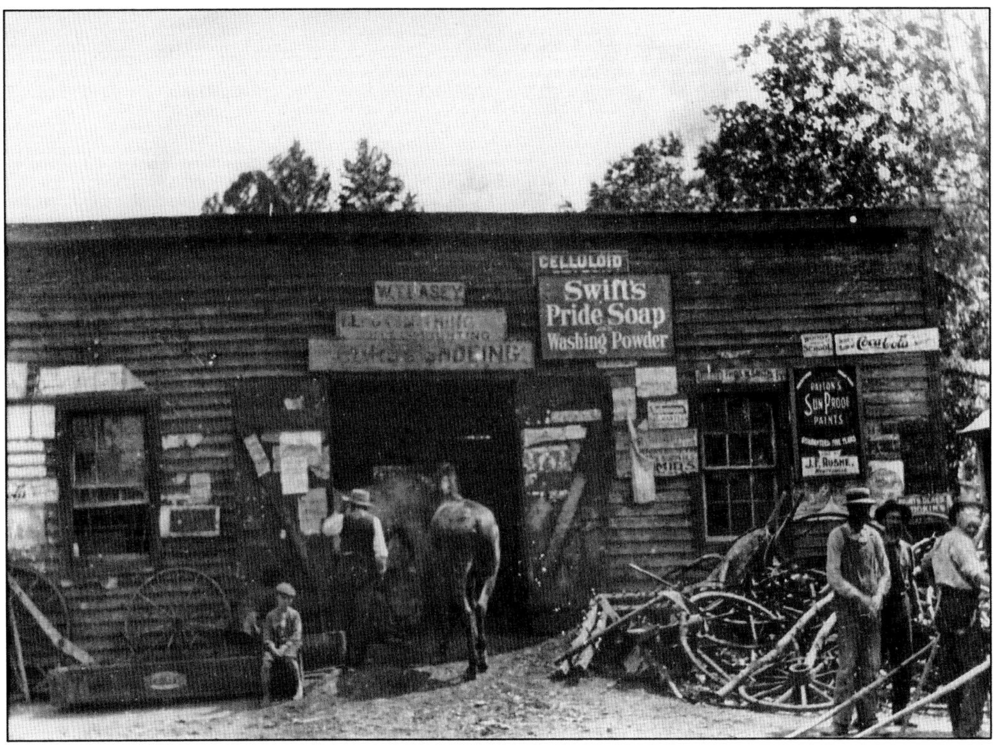

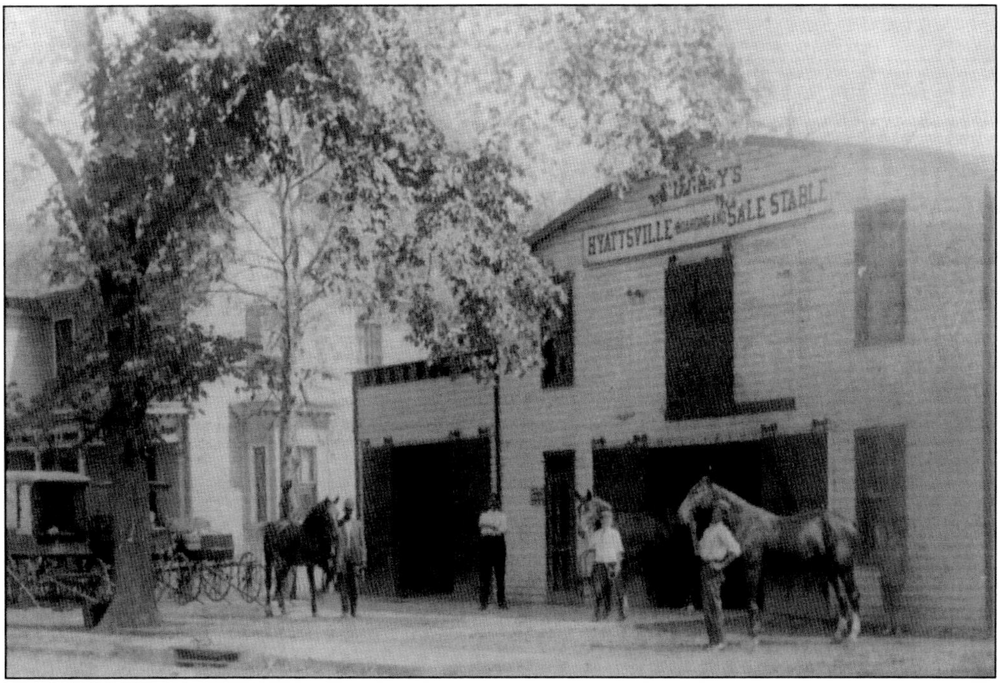

Forty-eight Maryland (Baltimore) Avenue at Guy Avenue (Emerson Street) was the location of Hyattsville Livery Stable owned by Lemuel Gray at the beginning of the 20th century. The large building had many box stalls on the ground floor with hay storage above. A northern addition stored carriages and buggies. Many residents boarded their horses and vehicles here. Horses and vehicles were available also for rent, including hacks and hackneys for funerals. (HPA.)

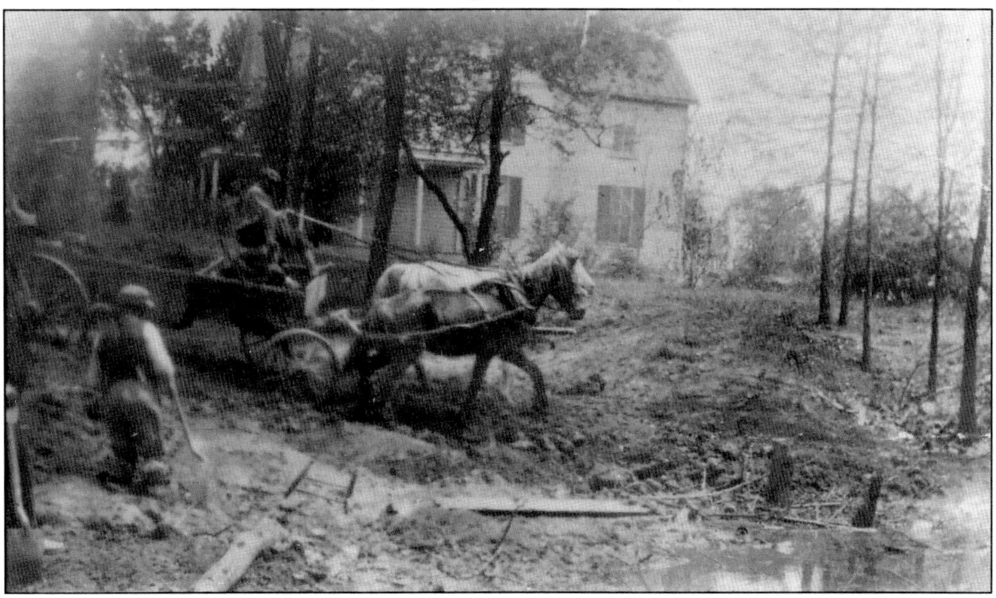

Local property names like Edgewood, Firwood, Ravenswood, and Wine's Woods aptly described the area's original tree-filled landscape. As development spread, clearing properties for construction was necessary. Man and horse labored in tandem in the 1900s, removing trees from Wine and Johnson's First Addition in the 4100 block of Hamilton Street. (PGCHS.)

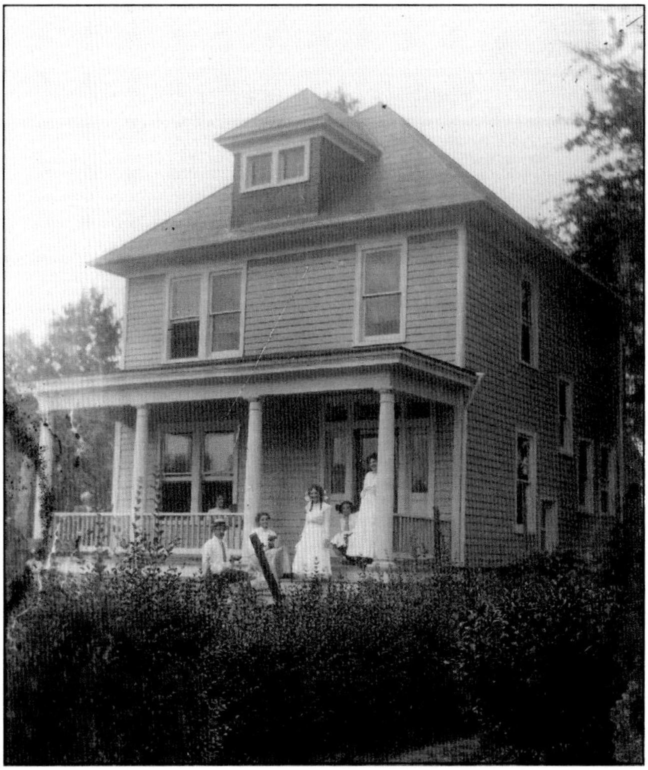

The Piozets, Emile (born 1850 in Switzerland) and Bertha (born 1872 in Germany) immigrated to the area in 1894. Here they stand on the steps of their Baltimore Avenue home in 1900 with children Charles, Clara, Annie, and Robert. When Emile died about 1912, Bertha sold fresh-cut flowers from her home for income. (PGCHS.)

Few little girls could resist a new doll found under the Christmas tree. Perhaps Clara and Annie Piozet had admired the toys at Deitz's Department Store, recently opened by a fellow immigrant. This 1900 scene shows that some holiday traditions have not changed. (PGCHS.)

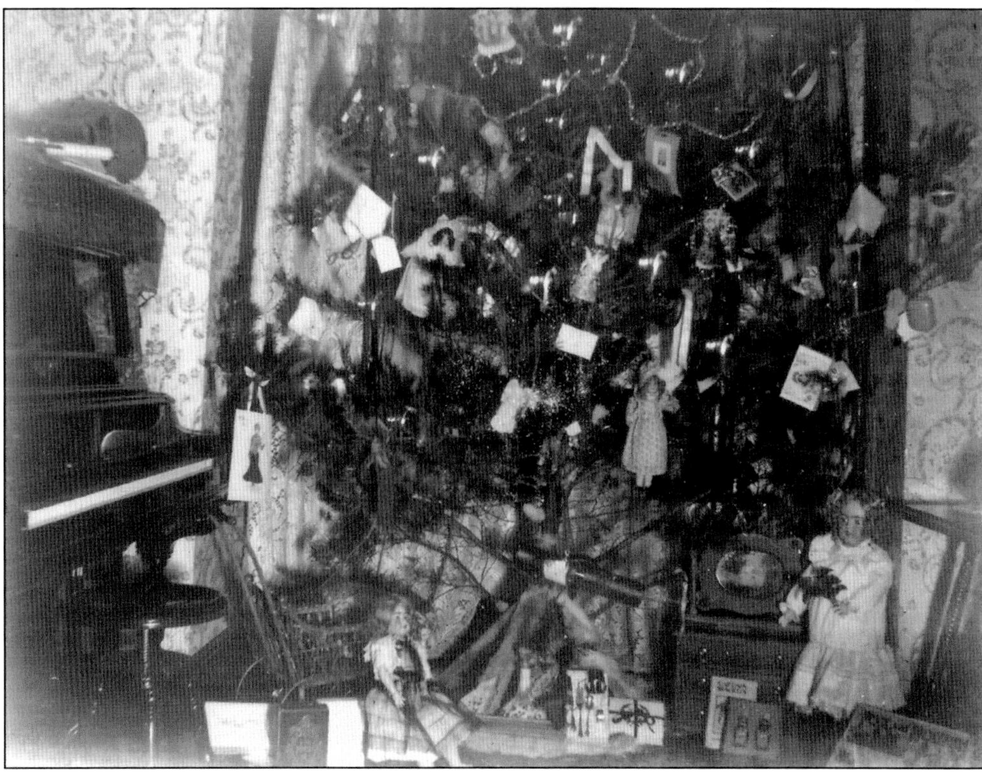

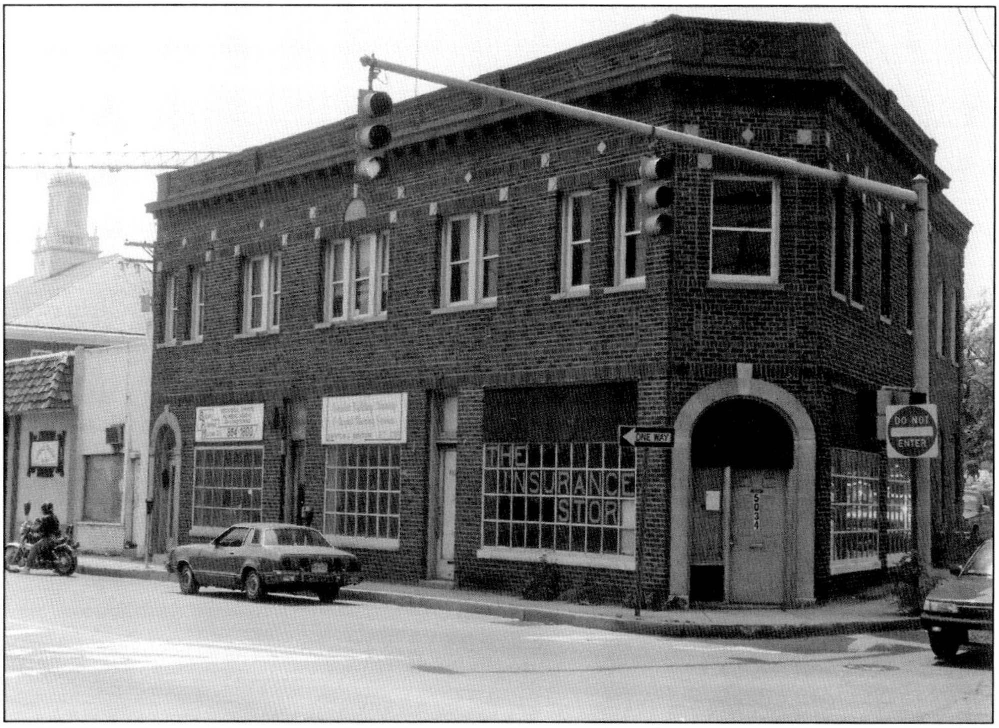

German immigrants Max (born 1878) and Rosie Deitz opened Deitz's Department Store about 1900 at Baltimore Avenue and Spencer (Gallatin) Street. The store sold dry goods: bolts of cloth on shelves against the wall, ribbons in the glass display cases, and toys in any open space. (Both PGCHS.)

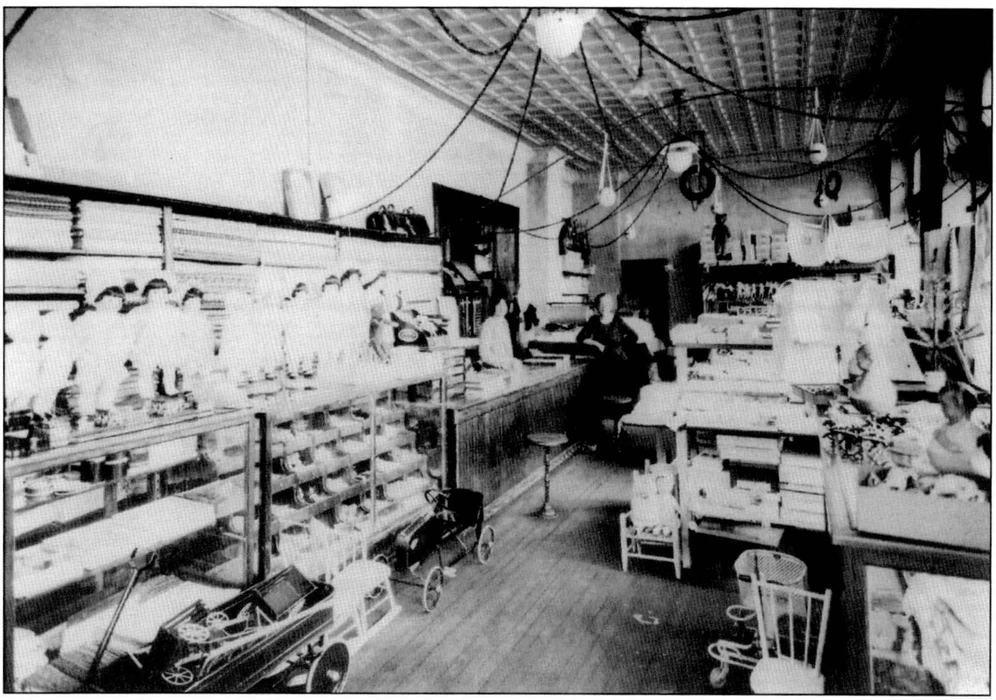

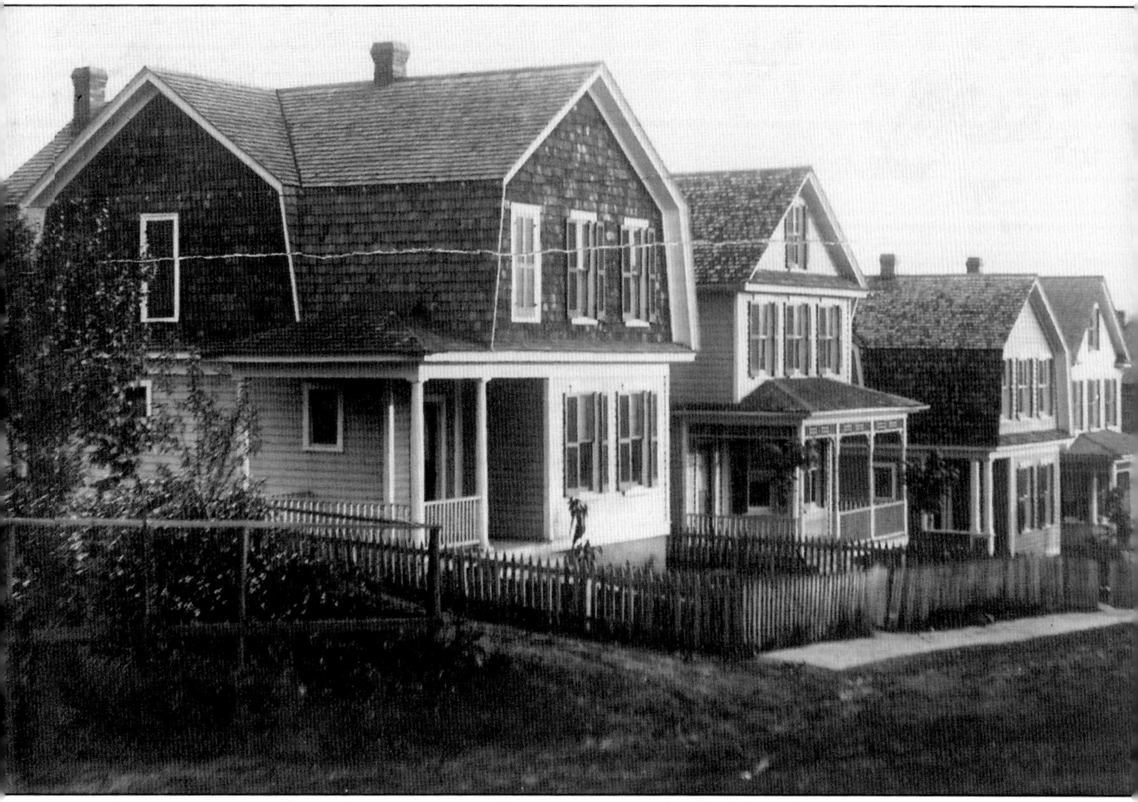

Streetcar access from downtown Washington spurred a building boom, marketed to a broader economic audience and marked by more modest homes. Local builder Herbert Moffat constructed this Schley Avenue (Emerson Street) block of Dutch Colonial vernacular houses about 1906. Moffat applied building trade principles learned from a District firm to his local work. Moffat, like others, blended his work—assessor and justice of the peace—with his business contacts. (PGCHS.)

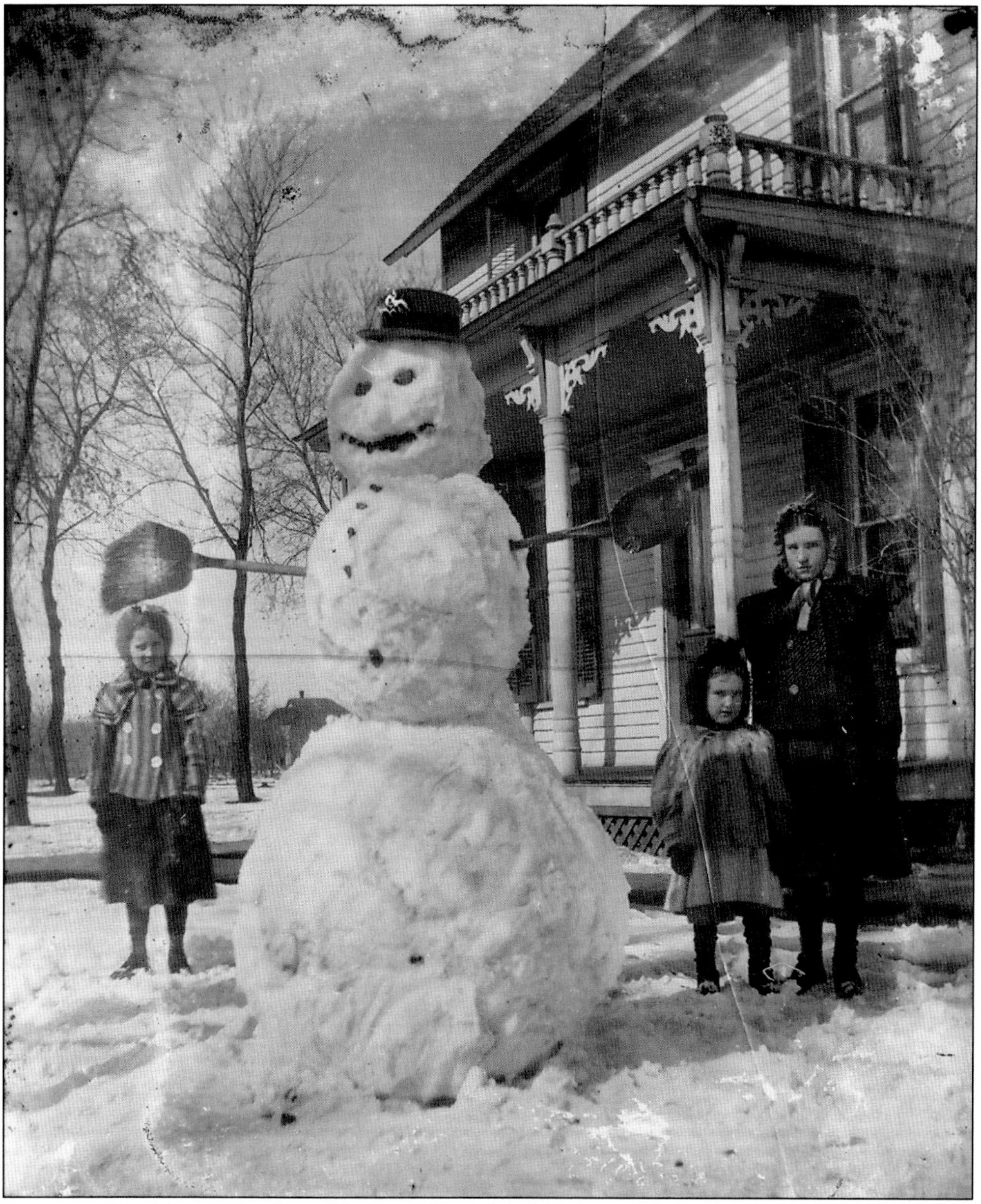

Benjamin Guy's house was located east of the railroad on Guy Avenue (Emerson Street). Herman and Catherine Burgess purchased the property and subdivided the land into improved lots. Winter was a favorite time for the family's children, who built a snowman seen here in front of their home around 1900. (PGCHS.)

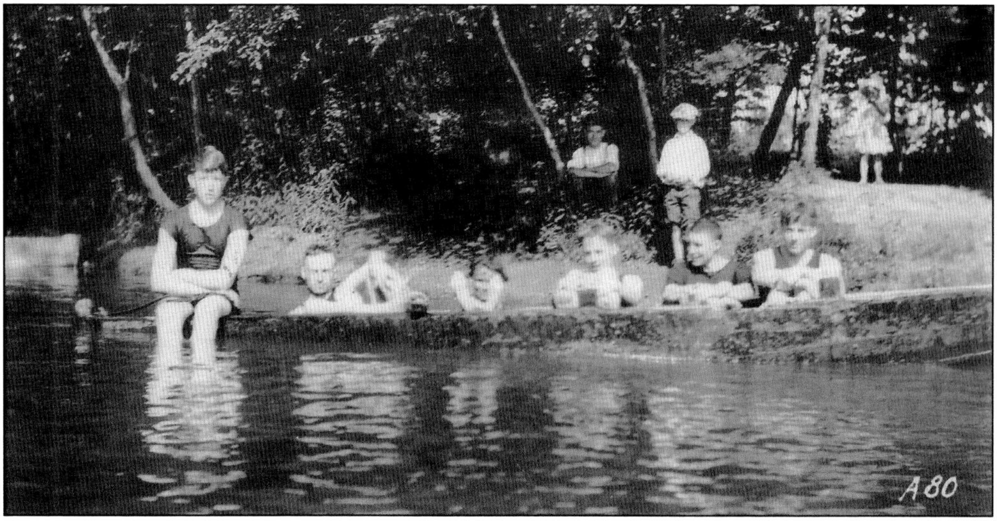

One of the local swimming holes in 1900 was near Carriage Road, now the 4700 block of Forty-first Avenue. This was a common route for area truck farmers bringing produce for sale. Heavily loaded wagons getting stuck in the muddy, unpaved road were often assisted by the swimmers. In reward for turning the wagon wheels, the boys received berries or other fruit from the farmer. (Above, PGCHS; below, Doug Dudrow.)

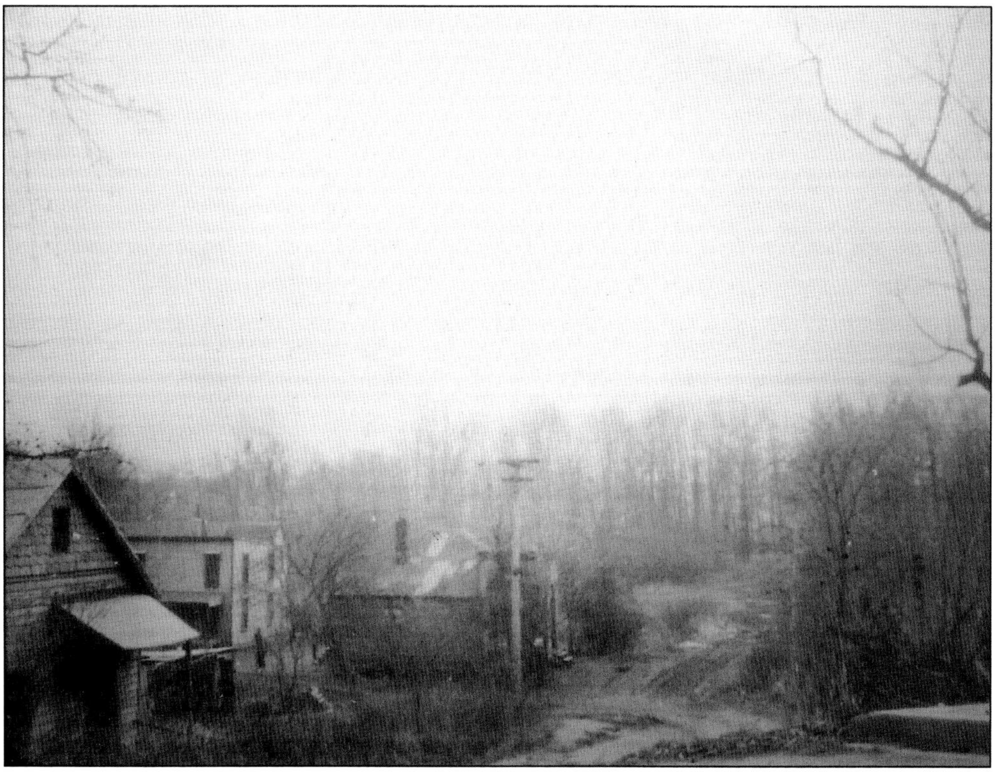

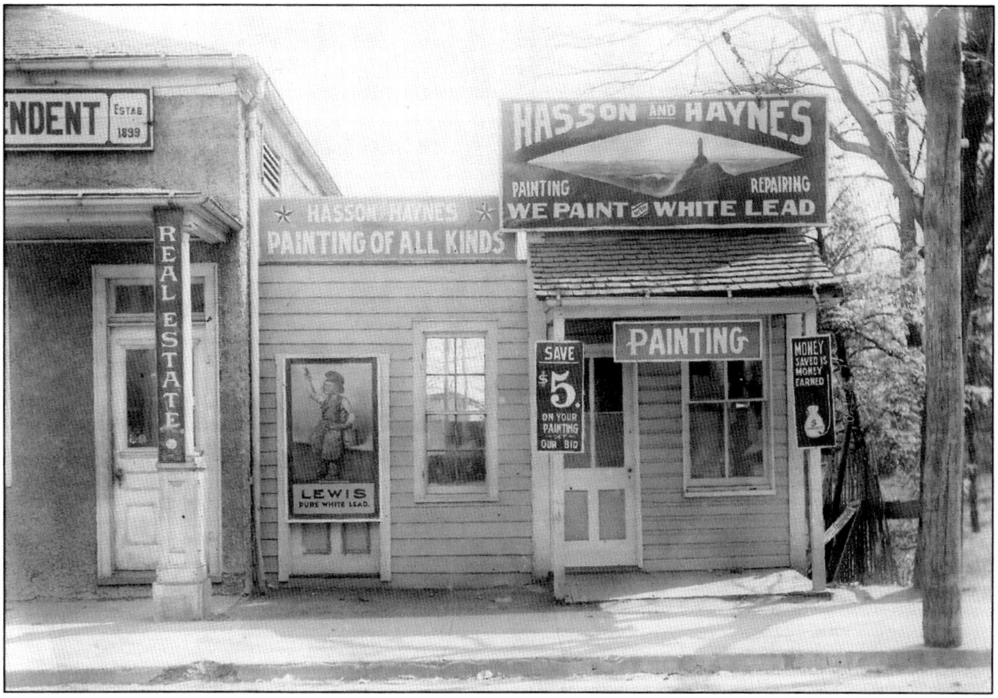

Small businesses proliferated around town in the 1900s. Hasson and Haynes painters and the neighboring real estate office were located on the south side of Johnson Avenue (the 4300 block of Farragut Avenue). The low wall between the buildings hid barrels of turpentine and oil from the street. These buildings are now demolished. (PGCHS.)

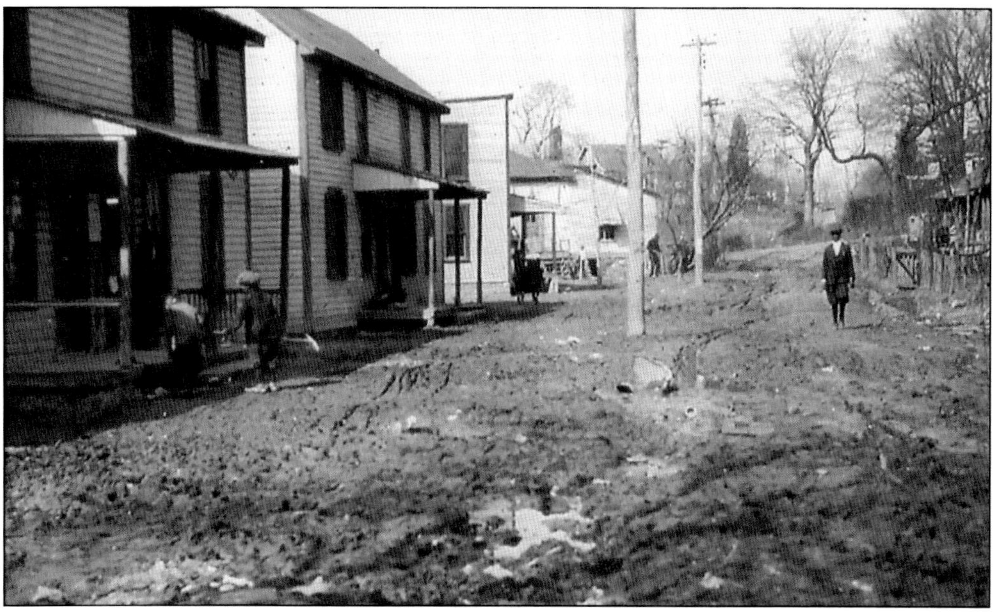

These Railroad Avenue homes were located in the Melrose section of town near the now-closed railroad crossing at Crittenden Street. The house on the left, 14 Railroad Avenue, belonged to Hyattsville High School custodian John Brown in this 1920s photograph. His wife, Mary, worked as a domestic until joining the high school cafeteria. (Doug Dudrow.)

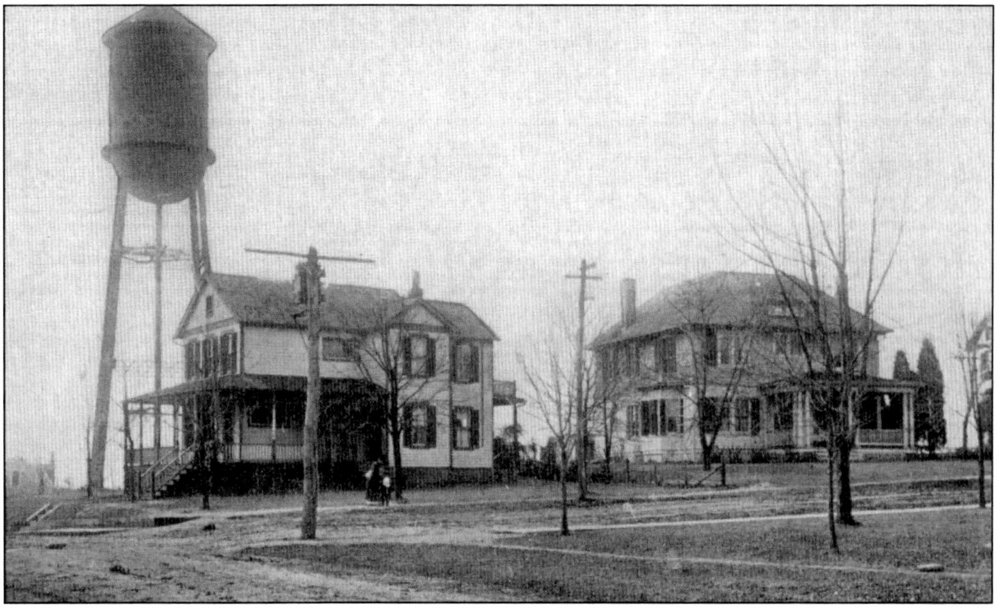

An 1898 drought dried many individual wells and focused the need for a public water system. In April 1901, $30,000 in bonds was sold and work began immediately. A well was drilled east of the railroad on Wells (Decatur) Avenue with a 100,000 gallon in-ground reservoir alongside. Water was pumped from the well to the reservoir and into the standpipe, seen here, located on Wine (Forty-second) Avenue and Franklin (Jefferson) Street. (PGCHS.)

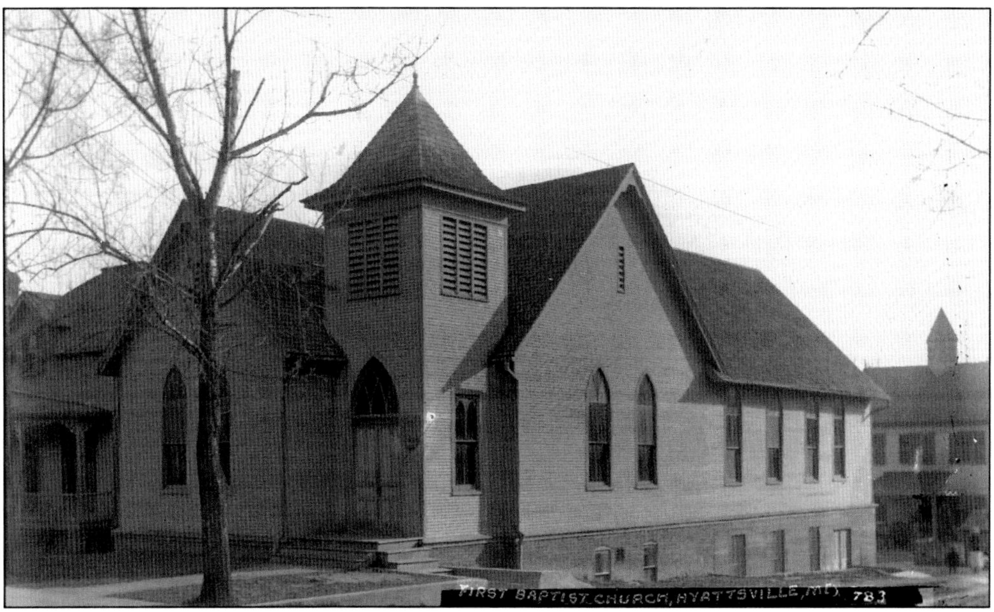

Rev. G. S. Williams of Washington's Metropolitan Baptist Church organized area Baptists in 1897. Rev. Franklin Rattray began services in January 1898 in the Methodist Episcopal Church South. Members purchased a $452 lot at Spencer (Gallatin) Street and Ravenswood (Forty-third Avenue) in February 1899. Contractors Dozier, Poppleton, and Pound were hired in July 1901 for $2,450 to complete the light-yellow clapboard and green-trimmed church. The first service conducted there was November 10, 1901. (HSWDC.)

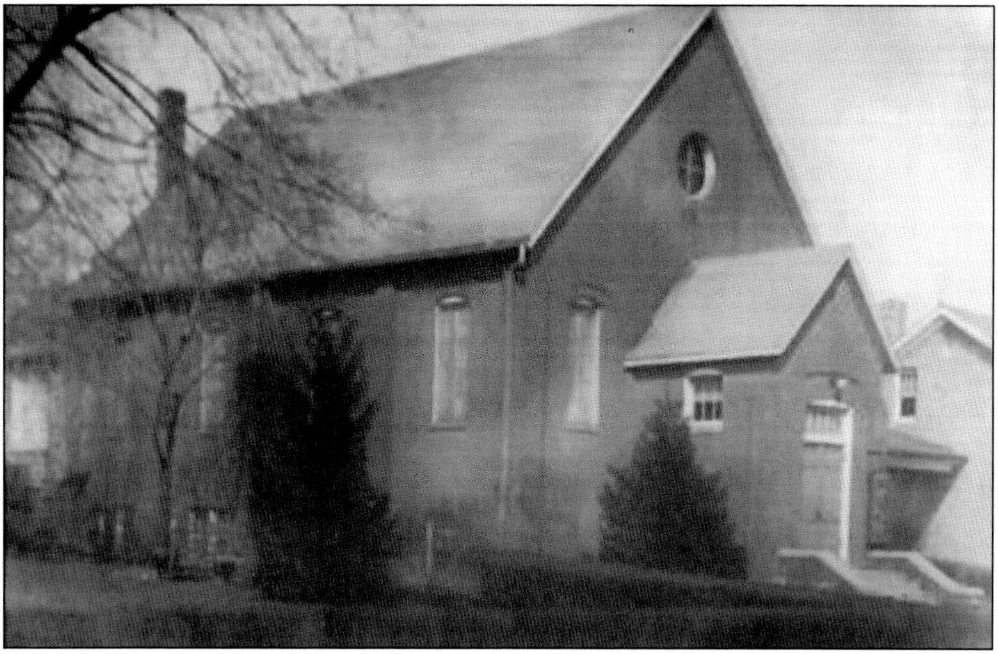

Roger Bellis built Memorial Methodist Church in 1902 at his own expense in memory of his wife, Rebecca, and deeded it to the church's Baltimore Conference. The congregation moved to its new Johnson Avenue (4300 block of Farragut Avenue) location from Bladensburg, where the Southern sympathizers had been dispossessed. The congregation moved in about 1950 to College Park. (Marion Robinson Dorn.)

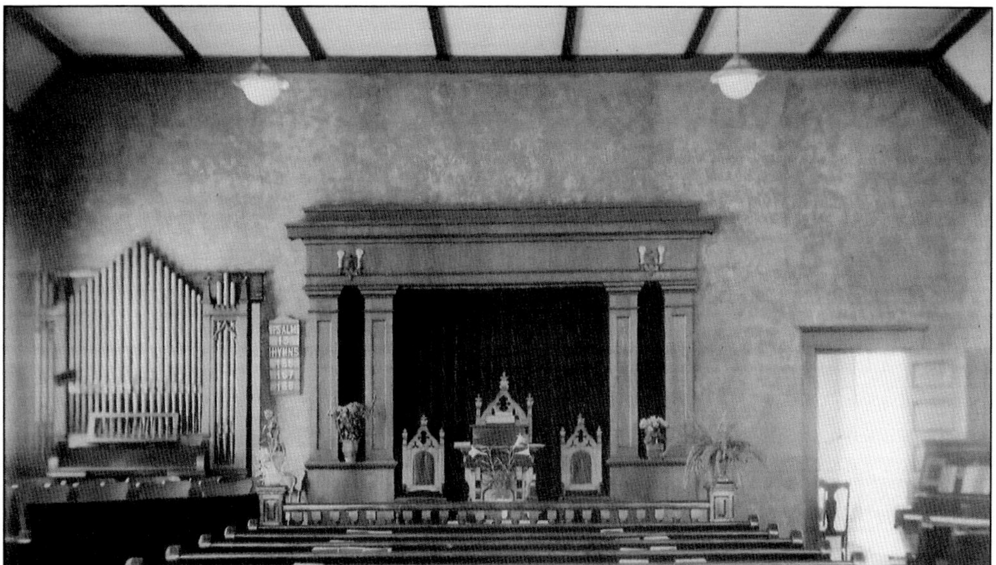

Resident Franklin Robinson helped construct Memorial Methodist Church shortly after moving to town. Robinson, honored for more than 40 years of trusteeship to the church, had dedicated to him the Robinson Bible Class room to the right of the sanctuary. The church was moved down the street from its original location, used for storage, and eventually burned. (Marion Robinson Dorn.)

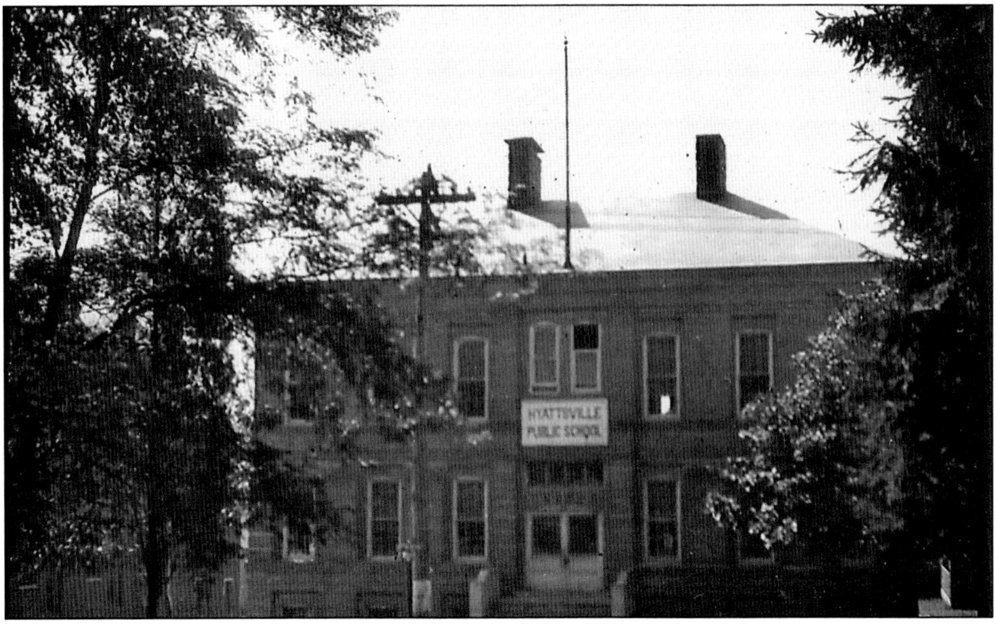

By May 1904, the school was too small and citizens petitioned the county again for a new building. Architects Walker and Webb designed a 50-student-capacity, eight-room brick building with basement, hot-air furnace, toilets, and drinking fountains for the new Spencer (Gallatin) Street location. A $10,902 contract was awarded to Townsend Scott, who completed the school for its September 1905 opening. Miss Robey was the new principal. (Doug Dudrow.)

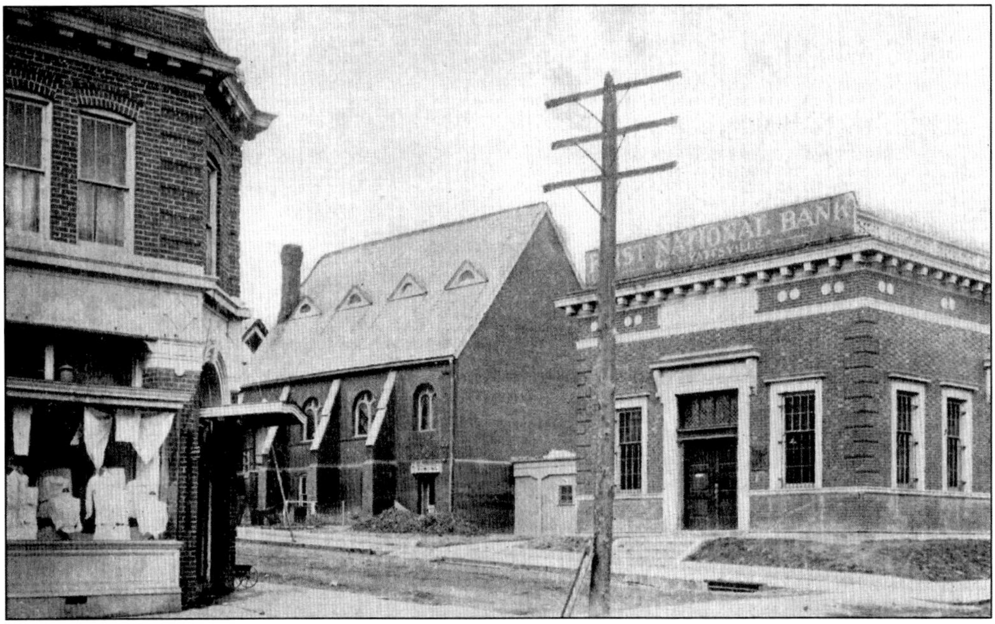

First National Bank opened on December 15, 1904, at Baltimore Avenue and Spencer (Gallatin) Street with $40,000 capital stock. Harry W. Shepherd, cashier, guaranteed three percent interest per annum on certificates of deposit of $50 or more left for six months. In 1915, the building was remodeled into its present form and electricity was installed. The bank failed in 1929, its accounts later secured by Prince George's Bank. (Kathy Albertson.)

The Hyattsville Gas and Electric Company was chartered in 1906 to make and sell gas and electricity for a 15-mile radius. Bartlett, Hayward, and Company of Baltimore organized the company with $50,000 capital stock with local A. S. Miller as its first president. Its electricity franchise was sold after its inauguration. Company offices were located at 5022 Rhode Island Avenue. (PGCHS.)

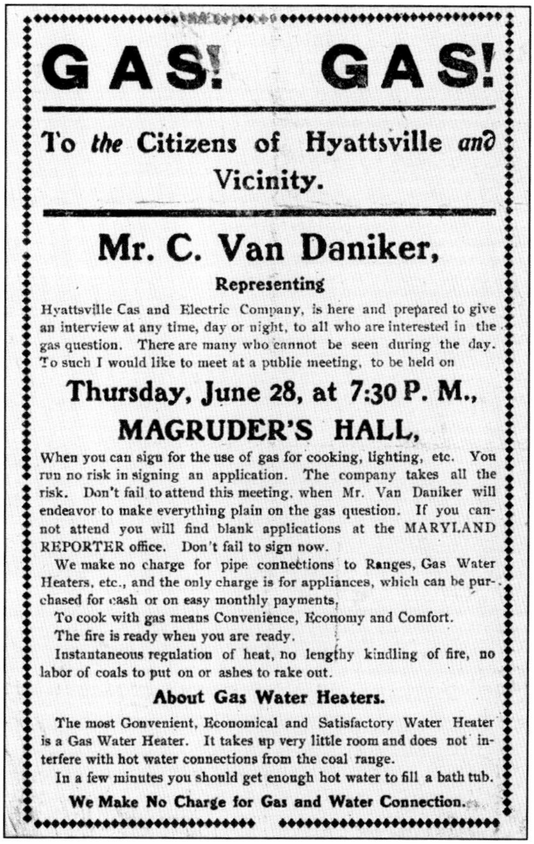

GAS! GAS!

To the Citizens of Hyattsville and Vicinity.

Mr. C. Van Daniker,

Representing

Hyattsville Cas and Electric Company, is here and prepared to give an interview at any time, day or night, to all who are interested in the gas question. There are many who cannot be seen during the day. To such I would like to meet at a public meeting, to be held on

Thursday, June 28, at 7:30 P. M.,

MAGRUDER'S HALL,

When you can sign for the use of gas for cooking, lighting, etc. You run no risk in signing an application. The company takes all the risk. Don't fail to attend this meeting, when Mr. Van Daniker will endeavor to make everything plain on the gas question. If you cannot attend you will find blank applications at the MARYLAND REPORTER office. Don't fail to sign now.

We make no charge for pipe connections to Ranges, Gas Water Heaters, etc., and the only charge is for appliances, which can be purchased for cash or on easy monthly payments.

To cook with gas means Convenience, Economy and Comfort.

The fire is ready when you are ready.

Instantaneous regulation of heat, no lengthy kindling of fire, no labor of coals to put on or ashes to rake out.

About Gas Water Heaters.

The most Convenient, Economical and Satisfactory Water Heater is a Gas Water Heater. It takes up very little room and does not interfere with hot water connections from the coal range.

In a few minutes you should get enough hot water to fill a bath tub.

We Make No Charge for Gas and Water Connection.

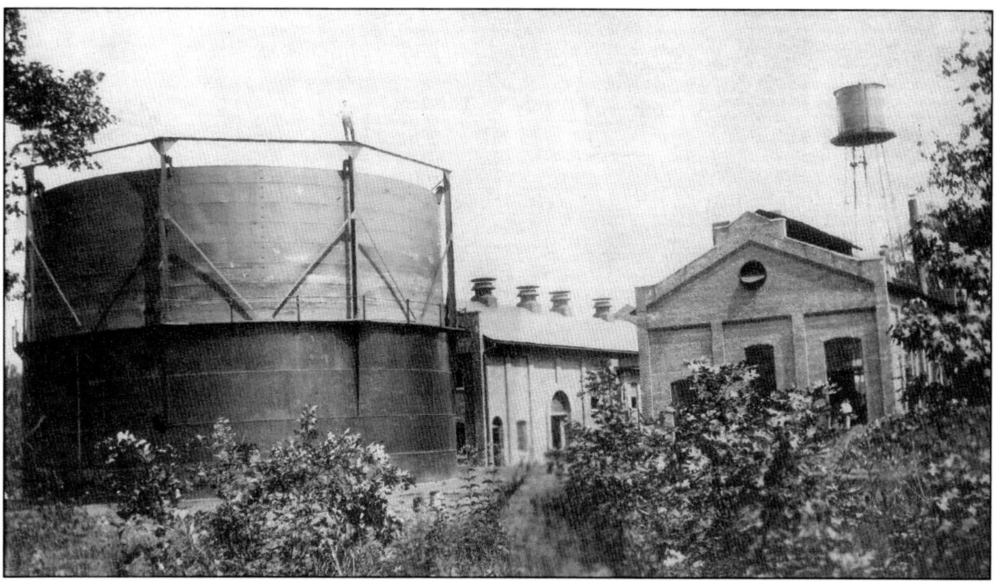

The new Edmonston plant had a container that stored 60,000 cubic feet and fed 6 miles of gas mains. Service began in October 1907 with 210 customers, including the water plant and Peter George for his confectionery store. Residents used the gas only for cooking and lighting. In one year, customers more than doubled. (PGCHS.)

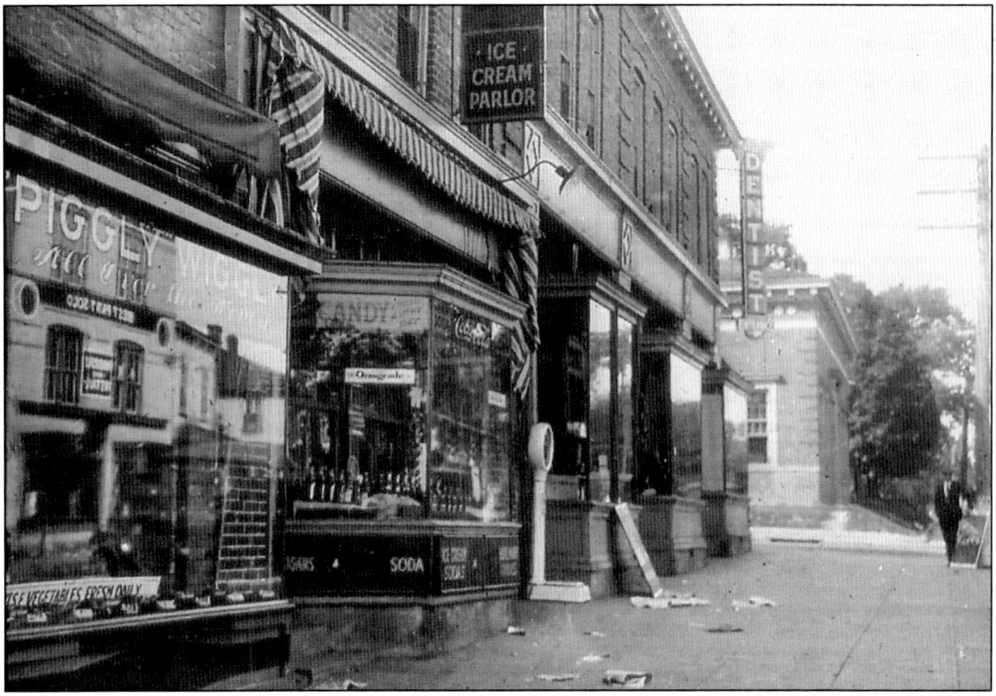

The Hyattsville Candy Kitchen was opened by Peter George on Baltimore Avenue around 1905. It was one of only a handful of businesses at the time. In the early days, a nickel would purchase a soda or other confectionery delights—handmade fresh every day. The store passed to his son Anthony and was one of the longest operating businesses in the city. Over the years, the name changed to George's Confectionary and later to George's Card Shop. (Doug Dudrow.)

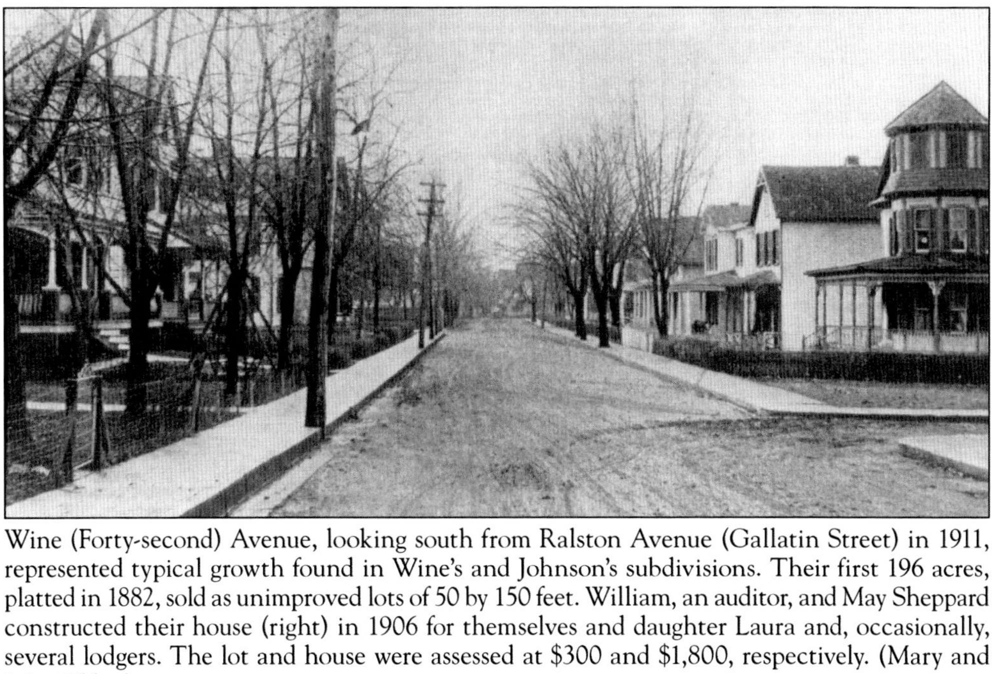

Wine (Forty-second) Avenue, looking south from Ralston Avenue (Gallatin Street) in 1911, represented typical growth found in Wine's and Johnson's subdivisions. Their first 196 acres, platted in 1882, sold as unimproved lots of 50 by 150 feet. William, an auditor, and May Sheppard constructed their house (right) in 1906 for themselves and daughter Laura and, occasionally, several lodgers. The lot and house were assessed at $300 and $1,800, respectively. (Mary and John Sibley.)

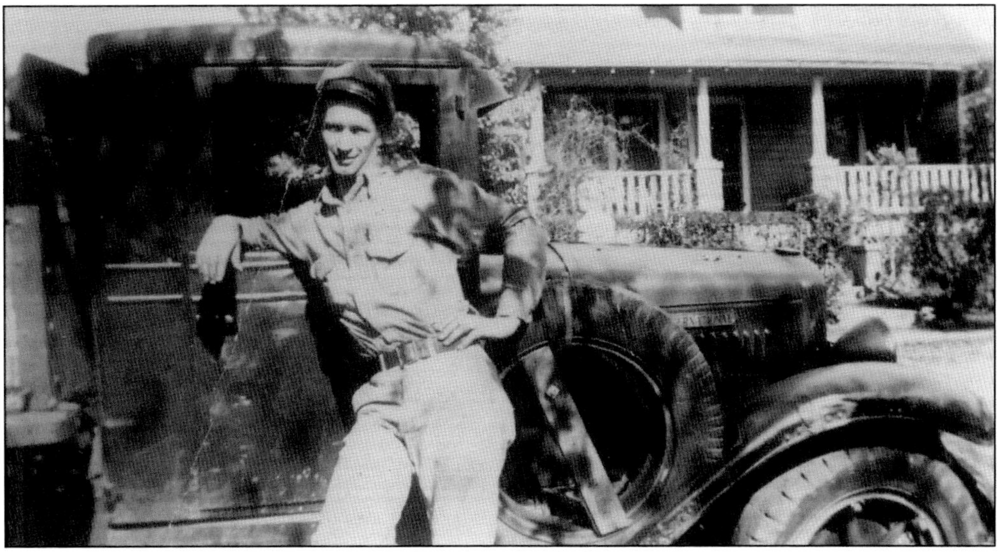

The Equitable Ice Company initially offered ice made from Spa Springs water in June 1908. It was the first ice manufacturer in the area, using a coal-fired steam boiler to power a compressor. At 30¢ per 100 pounds, customers were encouraged to specify a quantity and delivery would be prompt. Iceman Eddie Thorpe provided home deliveries from the company's plant near the Anacostia and the Point Lookout Railroad. (PGCHS.)

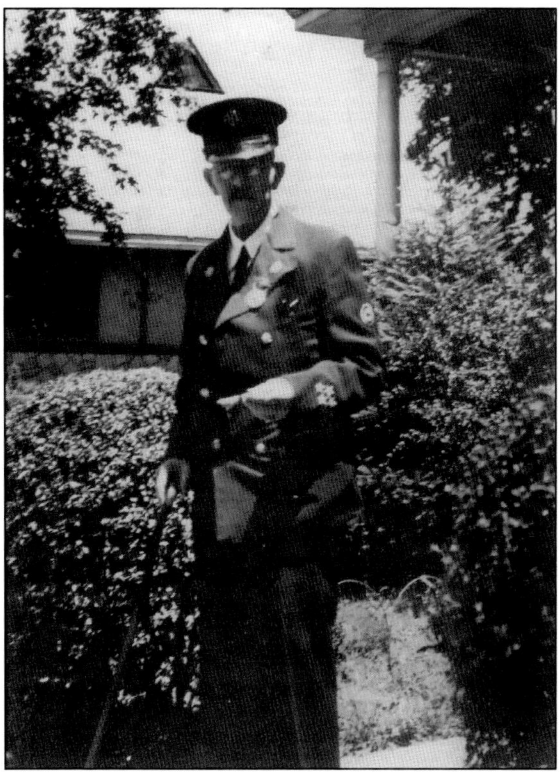

John and Mary Fainter moved to Sibley (Buchanan) Avenue in 1896. John began work immediately with the fire department, serving as chief in 1906 and 1916, before resigning to become city inspector. Mary was involved actively in the ladies' auxiliary. John was also councilman, 1902–1916; interim mayor, 1908; and justice of the peace, beginning in 1921, for more than 15 years. (City of Hyattsville.)

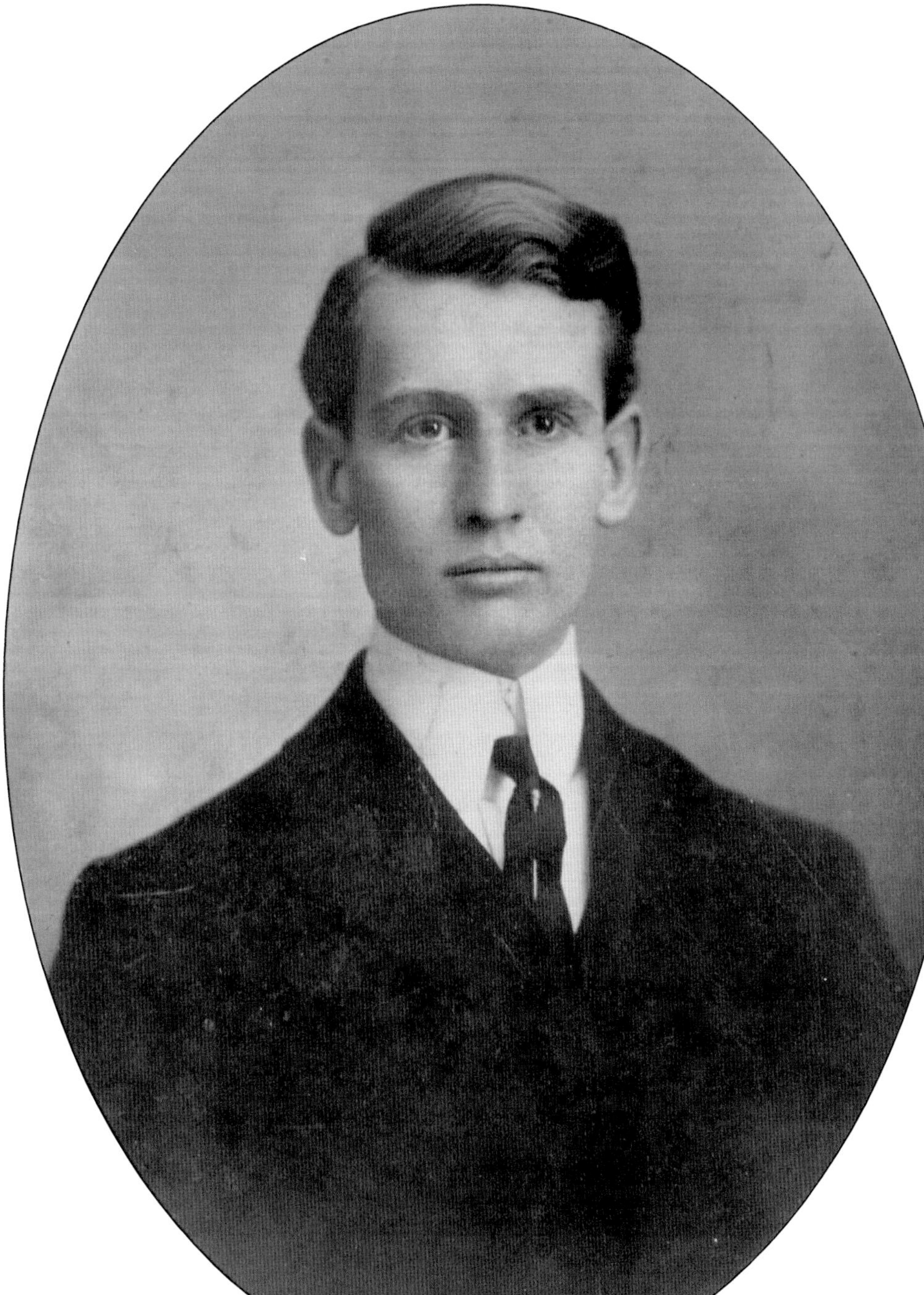

Rexford M. Smith (pictured) and partner Anthony Jannus, representing the Emerson Engine Company of Alexandria, Virginia, were local pioneers of aviation, testing their planes at the nearby College Park Airport. (City of Hyattsville.)

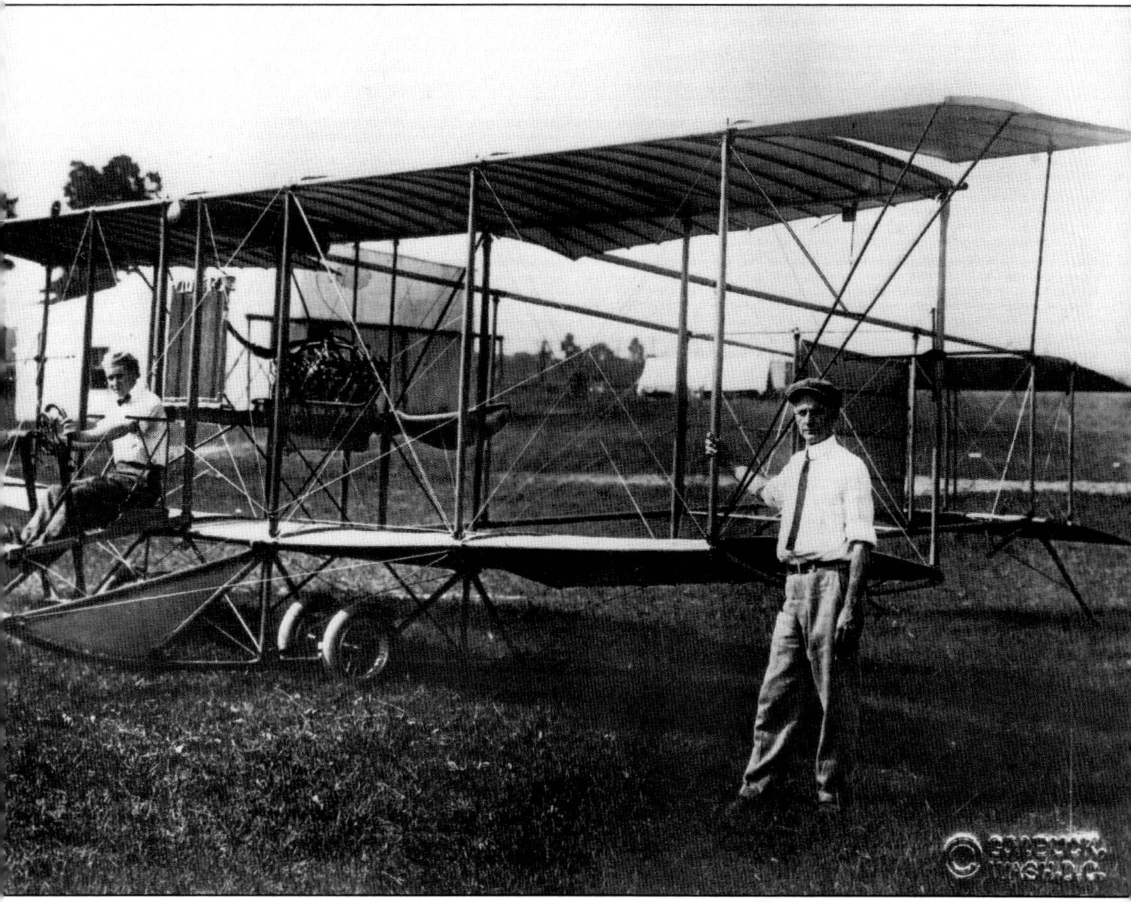

In 1910, some 100 spectators gathered to watch Smith's handcrafted 100-horsepower biplane circle the airfield, 1.5 miles, at 100 feet altitude—a height and distance set by the Wright brothers the previous year in College Park. (College Park Aviation Museum.)

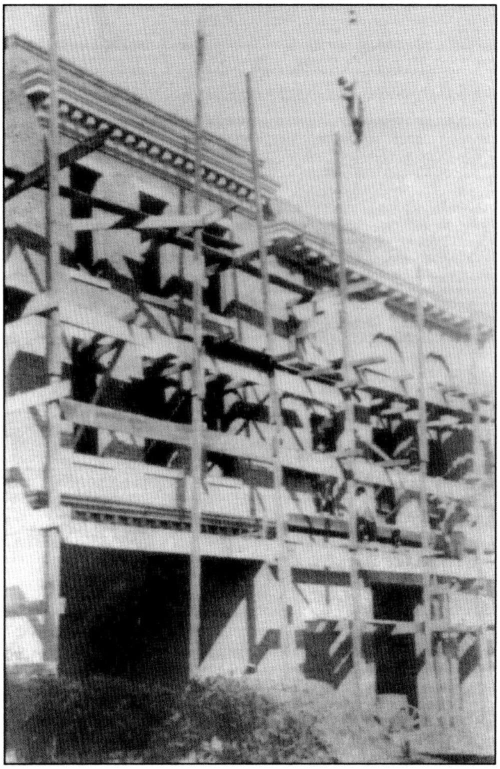

The city rented space for meetings and firefighting equipment storage since its incorporation nearly 25 years earlier. Council discussions began in early 1911 to construct the first municipal building and firehouse. Two sites were suggested, the council selecting Dr. H. T. Willis's property, 23 Johnson (4334 Farragut) Avenue, for $1,000 next to the post office. Former councilmen J. Frank Rushe and William A. Brooks enjoined the city to stop the purchase, causing nearly a year of litigation. On February 23, 1912, the city passed an act authorizing erection of the building. A sum of $2,400 was borrowed from the Hyattsville Building Association, and a $6,555 contract was let to Burgess and Parsons on August 5, 1912. Alex Hasson worked hanging from the flagpole during these various stages of construction. (Both PGCHS.)

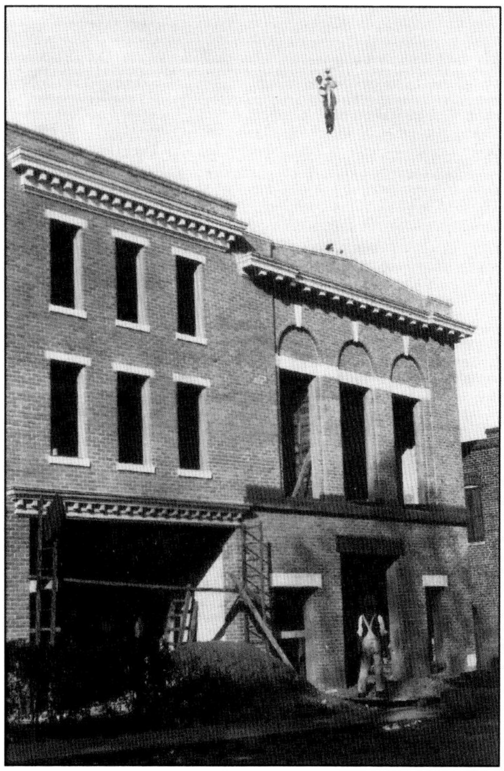

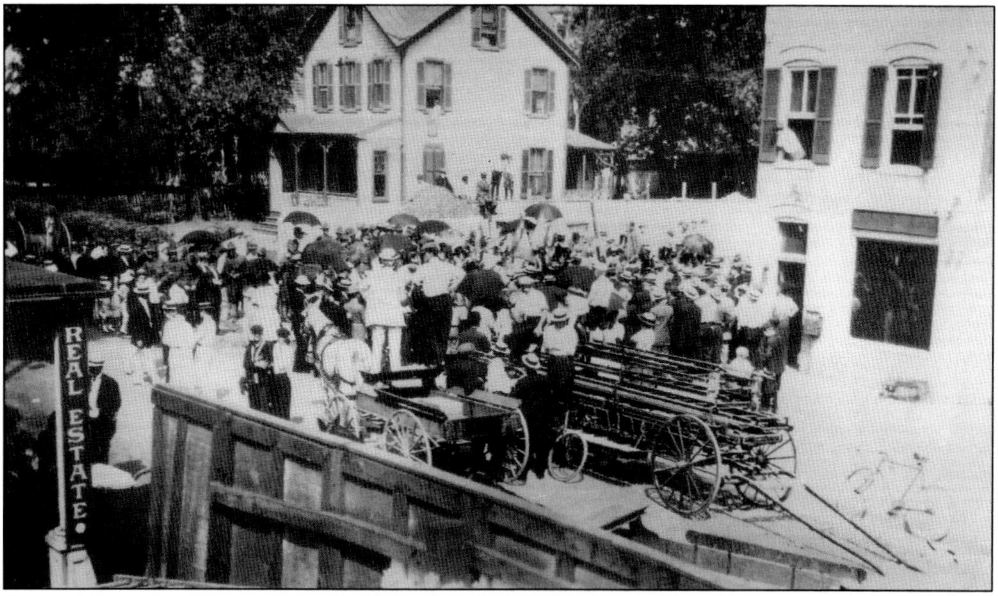

Despite the controversy, a crowd gathered on this sunny September 2, 1912, day for the elaborate cornerstone-laying ceremony. A house was moved recently from the property to make way for the new construction. Volunteer fire department members rode to the gathering on the ladder truck seen in the foreground. (PGCHS.)

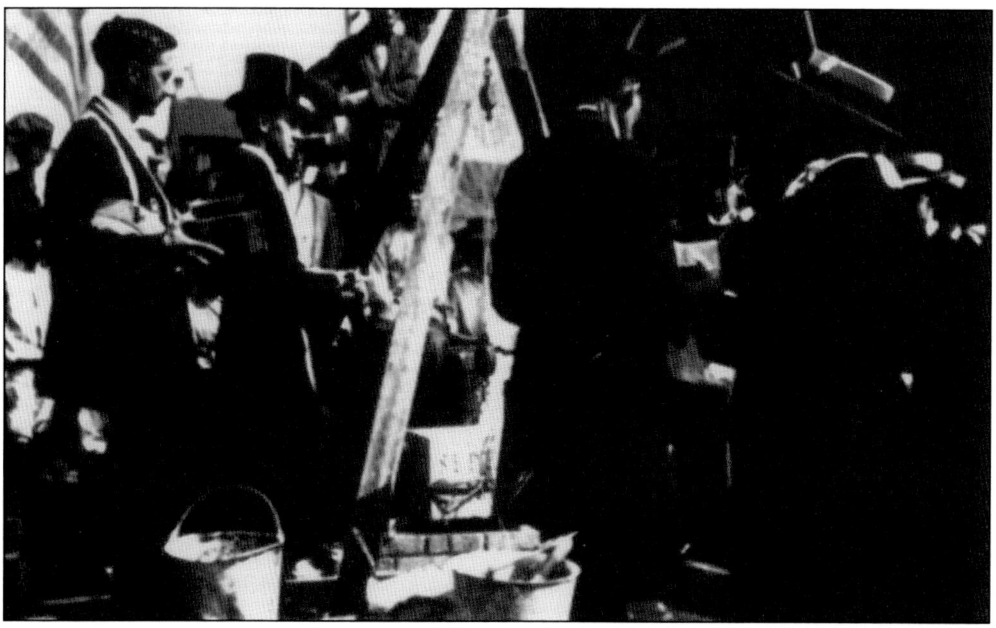

Mount Hermon Lodge members conduct the ceremonies around the cornerstone suspended by a wooden tripod. From left to right, members G. Hodges Carr, Elmer Hutchinson, Dr. McMillan, and Herman Burgess (in straw hat) perform the dedication while Mayor Harry W. Shepperd watches in the background. The building was accepted officially December 23, 1912. (City of Hyattsville.)

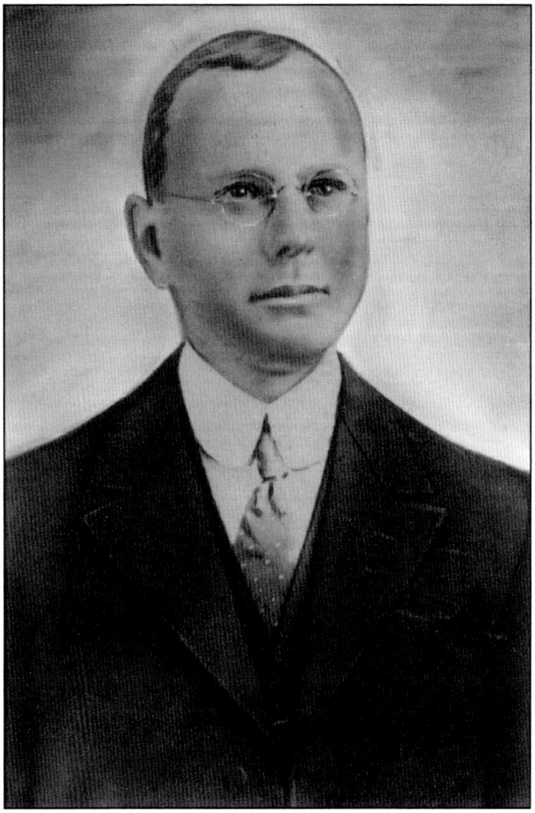

Company F, First Infantry, Maryland National Guard, was mustered into service May 8, 1912, with 54 men. The company won marksmanship competitions in 1912, 1914, and 1915, including the War Department's National Trophy. Without an armory, guardsmen met in the Municipal Building. Oswald Granger organized the guard and was elected its first captain. Granger was mayor from 1914 to 1915. (City of Hyattsville.)

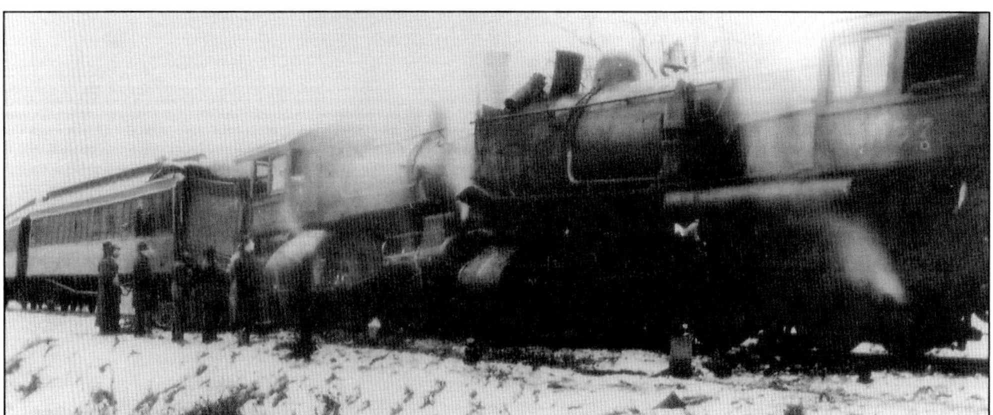

Hyattsville witnessed its share of train accidents over the years. This December 12, 1912, crash caused little damage other than to the two engines involved. Comparatively, an August 11, 1917, derailment destroyed the B&O switching tower. (City of Hyattsville.)

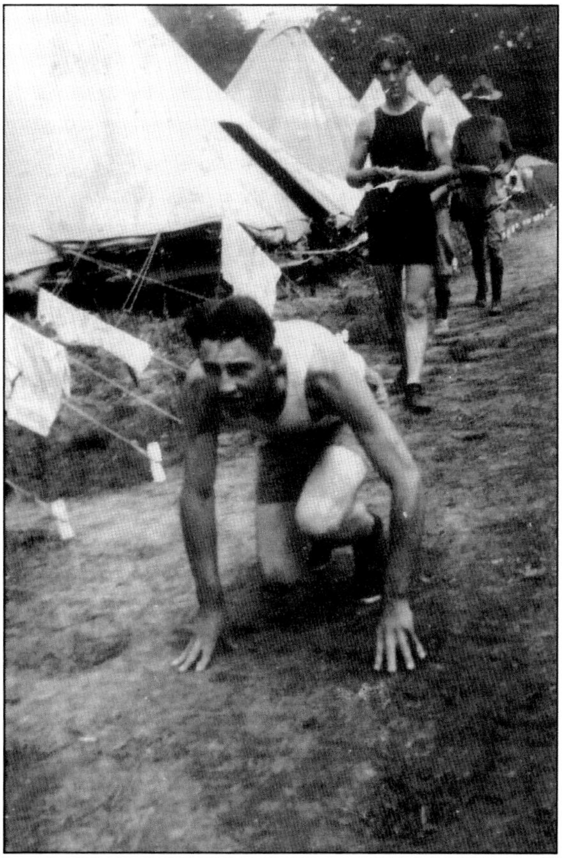

On July 25, 1917, Company F was called to service in World War I. As part of the 29th Infantry Division during the Meuse-Argonne Offensive, Company F's strength was vital in the German defeat. Veterans formed the Snyder-Farmer American Legion Post No. 3, honoring two of their fallen comrades. Shortly after returning from the war, Company F continued its training at Camp Ritchie in western Maryland. Wells Fainter (right) prepares to run a race. (Both City of Hyattsville.)

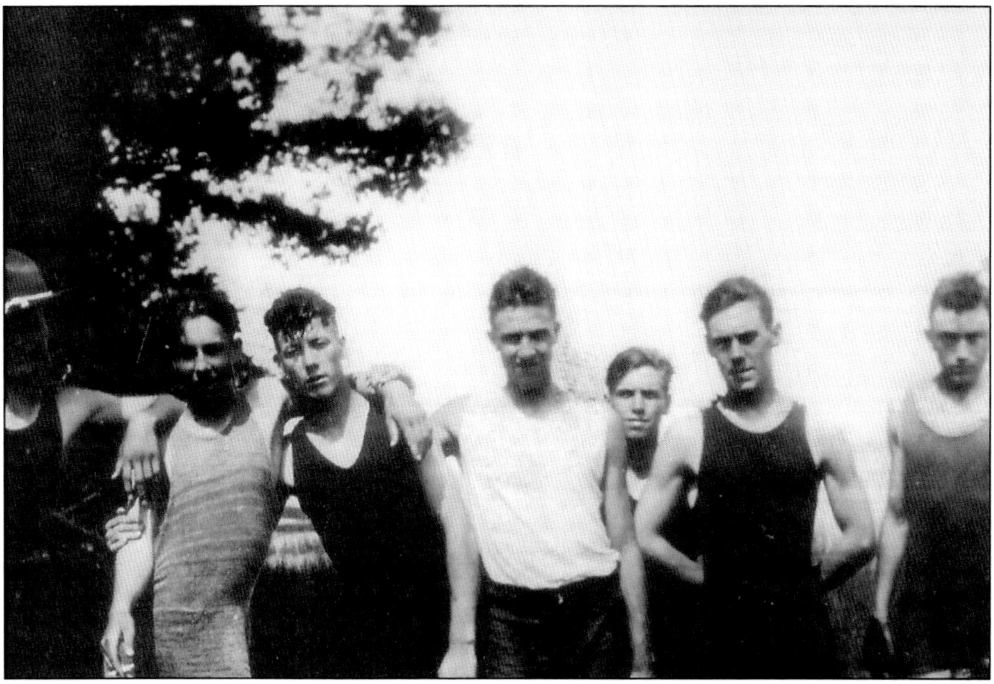

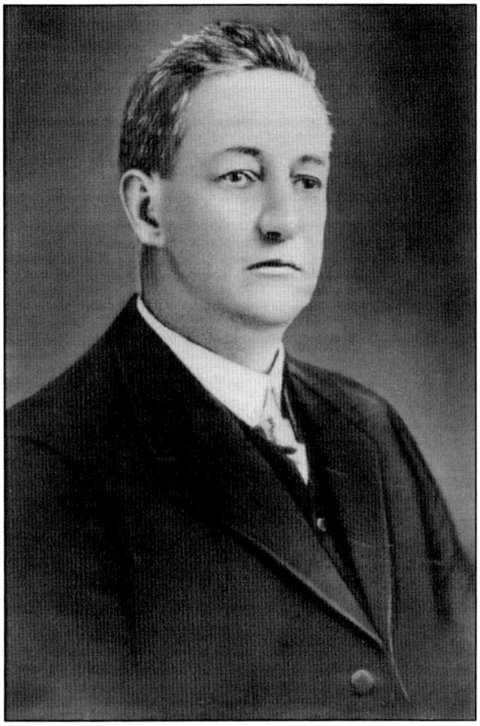

Mayor Harry Shepperd (1913–1914) welcomed the National American Woman Suffrage Association (NAWSA) delegation on July 31, 1913. More than 60 automobiles brought suffragists to the 10:00 a.m. rally in support of the Susan B. Anthony amendment to give women the constitutional right to vote. Shepperd welcomed all and presented NAWSA executive director Mary Ware Dennett a key to the city. (City of Hyattsville.)

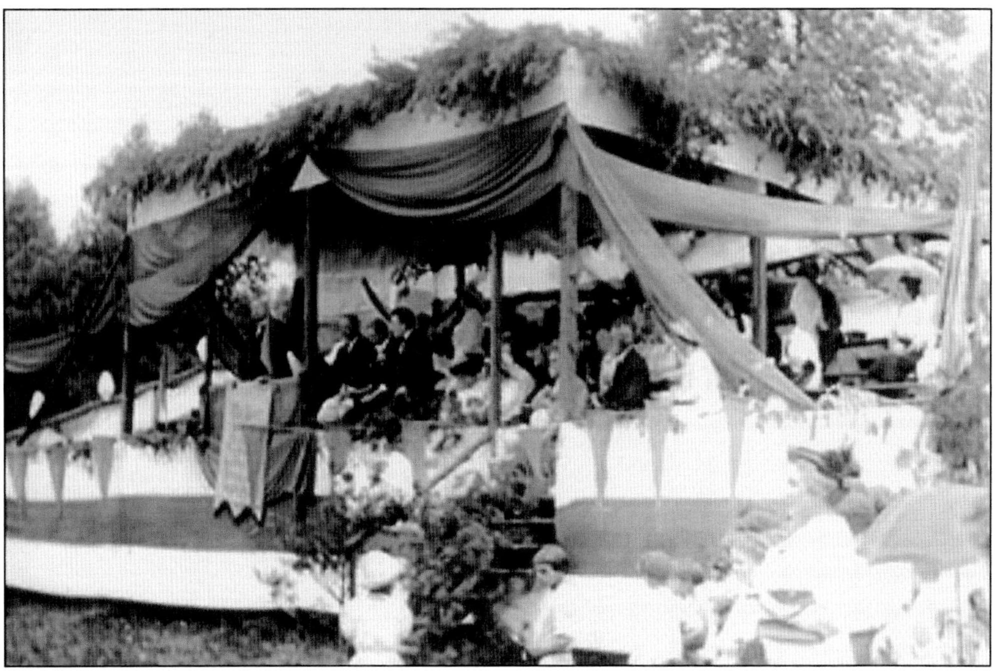

This rally was NAWSA's third largest event to date. Alice Paul, NAWSA's legislative committee chair, and Senate Woman Suffrage Committee members gave speeches. Suffragists from every state carried amendment petitions bearing 85,000 men's and women's signatures. Once entered into the official Senate record, this would be the first congressional debate on suffrage since 1887. (VintagePostcards.com.)

Dr. Cora Smith King (1867–1939) was a prominent figure in winning suffrage in Washington state. She transferred her medical practice to Washington, D.C., living in Hyattsville. She organized NAWSA's July 31 activities. King was the first woman to take and pass the North Dakota medical board examination and was licensed to practice on October 13, 1892. (Library of Congress, Manuscripts Division.)

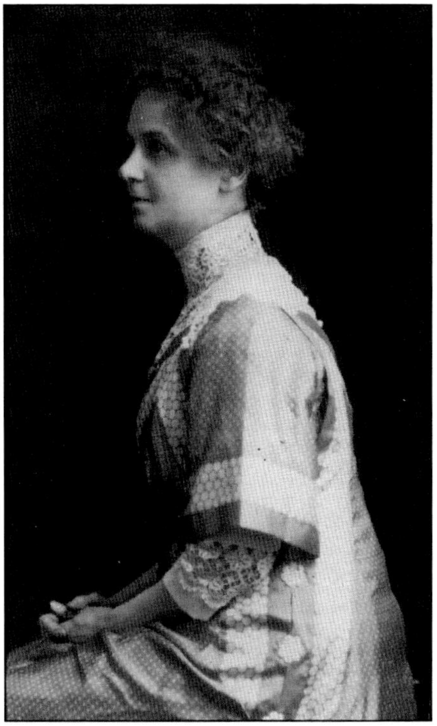

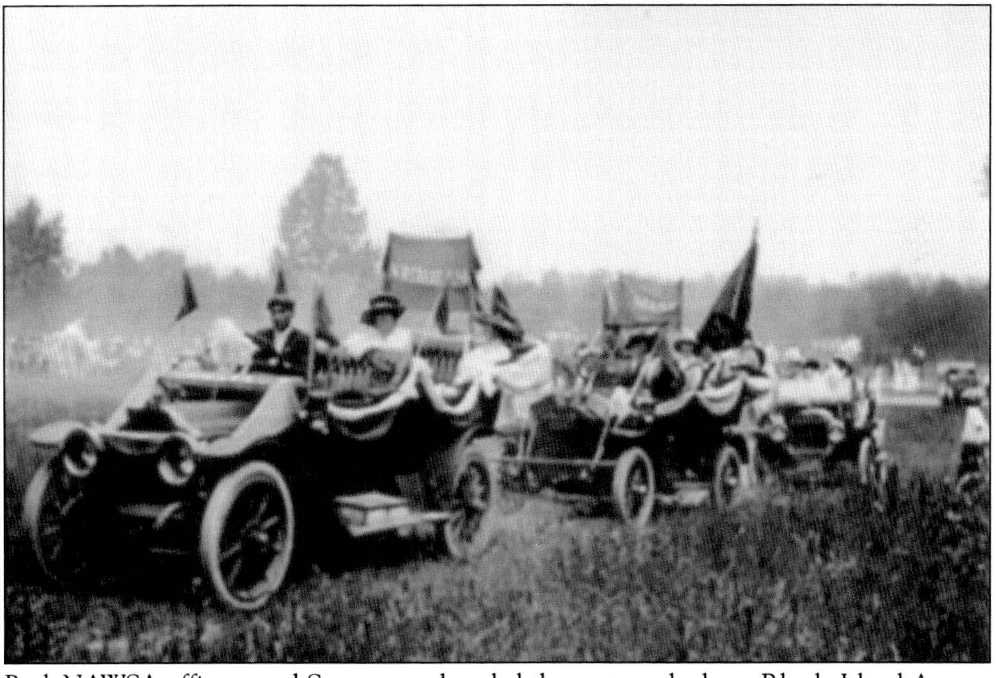

Paul, NAWSA officers, and Senate members led the motorcade down Rhode Island Avenue towards the Capitol. Fluttering flags and pennants announced each delegation's name. Upon arrival, a *Washington Post* report claimed the "suffrage army . . . besieged the Senate chamber and bombarded [s]enators with petitions," sparking a two-hour debate. The 19th Amendment was not ratified until August 18, 1920. (VintagePostcards.com.)

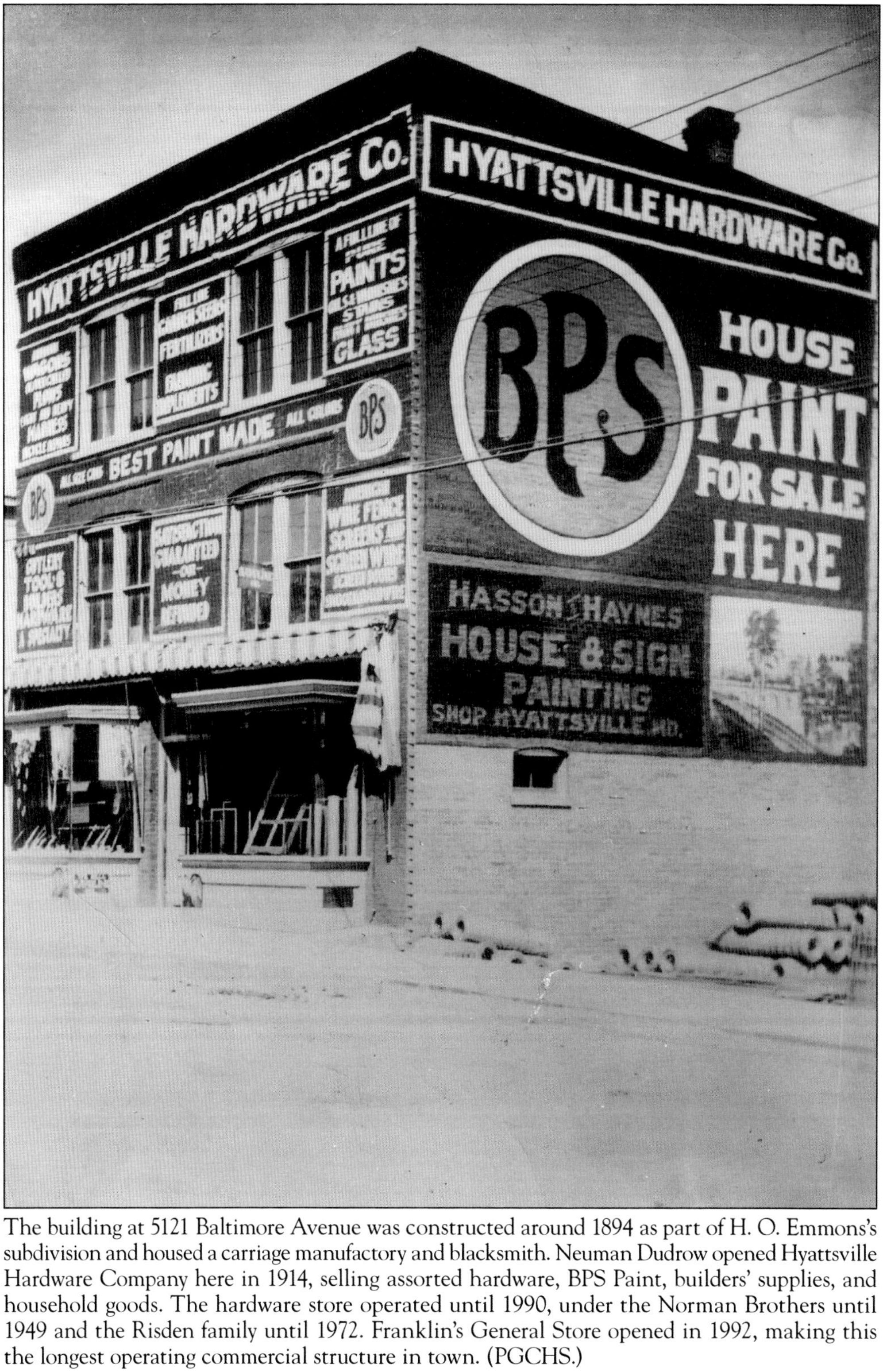

The building at 5121 Baltimore Avenue was constructed around 1894 as part of H. O. Emmons's subdivision and housed a carriage manufactory and blacksmith. Neuman Dudrow opened Hyattsville Hardware Company here in 1914, selling assorted hardware, BPS Paint, builders' supplies, and household goods. The hardware store operated until 1990, under the Norman Brothers until 1949 and the Risden family until 1972. Franklin's General Store opened in 1992, making this the longest operating commercial structure in town. (PGCHS.)

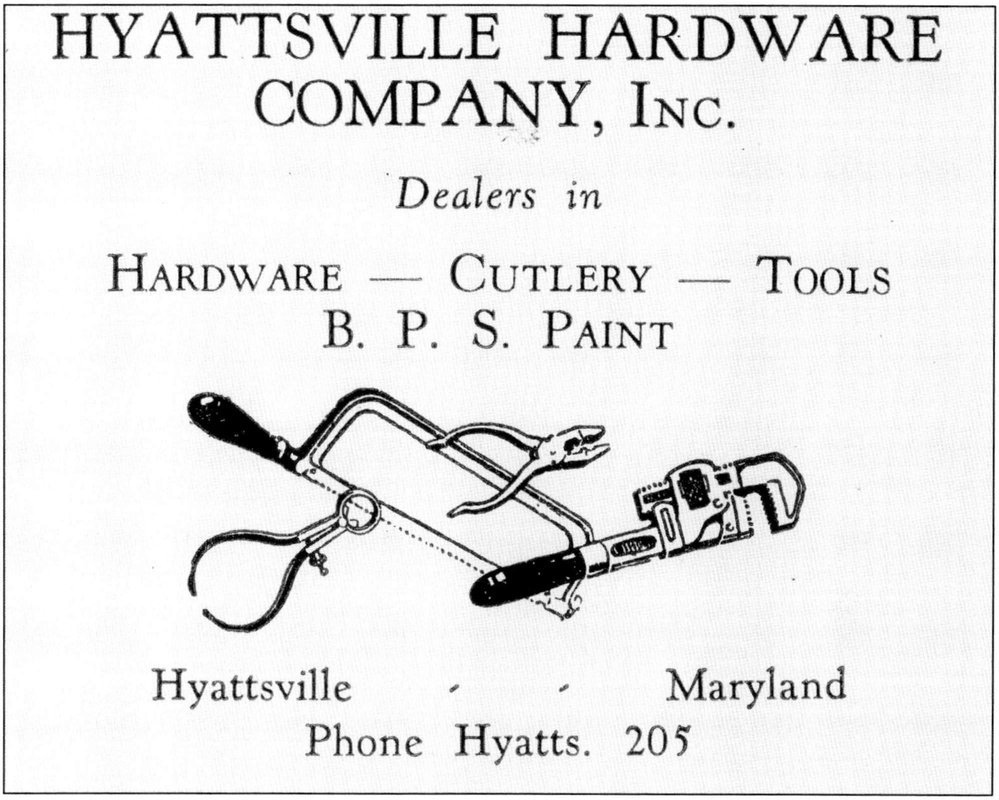

In this 1926 advertisement, Hyattsville Hardware announces its specialties—BPS Paint, tools, cutlery, and hardware. (City of Hyattsville.)

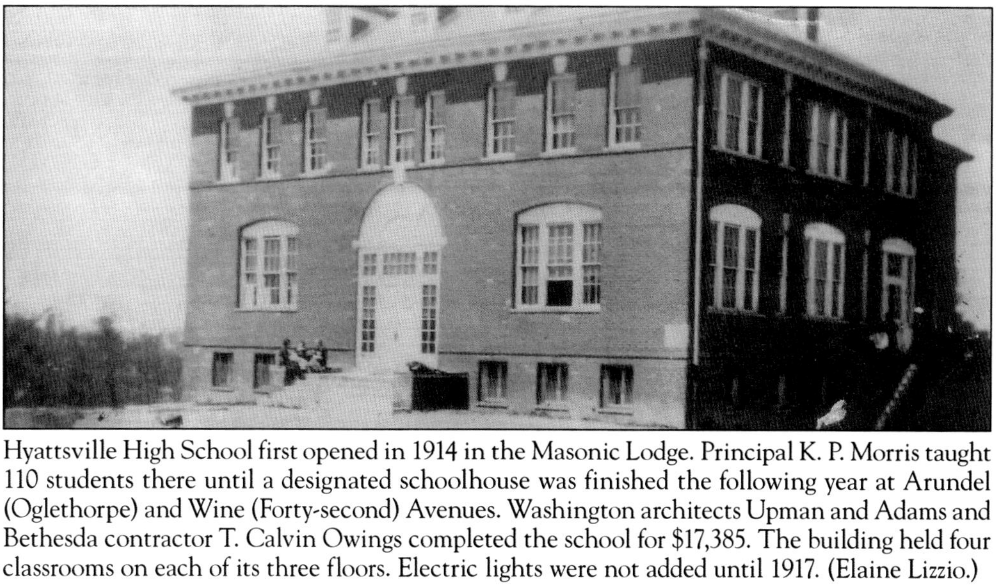

Hyattsville High School first opened in 1914 in the Masonic Lodge. Principal K. P. Morris taught 110 students there until a designated schoolhouse was finished the following year at Arundel (Oglethorpe) and Wine (Forty-second) Avenues. Washington architects Upman and Adams and Bethesda contractor T. Calvin Owings completed the school for $17,385. The building held four classrooms on each of its three floors. Electric lights were not added until 1917. (Elaine Lizzio.)

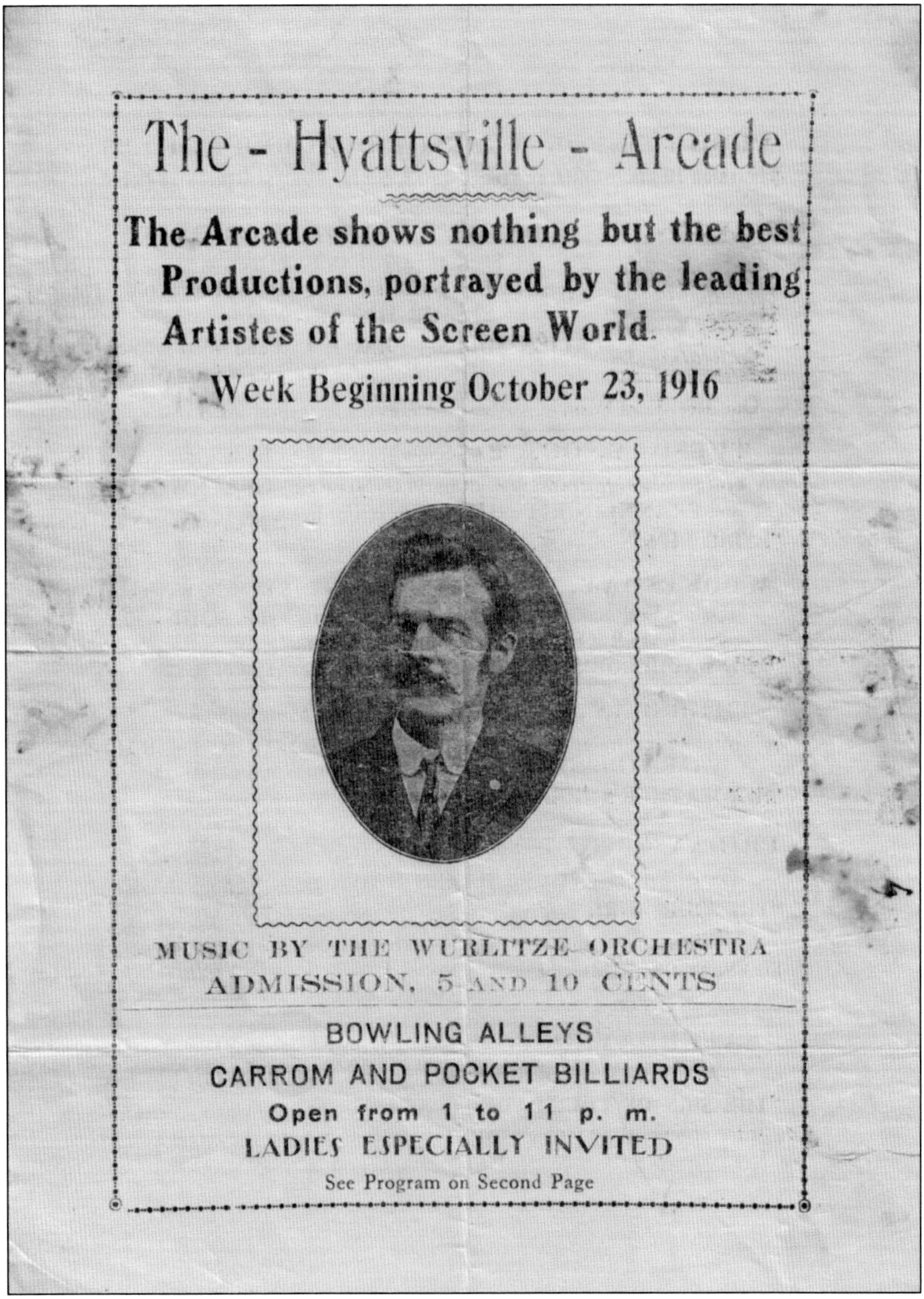

Frank Rushe purchased the first Pinkney Memorial Church after its 1913 move. He opened a remodeled and extended complex known as the Arcade. The basement accommodated four regulation bowling lanes. A cashier, refreshments, and three billiard tables were on the ground floor. The sanctuary was now an auditorium showing Paramount Photoplays every evening at 7:00 p.m. for 5¢ or 10¢ admission. Two storefronts housed a barbershop and ice cream parlor. (PGCHS.)

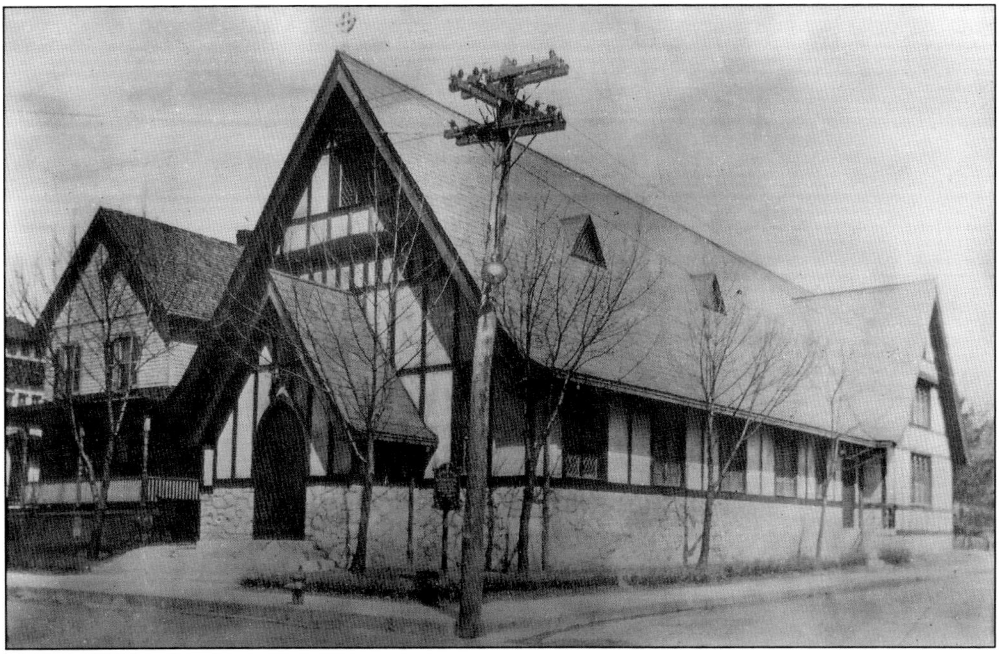

The Pinkney Memorial congregation, under Rev. Henry Thomas, outgrew its first church, so new property was purchased at Spencer (Gallatin) Street and Wine (Forty-second) Avenue in 1913. While in transition, parishioners worshipped at the Masonic Lodge. Ground was broken September 1915 and the first services held on June 11, 1916. The church was consecrated when the mortgage was burned in 1940. A fire destroyed the building in 1993. (Both Kathy Albertson.)

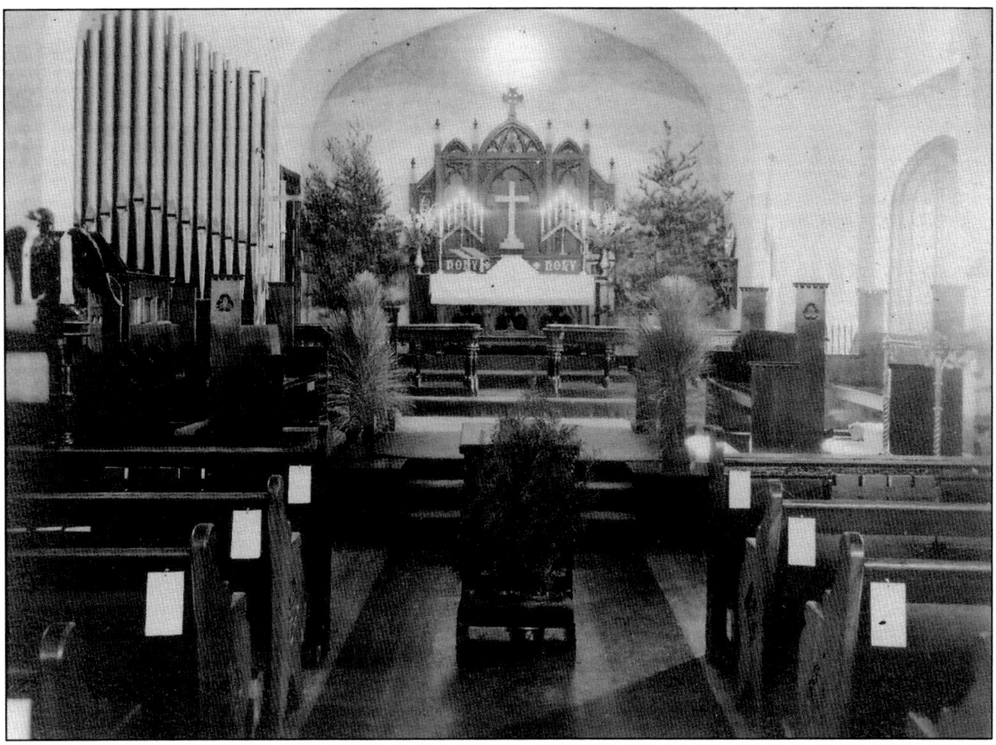

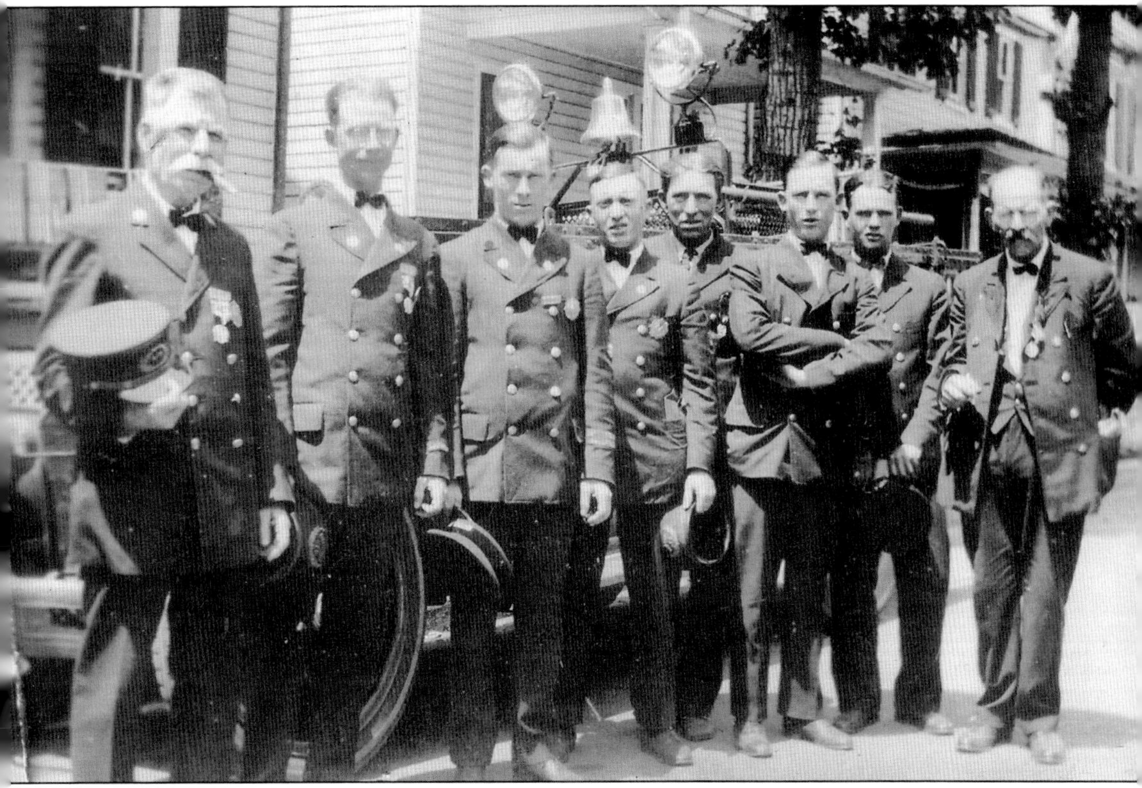

Volunteer fire department members stand in front of the city's first motorized fire engine, a Model T Ford, in 1918. Until this purchase, the fire engines were pulled by horse. The importance of motorized equipment was made clear during the November 30, 1912, fire at the Maryland Agricultural College, when a horse was harnessed to the equipment and died. Two buildings were lost in that fire. (City of Hyattsville.)

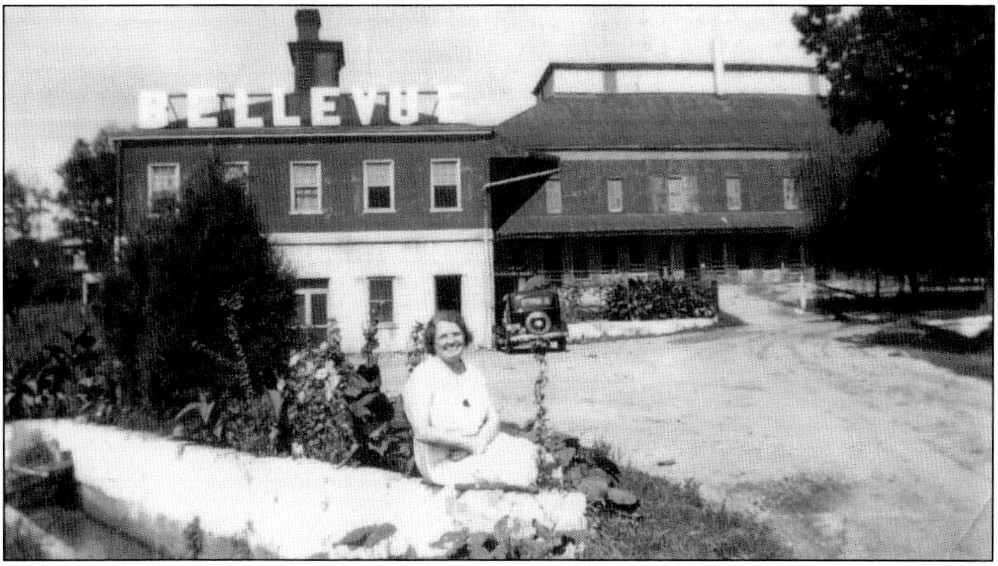

Christian Heurich brought his family to Bellevue Farm during Prohibition and World War I when anti-German sentiment peaked. His dairy barns, here, employed the latest technologies, including cement floors. Heurich was accused that these were bunkers from which to launch bombs at the Capitol. (City of Hyattsville.)

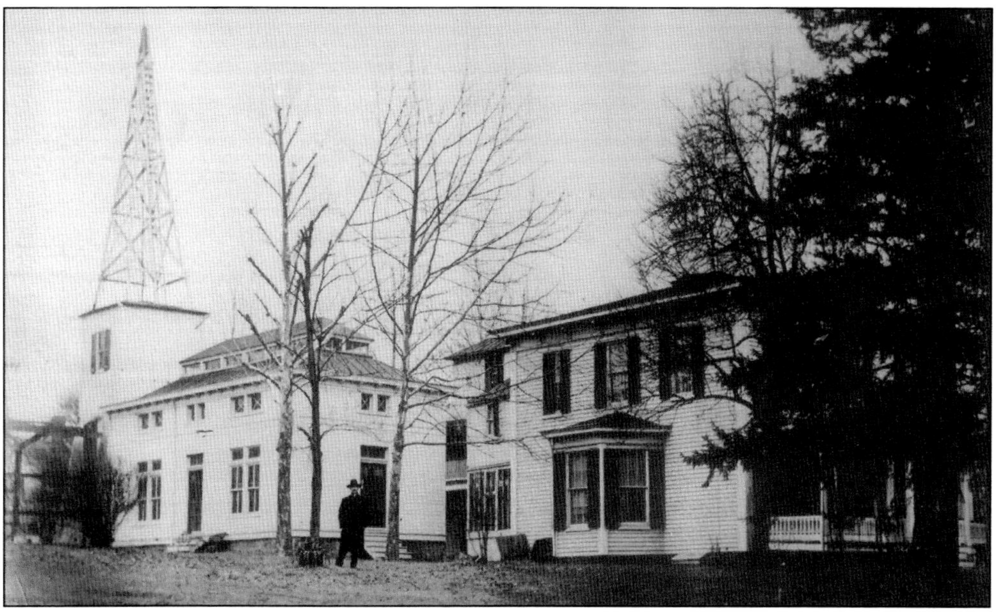

Dr. James Harris Rogers (1850–1929) was an internationally known inventor. Born in Franklin, Tennessee, Rogers was educated by private tutors and attended St. Charles College, London. The family moved to Bladensburg in 1877, at which time Rogers was chief electrician at the U.S. Capitol. In 1895, he purchased his home Firwood, seen here, on Baltimore Avenue (current site of the justice center). (PGCHS.)

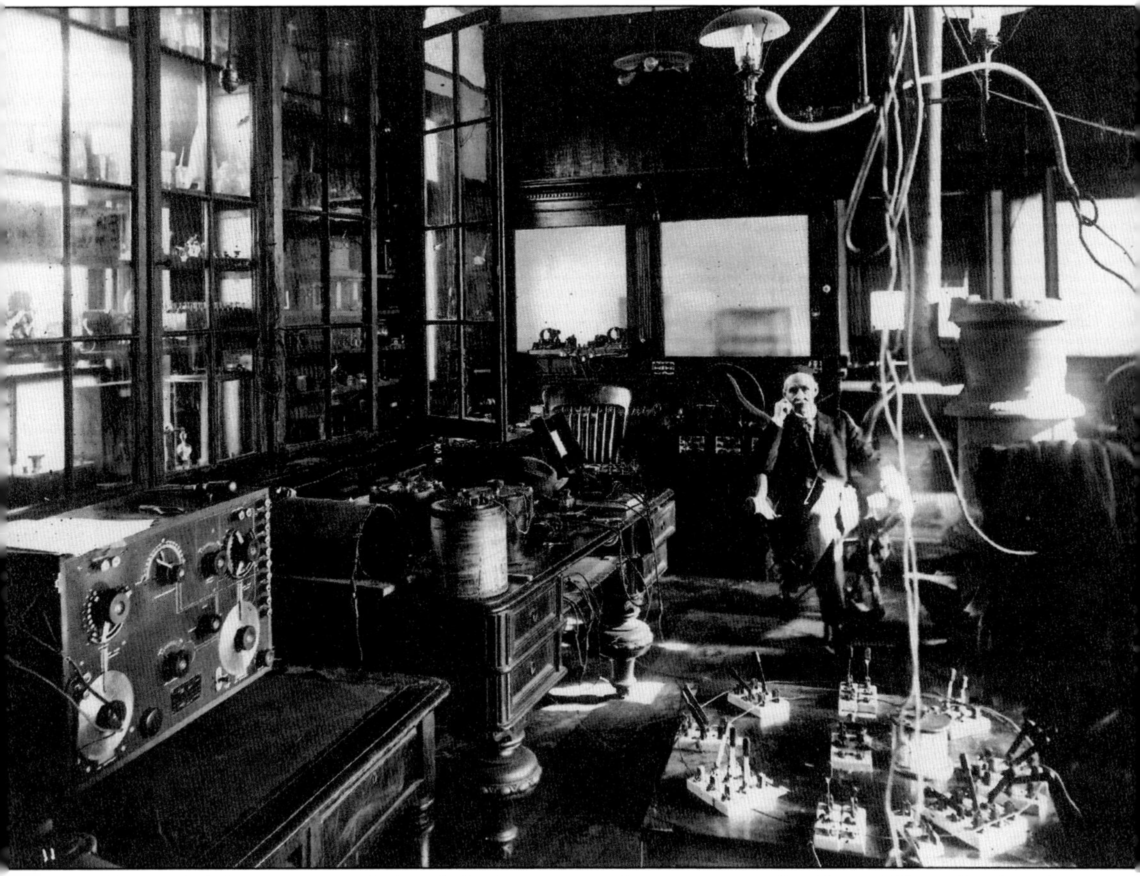

Rogers's laboratory was behind the house in a large separate building. The tall glass doors encased working models of his more than 50 patents, including improved electric lights and telephone system. In March 1895, his printed telegraph system transmitted successfully between Washington, D.C., and Baltimore, Maryland, at 200 words per minute. The Wright brothers visited after Rogers devised a plane with better stability in 1909. (Georgetown University Library, Special Collections.)

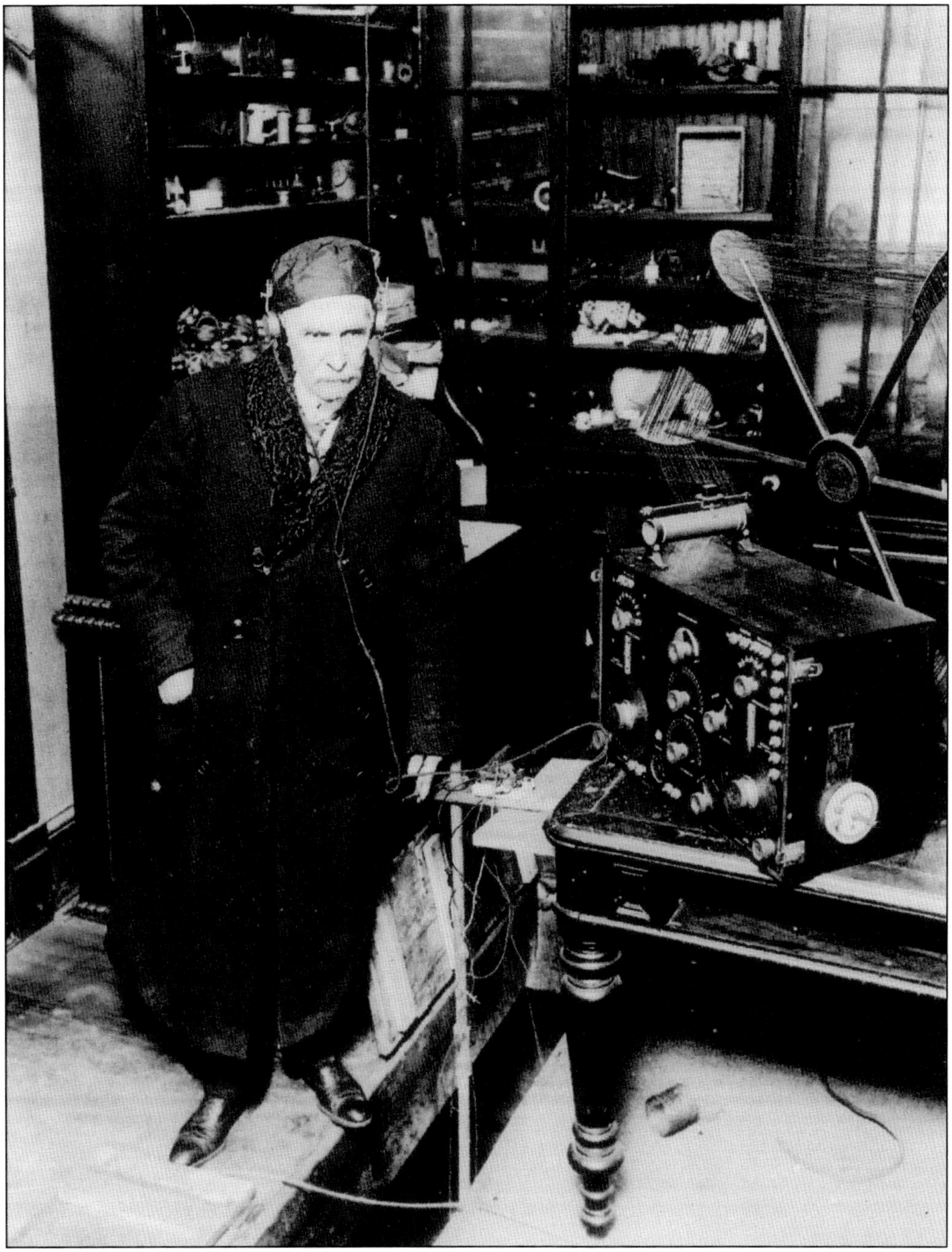

Rogers worked in 1908 on an undersea and underground wireless telegraphy system. He realized its importance at the start of World War I and offered it to the government. After an investigation, Secretary of the Navy Joseph Daniels expedited patents. Receiving stations were installed at Rogers' lab and at several naval stations. Messages from Germany detailing official battle reports and submarine operations were intercepted around the clock. Firwood was guarded, and U.S. and Allied military visited secretly. (Georgetown University Library, Special Collections.)

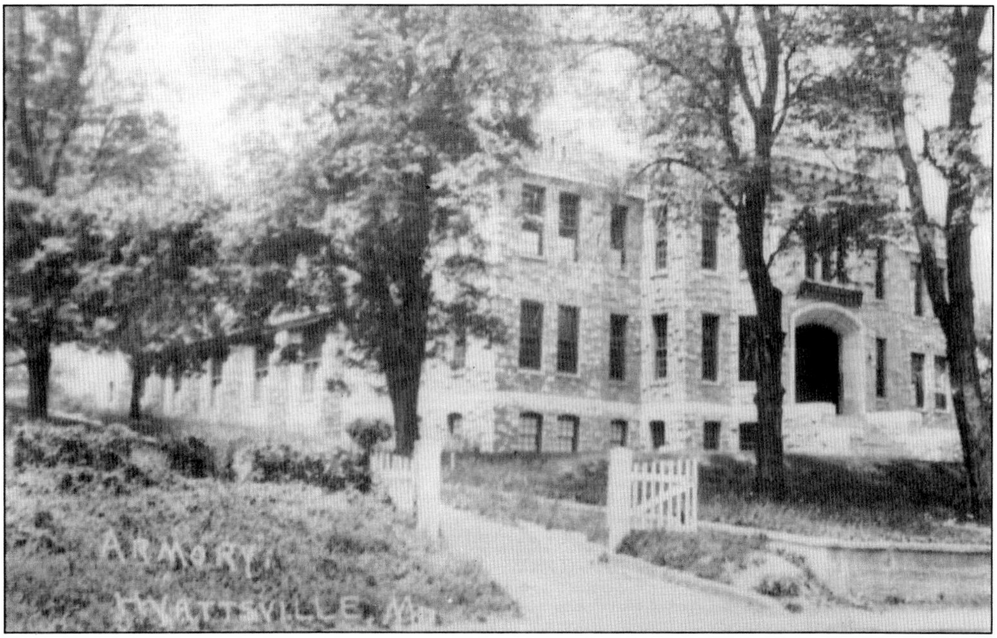

Company F returned from World War I to find a new armory—the first in the county. Robert Lawrence Harris, Maryland state architect, designed the formidable, castellated stone building. Harris later worked on the Pentagon. The head shed contained offices and the drill shed a large auditorium. The basement housed 150 men, an armory, and a target range. It was the town's largest building and served as a civic center. (PGCHS.)

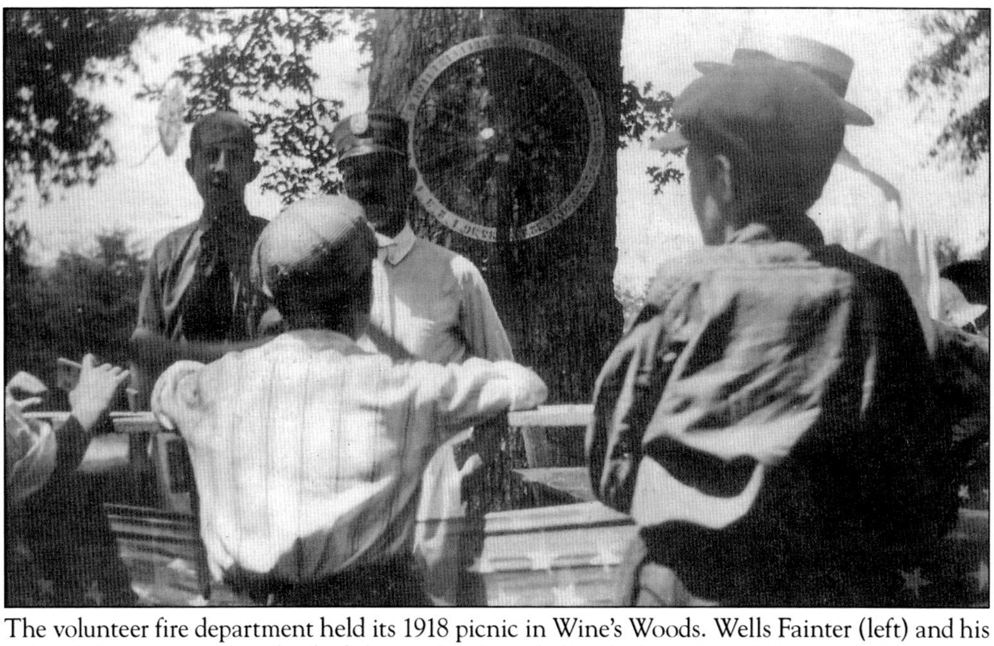
The volunteer fire department held its 1918 picnic in Wine's Woods. Wells Fainter (left) and his father, John, operate the wheel of chance for those feeling lucky. (City of Hyattsville.)

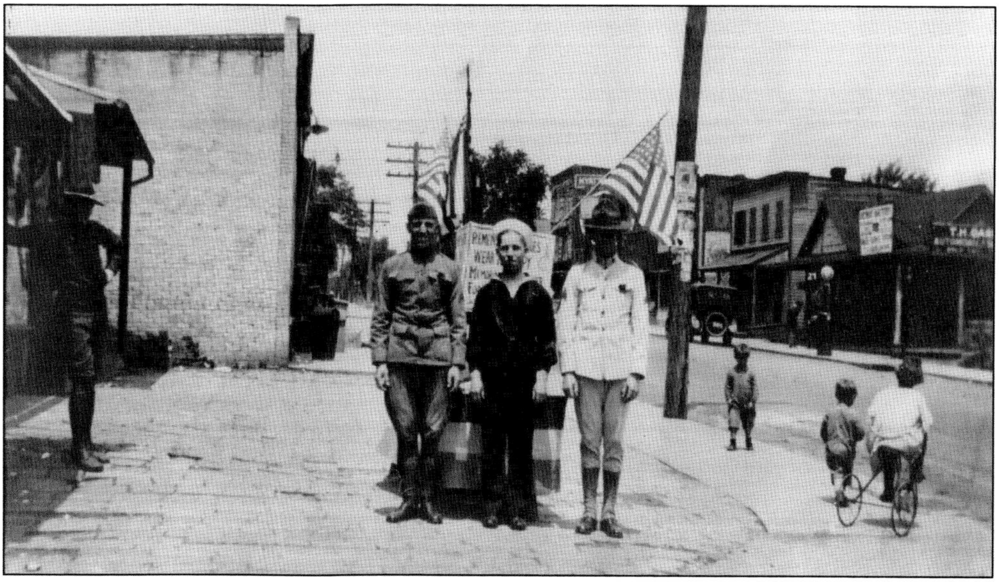

Veterans of Foreign Wars gathered on Baltimore Avenue in the early 1920s for one of the first Buddy Poppy sales. The year 1922 marked the first Memorial Day poppy sales, assembled by disabled and needy veterans who were paid for their work to provide them financial assistance. The VFW's memorial flower was selected from Col. John McCree's 1915 wartime poem *In Flanders Field*: "the poppies blow / Between the crosses row on row." (PGCHS.)

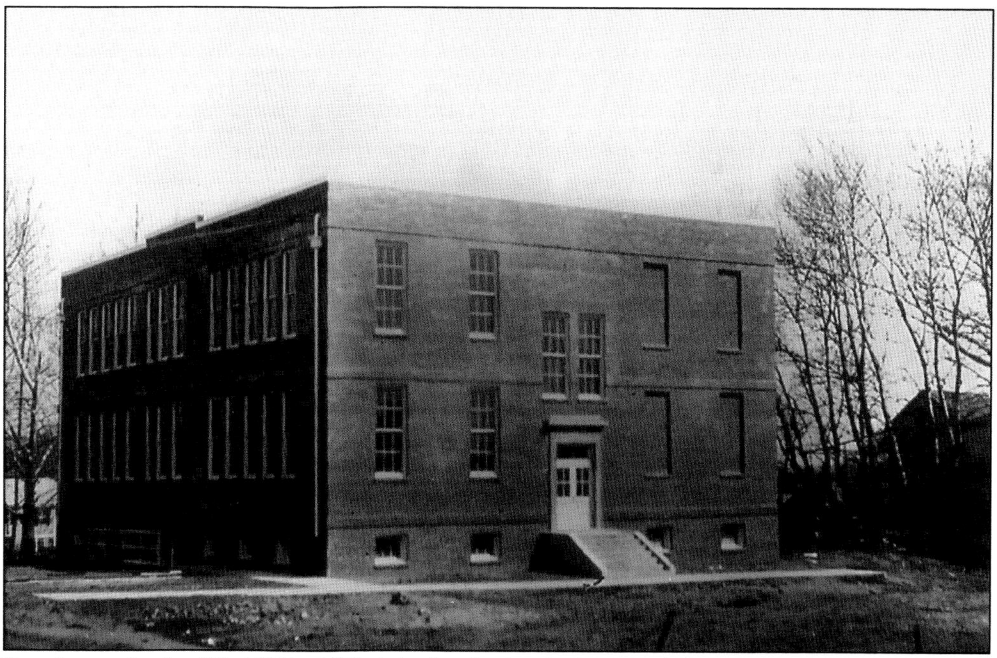

Rapid growth after World War I filled the local schools. A second elementary school was planned at Olive (Forty-third Avenue) and Franklin (Jefferson) Streets. In September 1925, the board of education approved $50,000 in 30-year bonds sold by the First National Bank of Southern Maryland. Grades four to seven were moved to the new Olive Street School under Principal Mary Petty. Additions were made in 1935, 1954, and 1961. (Doug Dudrow.)

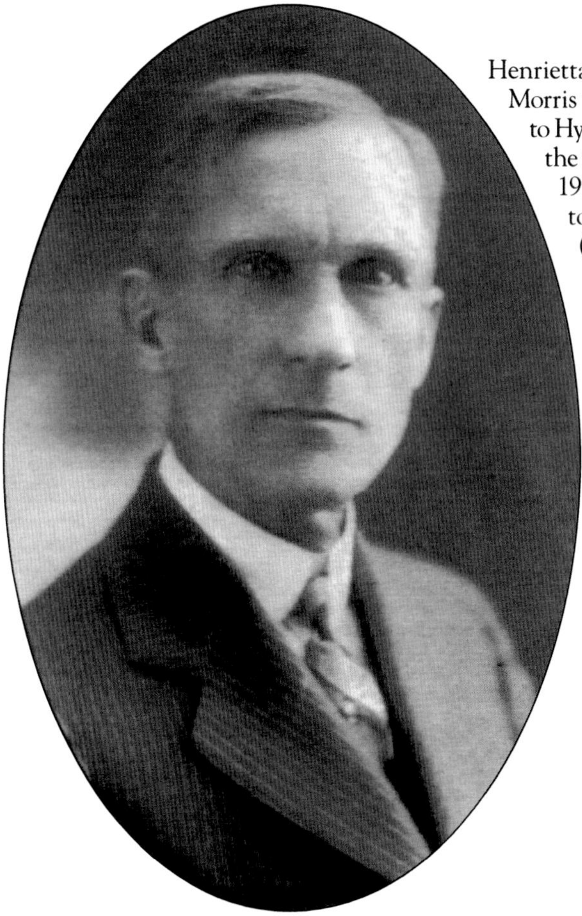

Henrietta "Rhetta" (below) and Prof. K. J. (left) Morris were originally from Kentucky, moving to Hyattsville about 1914. K. J. (born 1864) was the first high school principal, teaching from 1914 to the 1930s. He was fondly referred to by his students as "Kill Joy." Rhetta (born 1870) worked for the National Democratic Party and participated in the Hyattsville Women's Club. She was appointed Maryland's first female justice of the peace, serving the 16th District during Prohibition. Morris worked from her Baltimore Avenue office with Constable Claude "Two Guns" Reese and local deputies George Buckholtz, Andy Gasch, Jack Wilson, and Will Flerstien, reportedly making it "hot for bootleggers and scofflaws." (Left, Doug Dudrow; below, PGCHS.)

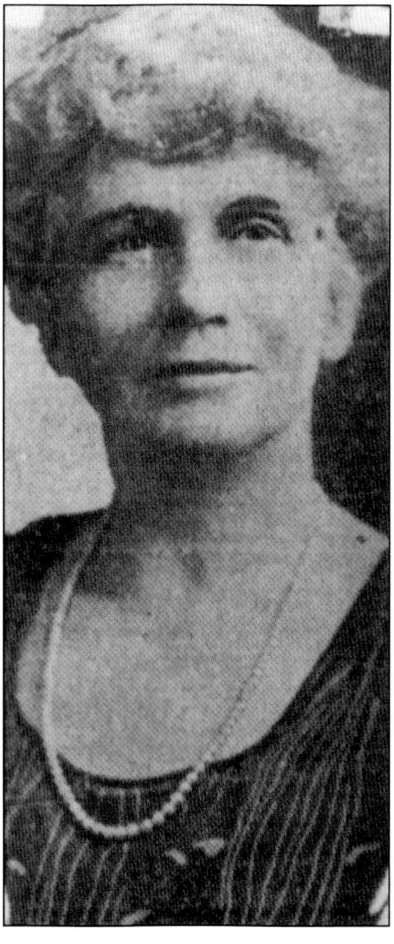

Three

Route 1 and the Automobile

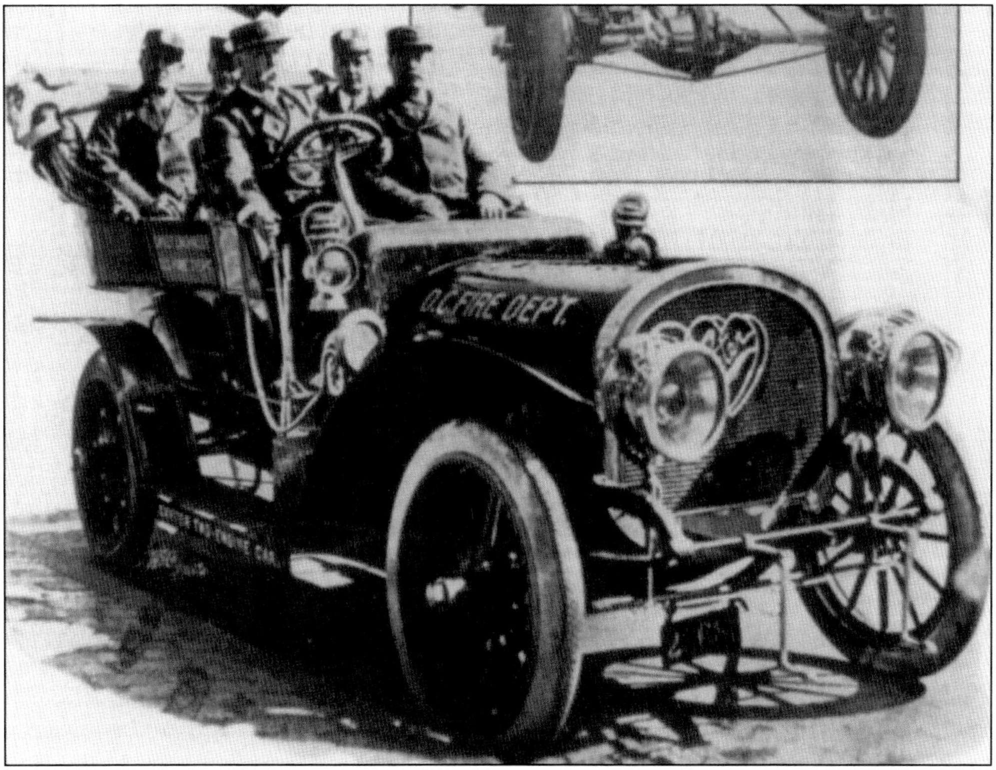

Carter Motor Car Corporation was an established company before coming to town in 1907, with Baltimore, Detroit, New York, Philadelphia, and Washington, D.C., offices. A "modern" manufacturing facility was completed by June 1908, with the first cars, trucks, ambulances, and fire trucks listed as 1909 models. The first cars—roadsters, tourings, and limousines starting at $4,000—had two separate four-cylinder engines with their own ignition and cooling systems. (*Road and Track*.)

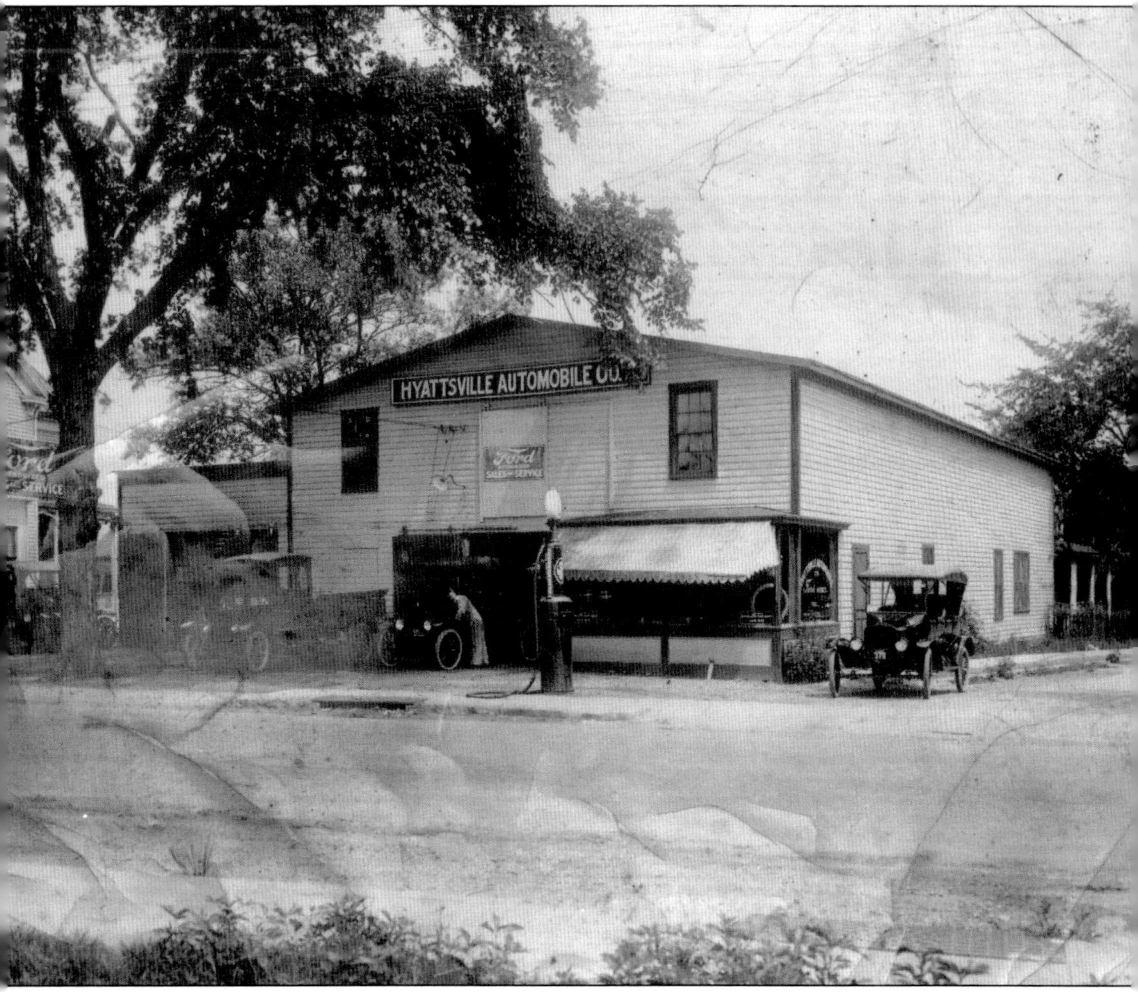

Lem Gray moved his livery and sold this property to Hervey "Herb" Machen around 1915. Machen converted the building into Hyattsville Auto Company, one of the earliest in the area. Machen was a sales and service agent for Mitchell and Ford motor companies, specializing in the Model T and later the Fordson's farm tractor. A 1909 touring car cost $850, advertised as "high priced quality in a low priced car." (PGCHS.)

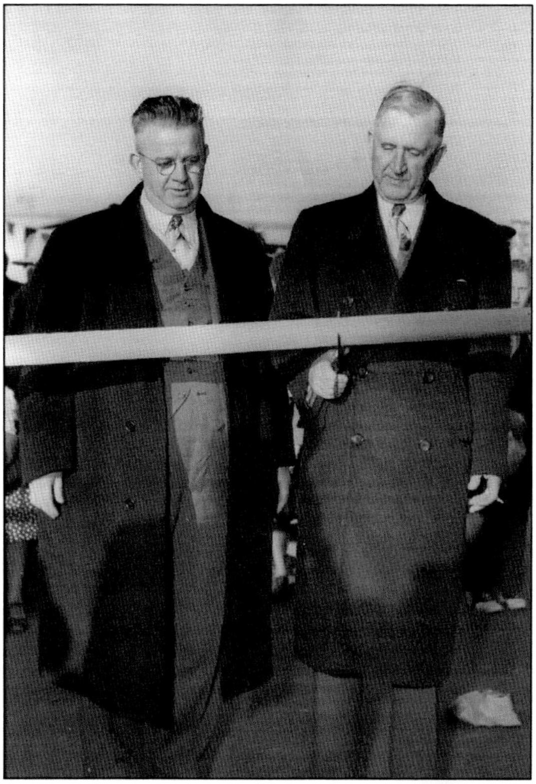

The Washington Suburban Sanitary Commission (WSSC) was legislated on May 1, 1918, to provide clean water and sewerage disposal for Washington, D.C., and its Maryland suburbs—one of the first regional systems in the country. Commissioner T. Howard Duckett (right), a local resident, was instrumental in locating the WSSC's first office building in the 4000 block of Hamilton Street in 1921. WSSC was one of the area's largest employers. (PGCHS.)

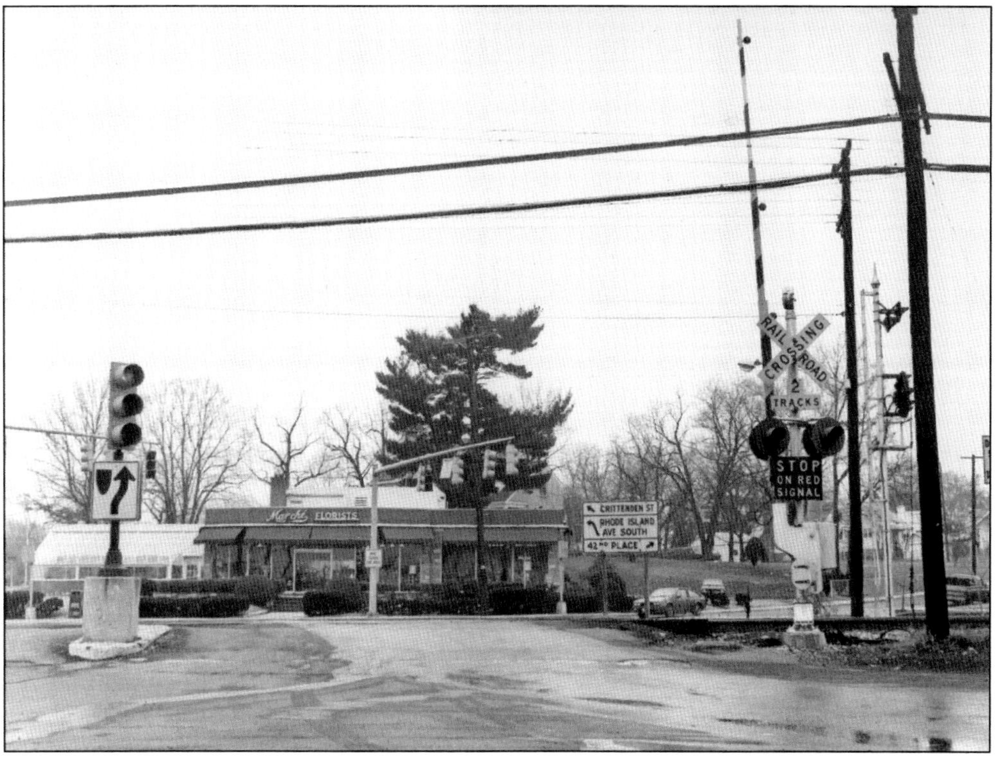

William and Augusta Marche purchased the girls' school at Columbia Road (Crittenden Street) and the railroad for their home in 1915. The Marches maintained their Washington, D.C., florist shop, supplying flowers grown in newly constructed local greenhouses. Augusta continued operations after William's 1919 death, with her son Billy helping as a teenager. In 1935, Augusta and architect John Robie Kennedy designed the house, and later shop, with its unique polychrome finish. (PGCHS.)

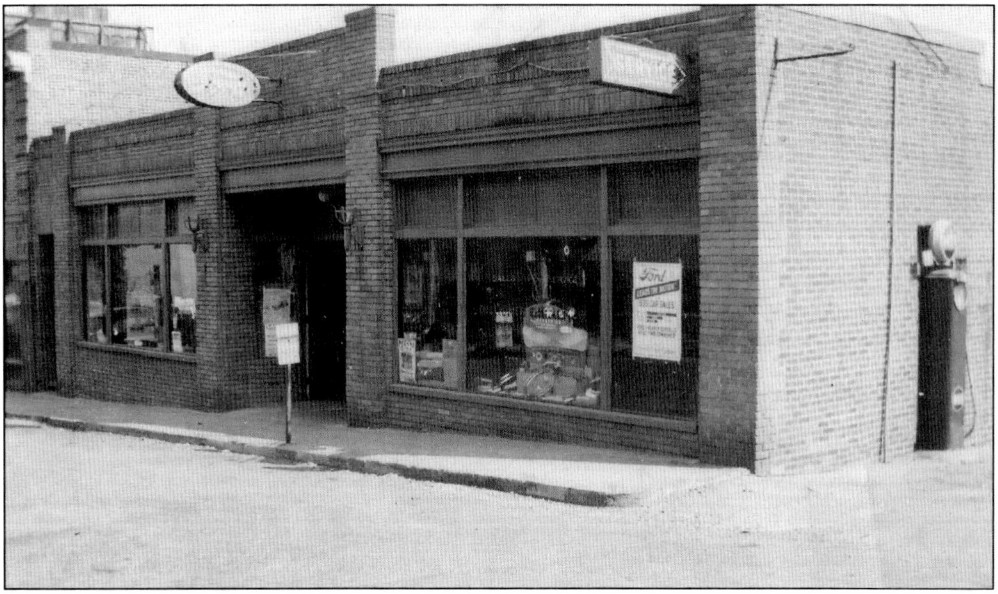

Palmer Ford, at 4327 Gallatin Street, opened in 1918—the first auto showroom in town. Its design adhered to an early "first-generation" formula of storefront with cornice. The establishment marked the emergence of Baltimore Avenue as a commercial corridor catering to automobile-related business. In the late 1940s, a sheet-metal dealership occupied the site and later a printing company. (PGCHS.)

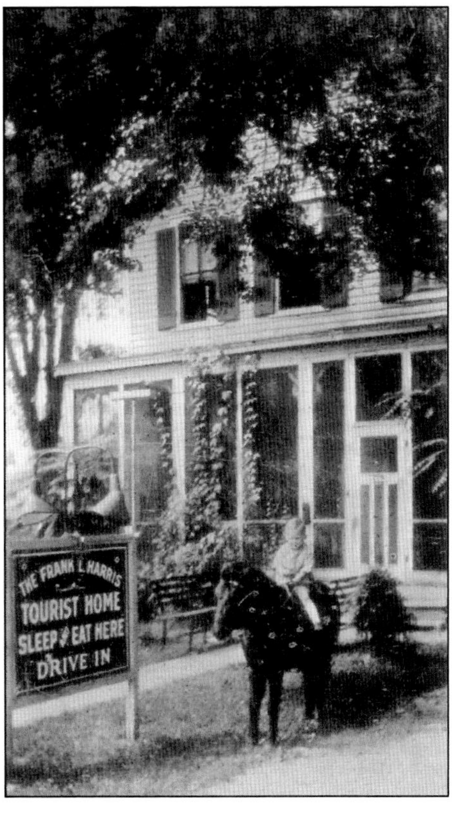

The Frank L. Harris Tourist Home, at 27 Maryland (4720 Baltimore) Avenue, provided lodging for $1 per night, meals for 50¢, and free parking. It was an "Approved National Wayside Home" with accommodations vetted by National Wayside Homes, Inc., of Canandaigua, New York. This organization capitalized on nascent auto travelers in the 1920s with regional guides highlighting their approved homes. Harris', Franklin's, Baker's, and one unnamed were early "motels" in the city. (PGCHS.)

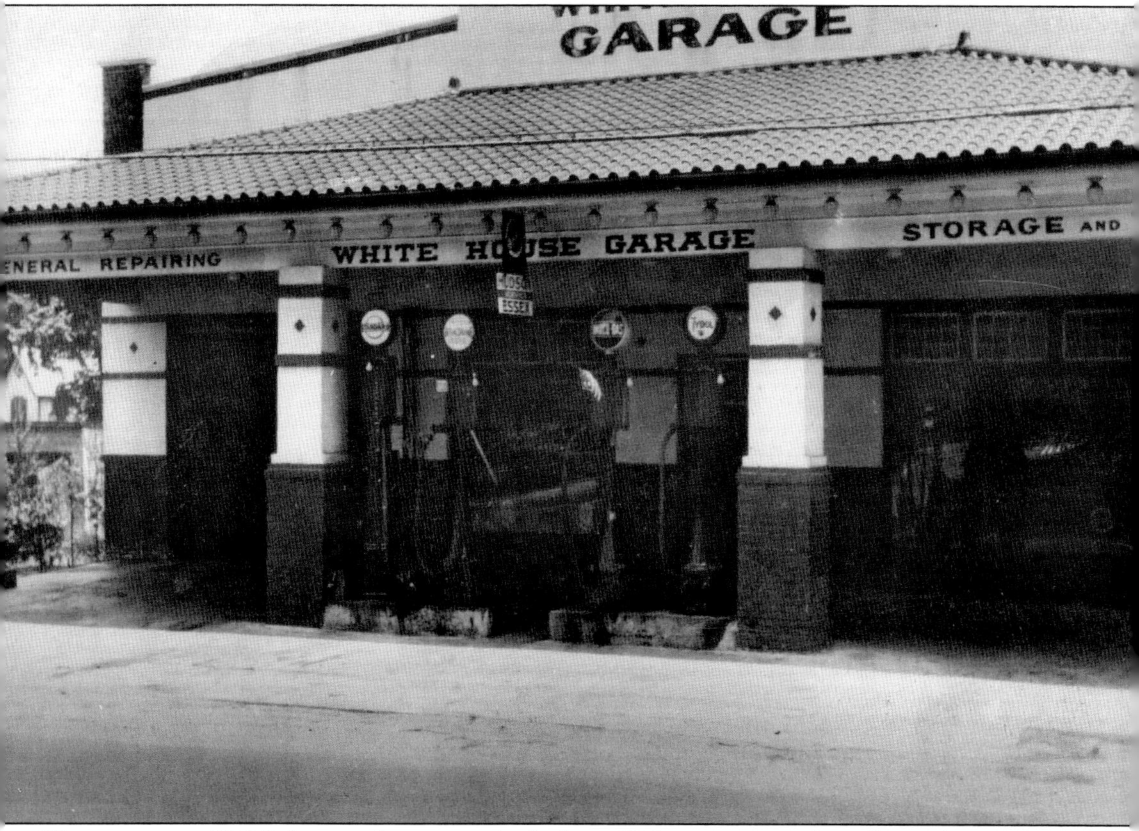

The structure at 5323 Baltimore Avenue was built about 1920 as a garage with no floor, submerged fuel tanks, and gasoline pumps adjacent to the Pike. It was known soon as the White House Garage and expanded to service up to 40 automobiles. By the 1930s, H. C. Fleming Motor Company sold and serviced Dodges there. More recently, Field's Buick used the front as offices and performed automotive repairs in the rear. (PGCHS.)

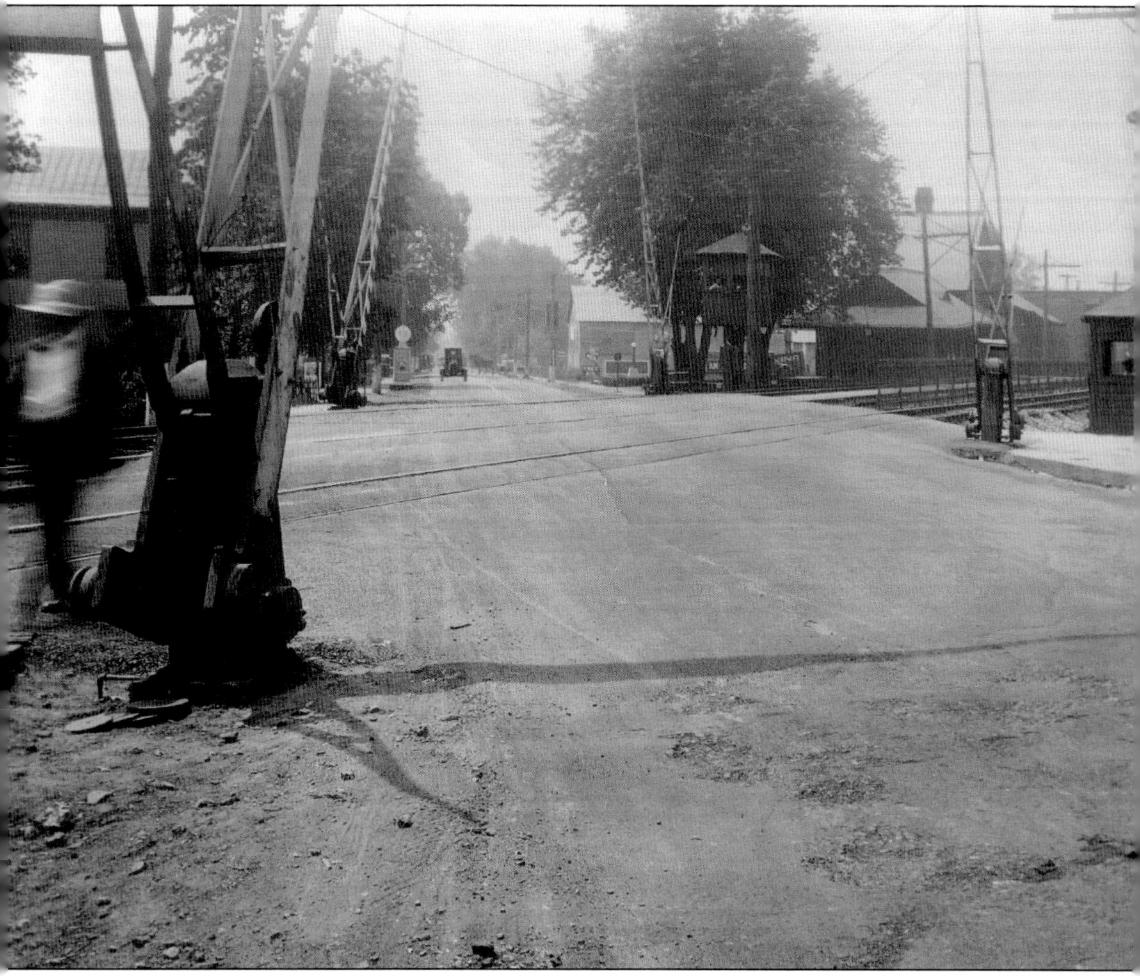

The train crossed local roads on grade at two locations, the Melrose Avenue (Crittenden Street) crossing and the Pike. Frequent accidents concerned citizens from the earliest days. At this latter crossing, towers were installed for a watchman who hand-lowered track barriers. The bridge overpass installed with the extension of Rhode Island Avenue in 1929 alleviated some of the traffic. It was not until 1950 that electronically operated barriers were installed. (PGCHS.)

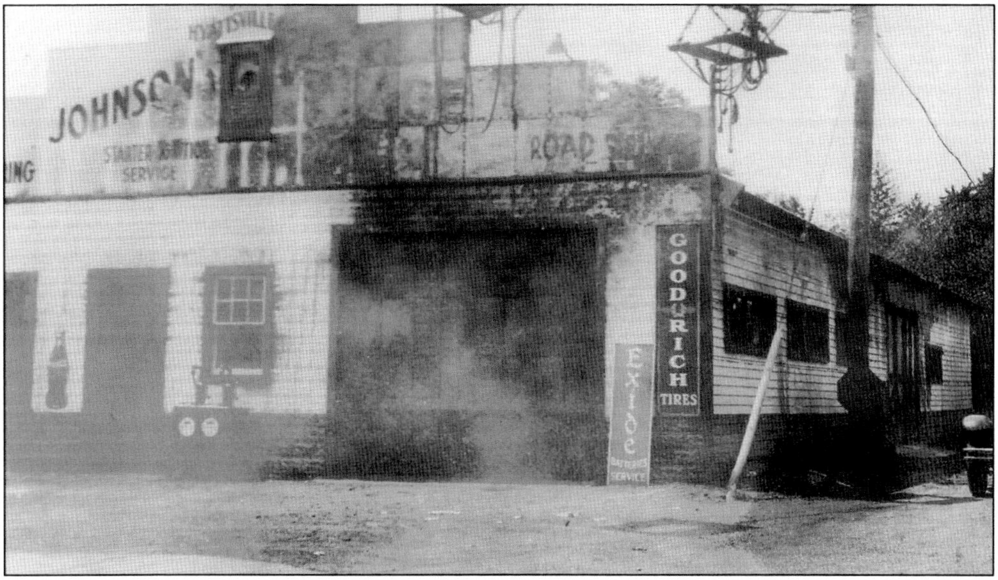

Johnson's Garage opened in the mid-1920s at Baltimore Avenue and Cottage Road (Crittenden Street). Johnson's was part of the local burgeoning auto business, providing gas and servicing. The garage was damaged by an August 6, 1932, fire (pictured), highlighting the flammability of auto materials. (PGCHS.)

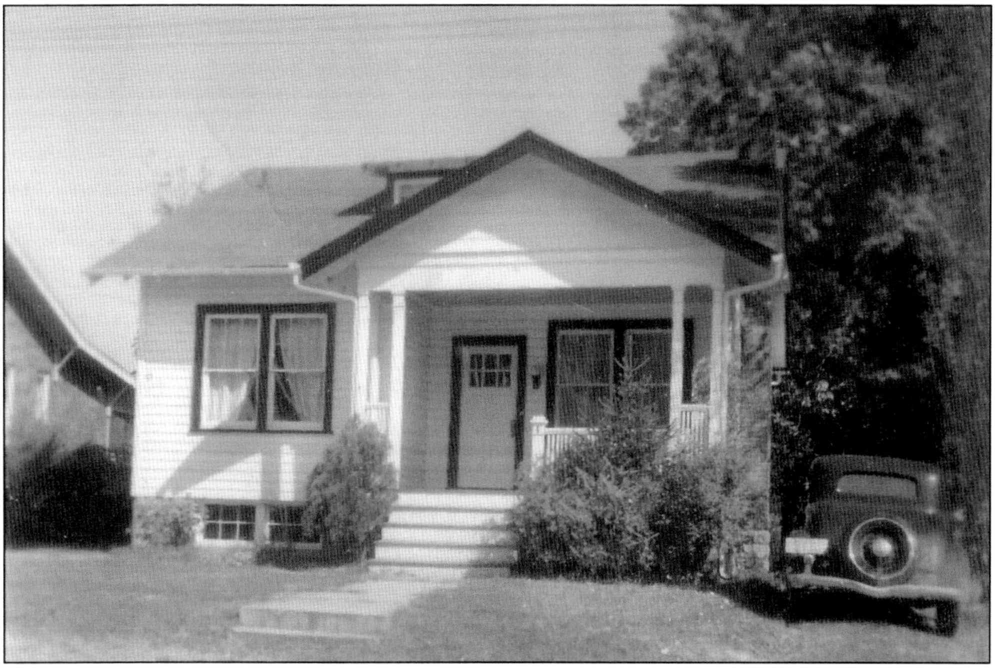

Hyattsville Hills was subdivided and available for sale in the spring of 1923. Four years later, an advertisement stated that over 250 homes were built and occupied by satisfied owners: "The Natural Lay of the Land and Ample Shade Trees Afford an Ideal Home Environment." Lots were as low as $300 with $5 down and $3 per month. Homes started at $3,500. The home at 4 McKinley (5403 Thirty-ninth Avenue) was still on a dirt street in this 1938 photograph. (Naomi and Thomas Behrens.)

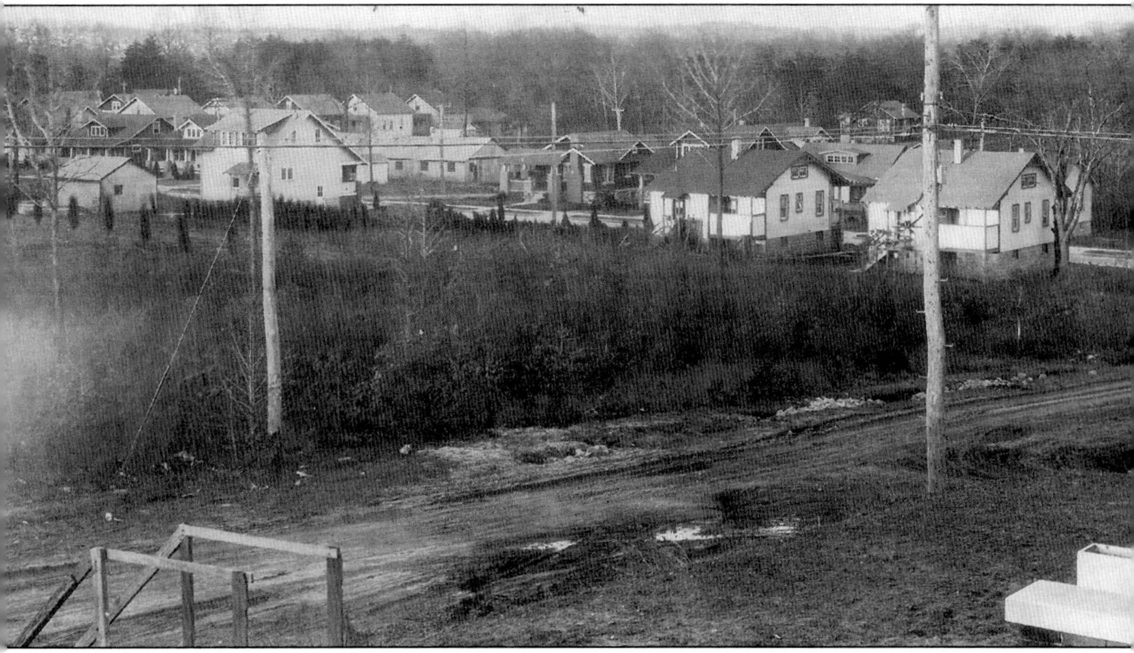

The post–World War I building boom claimed Wine's Woods. Smaller lot sizes, 50 by 115 feet, and the bungalow's popularity brought the suburban dream to the middle class. This view from Bayly Avenue (Longfellow Street), overlooking Oakwood Road (Fortieth Place), showed the rapidly developing Hyattsville Hills. Realtor O. B. Zantzinger re-subdivided Wine and Johnson's Third Addition, forming this rapidly expanding neighborhood. (PGCHS.)

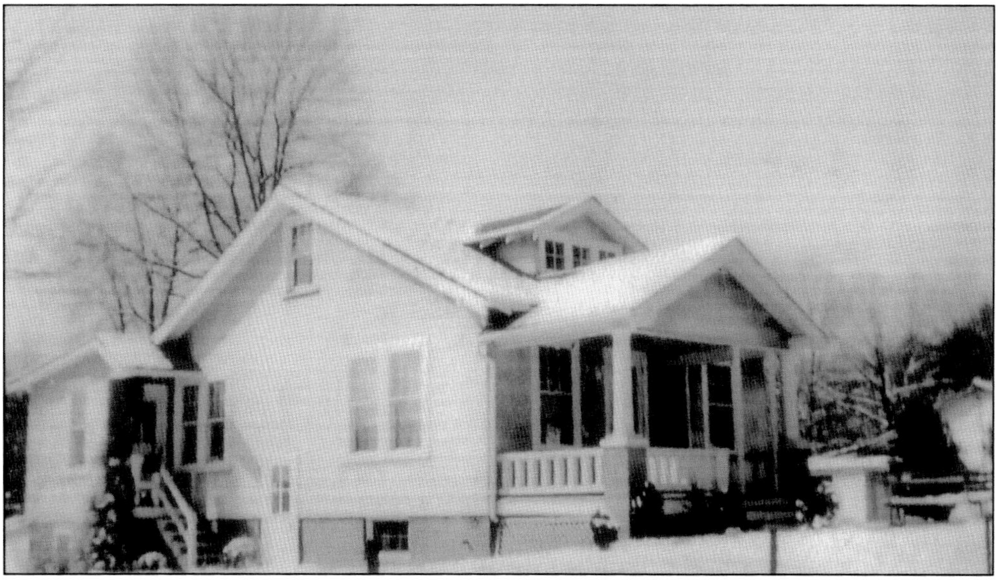

English immigrant Roland Read (1891–1937) came to the United States in 1906. He built 3909 Nicholson Street (Forest Drive) and two neighboring houses by hand, pouring four cement foundation blocks daily. Read was the city's first nighttime police officer, working from 7:00 p.m. to midnight. He also served as the first councilman from his section of Hyattsville Hills. (Mildred Ford.)

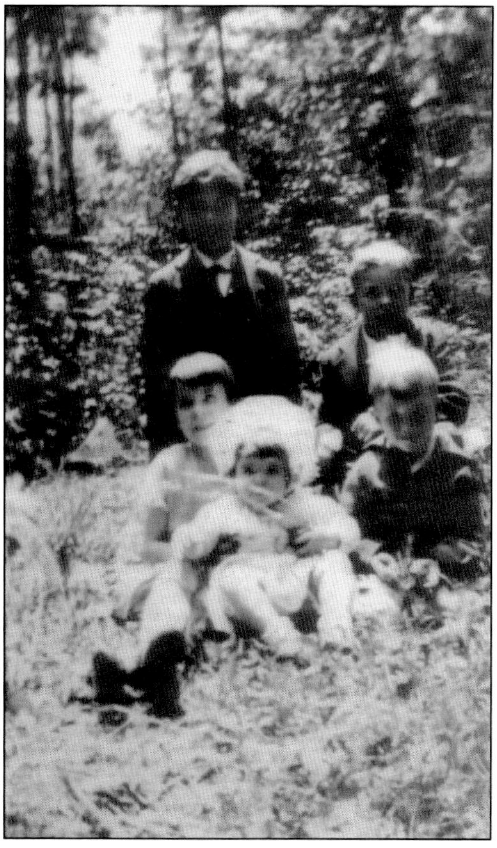

Roland and Alvirta (1898–1985) Read raised five children in the Nicholson home. Pictured here, they are, from left to right, (first row) Florence, Mildred, and Charles; (second row) Gilbert and John. The last children were born in the front room of the house. The family was Seventh-day Adventist, attending services in the Masonic Hall until a church was built in 1937. Johnny built the bungalow next to his parent's home. (Mildred Ford.)

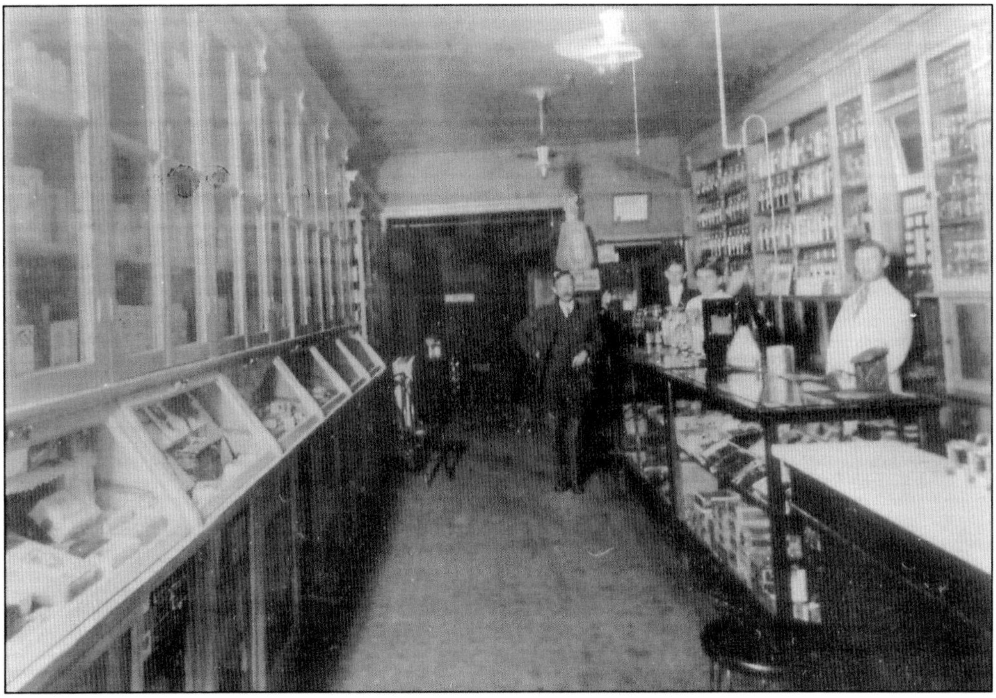

Dudrow's Drugstore opened on Baltimore Avenue and Anderson (Hamilton Street) on May 21, 1924. The staff of the family-run business included father Otis G., son Otis B. (left), pharmacist Dr. Ralph (right), and Dr. J. Dallas Erwin, who had dispensed pharmaceuticals in town since the 1880s. "More than a drug store . . . a neighborhood friend" was the store's early slogan. The business closed in 1949. (Doug Dudrow.)

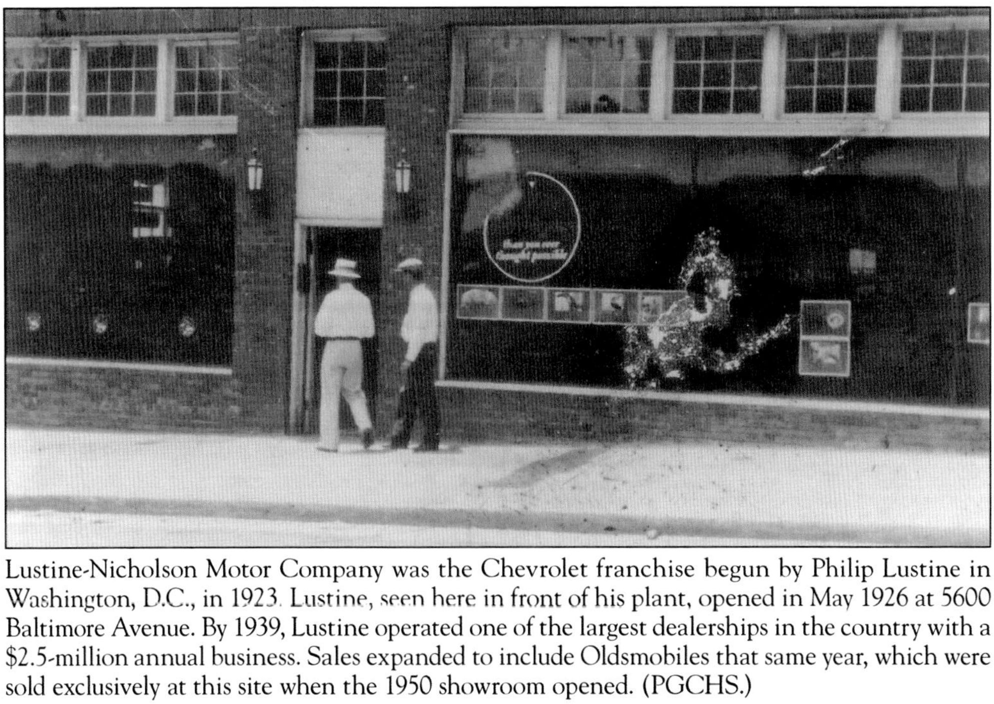

Lustine-Nicholson Motor Company was the Chevrolet franchise begun by Philip Lustine in Washington, D.C., in 1923. Lustine, seen here in front of his plant, opened in May 1926 at 5600 Baltimore Avenue. By 1939, Lustine operated one of the largest dealerships in the country with a $2.5-million annual business. Sales expanded to include Oldsmobiles that same year, which were sold exclusively at this site when the 1950 showroom opened. (PGCHS.)

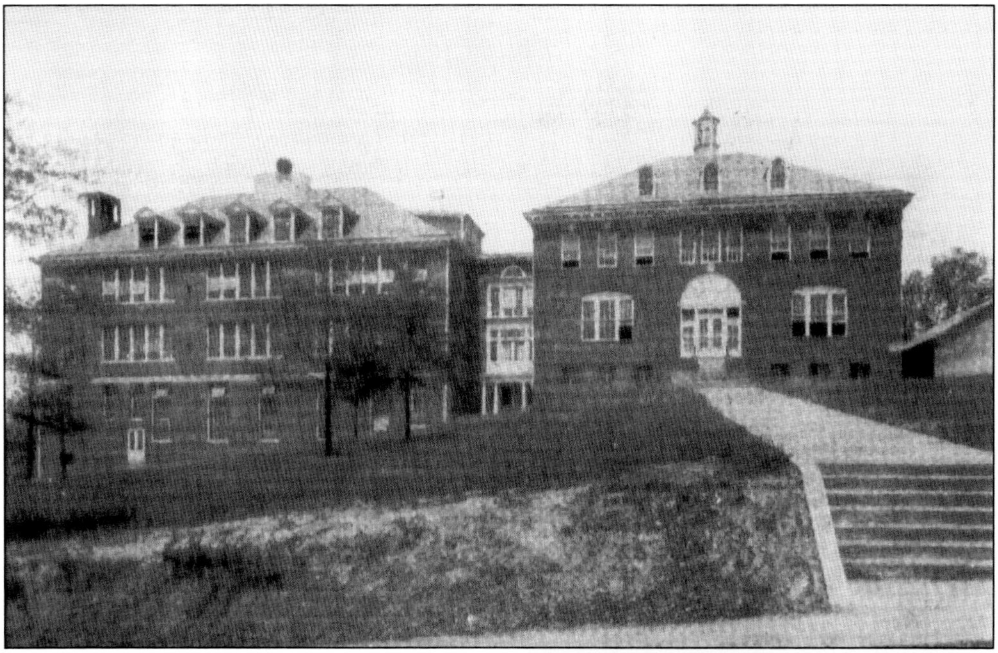

The high school was expanded in April 1925 when Washington builders Sylvester and Almutt received a $125,000 contract for a five-story building. Completed October 1925, it added 12 classrooms, a 700-seat auditorium, and a cafeteria—the first in the county. A $9,150 gymnasium followed. In 1951, the building became the junior high. All but the gymnasium was razed in the 1970s for construction of the current middle school. (Doug Dudrow.)

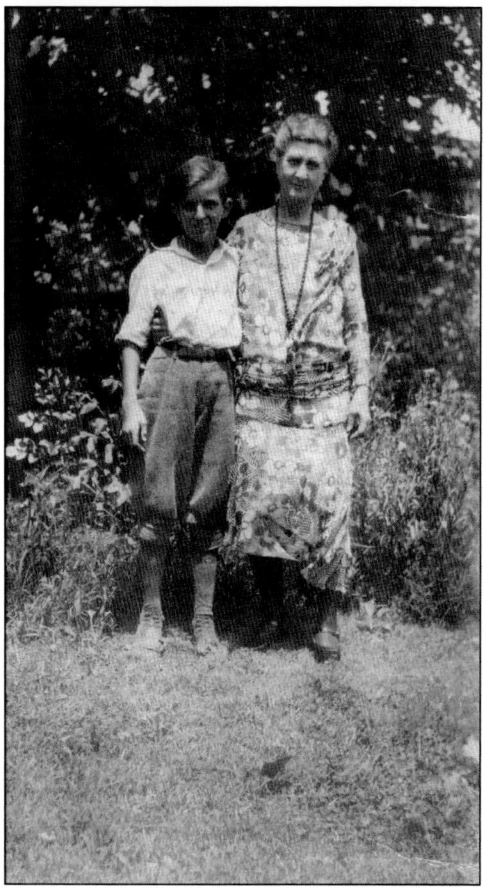

Jack Kaufman, 10, and his grandma stand in their 11 Sibley (Buchanan) Avenue backyard in 1927. Jack hitchhiked to the Beaver Dam Golf Course to earn money as a caddy. That summer, a club member gave him a dog he named Sandy. Sandy was famous for his gallivanting, following Jack's mother, Margaret, to Mass and Jack to school. (PGCHS.)

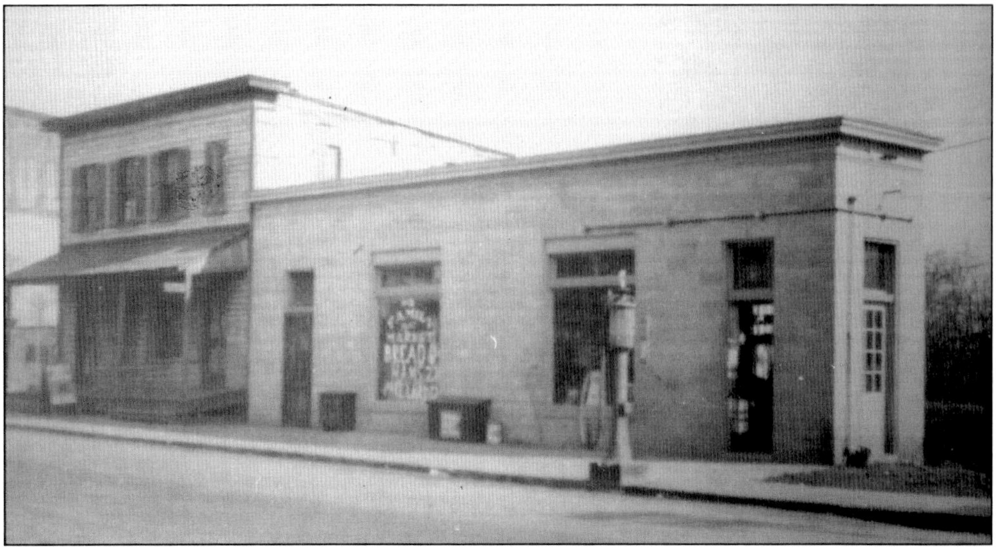

The triangular-shaped property formed north of the intersection of the railroad and turnpike was part of H. O. Emmons's 1894 subdivision. The unusually shaped parcel required a unique design to fully utilize the property. The "flatiron" building replaced earlier structures about 1920 and, in this 1927 photograph, was used as a market. W. P. Magruder reconstructed the building in the 1930s into its present form. (PGCHS.)

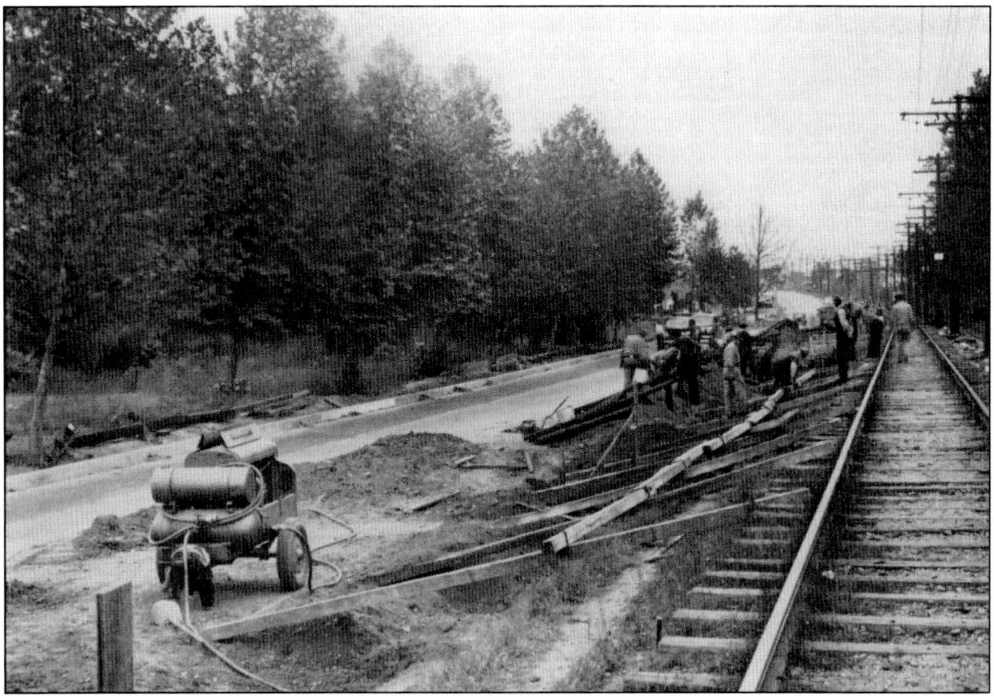

Fifteen years of increasing motor traffic on the Pike highlighted dangers of the on-grade B&O Railroad crossing before action was taken in 1926. The solution was the extension of Rhode Island Avenue from the District, pictured here under construction. Elsie Casey and Esme Reeder officially opened the avenue gates at 2:00 p.m., December 7, 1929, with a parade from Mount Rainier. (City of Hyattsville.)

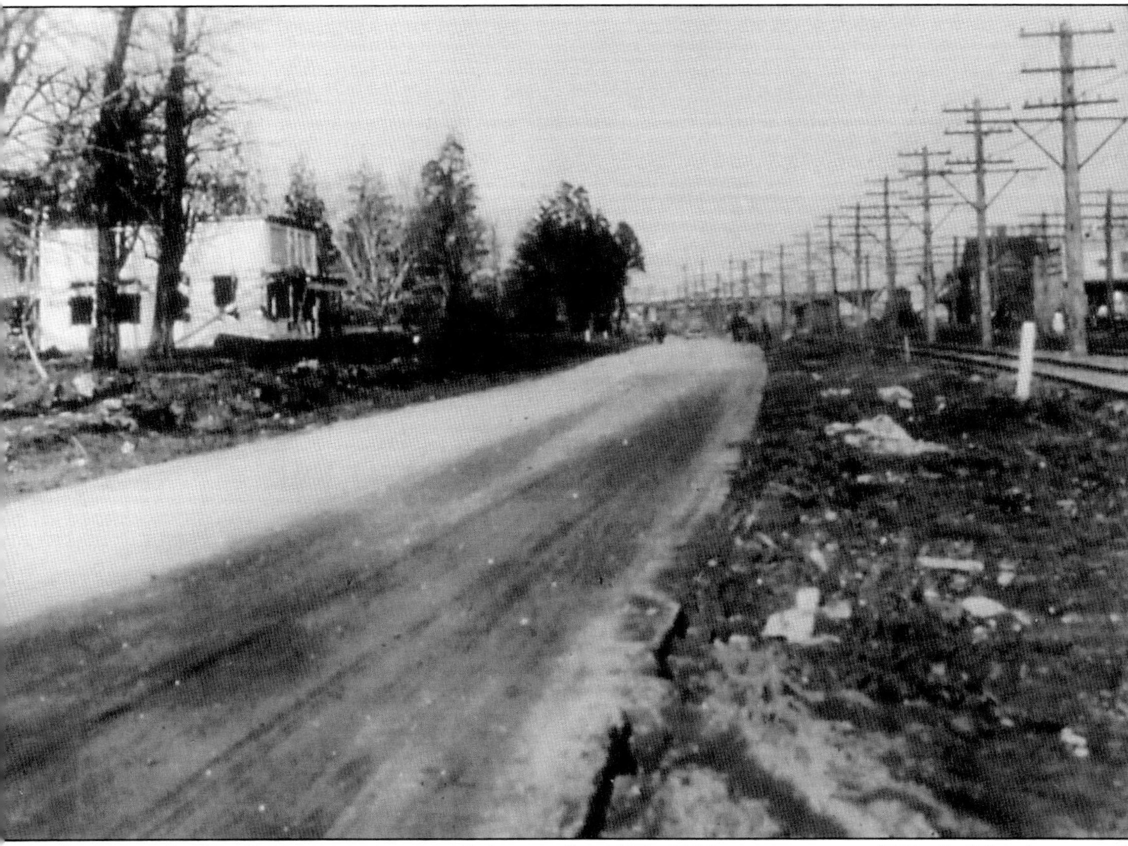

The Pig and Whistle Restaurant opened during the 1928–1929 construction of Rhode Island Avenue at its intersection with Ravenswood (Forty-third Avenue). (City of Hyattsville.)

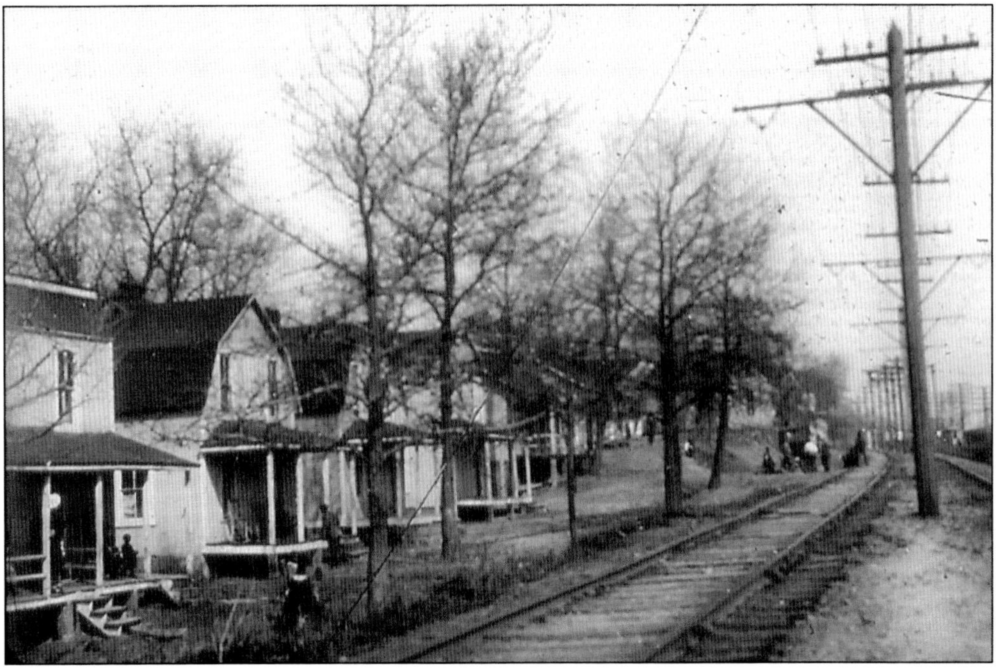

Purchase of properties for the Rhode Island Avenue right-of-way cost $50,000, which were paid for by the county. Houses were either moved to allow construction (above) or, like these duplexes, (below) were demolished. (Both Doug Dudrow.)

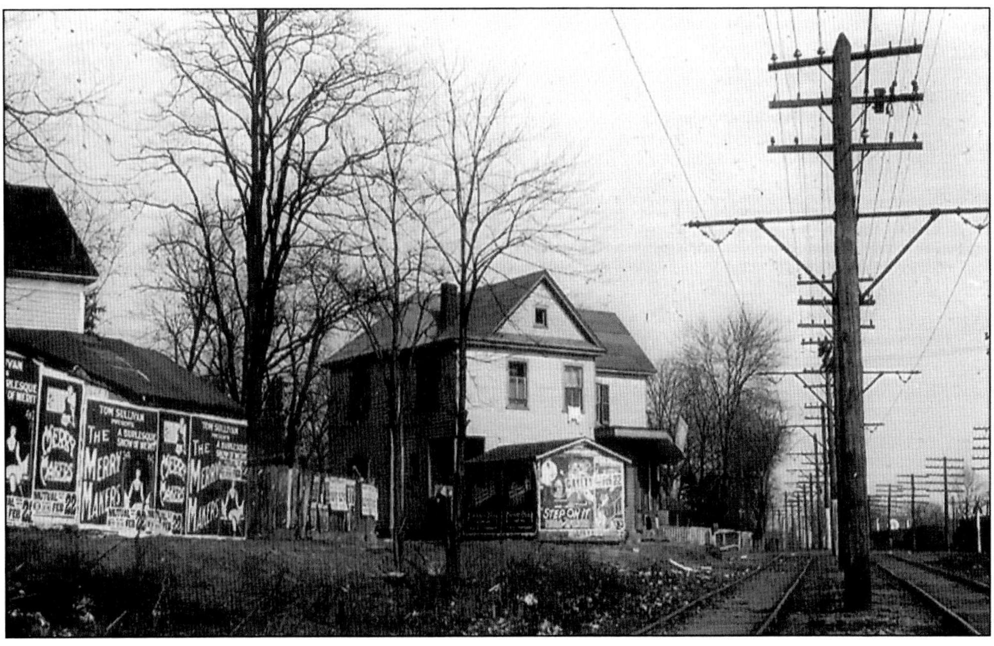

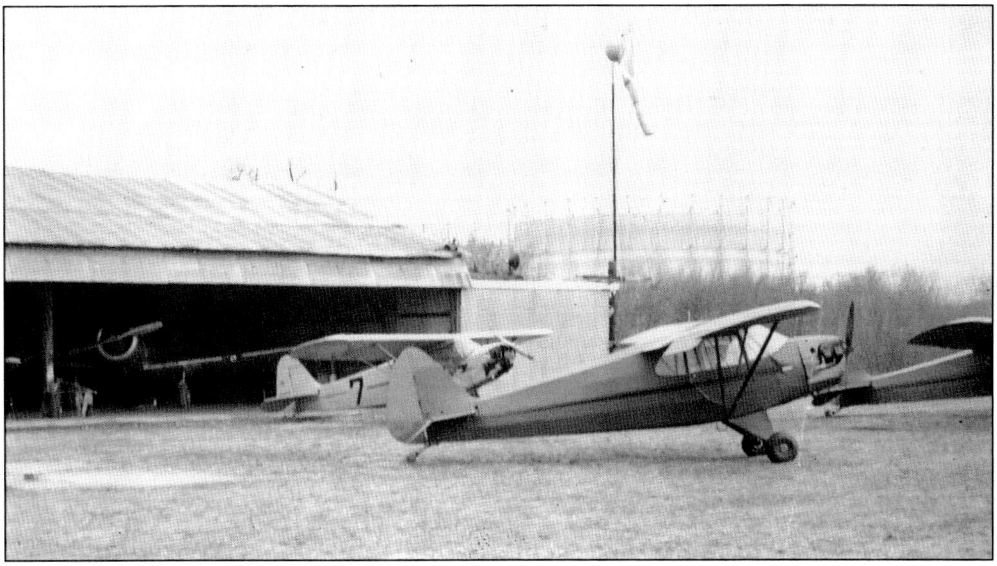

Queen's Chapel Airport opened in the mid-1930s at the current site of West Hyattsville Metro. It was owned by the Barrett brothers, and Bob Baber and Bill Henderson managed the general aviation field with one open grass airstrip and a single building (above). Pilots ate at the Greenwood Inn across the street. By 1941, the 21-acre establishment had two hangars and two sod strips, 2,000 and 1,500 feet long, and offered fuel and minor repairs. Security concerns closed the facility during World War II, but it reopened shortly after the war's end. In 1949, Maryland Flying Service purchased the property with manager John Dorr, who received major assistance from his wife, Debbie (below). Pilots who flew out of Queen's Chapel say it was a real eye-opener to get into and out of. The airfield closed in 1954. (Both College Park Aviation Museum.)

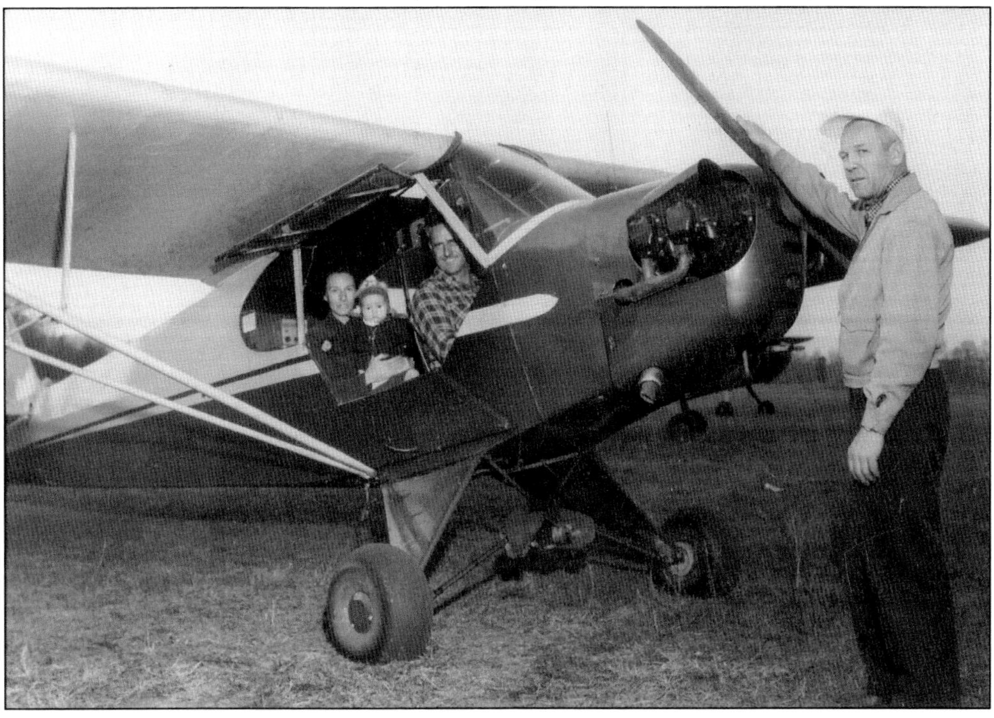

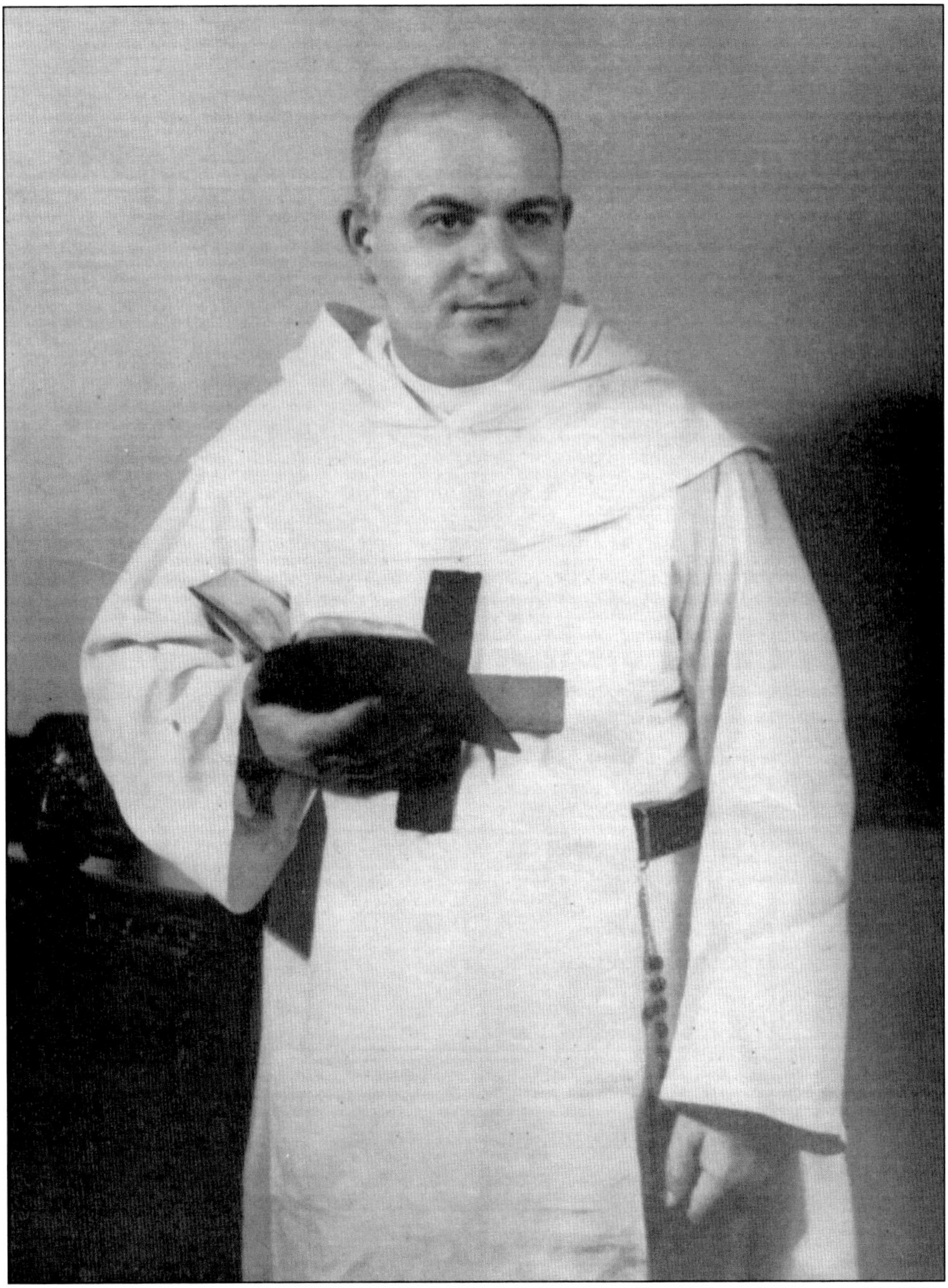

Fr. Michael Nardone arrived in Hyattsville on gray and misty, dull and dismal February 19, 1931, morning. He was charged with opening a house for clerical studies and a novitiate for the Order of the Most Holy Trinity. In the United States just over a month, Nardone felt ignorant of the language and customs. His first visitor resorted to Spanish in attempts to communicate, and his lunch consisted of his first American sandwich—bread and liverwurst. (DeMatha.)

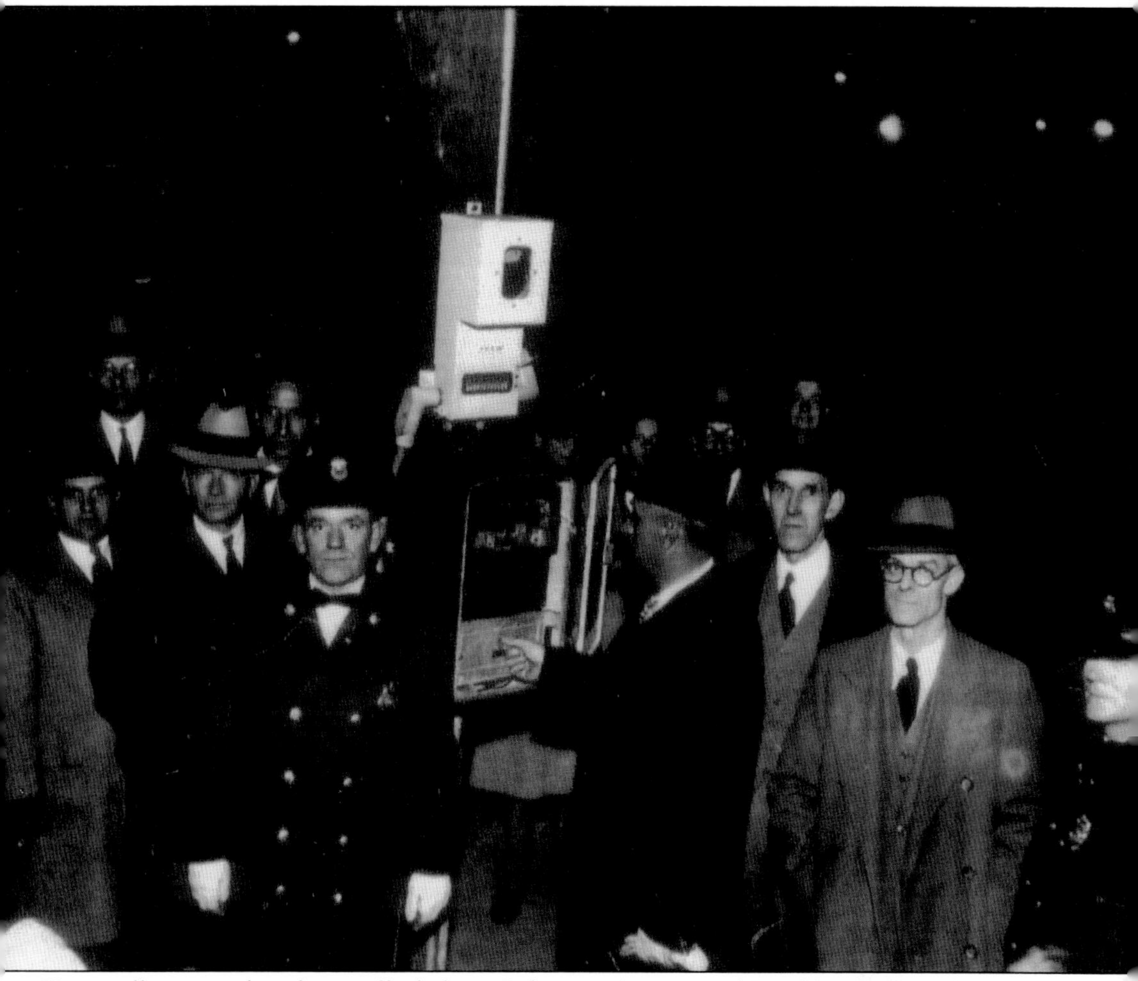

Hyattsville received its first traffic light at Baltimore Avenue and Franklin (Jefferson) Street about 1934. Mayor Hillary Willis stands at the light box ready to flip the switch, with policemen Howard Holmes to his left and Roland Read at the far right. (Mildred Ford.)

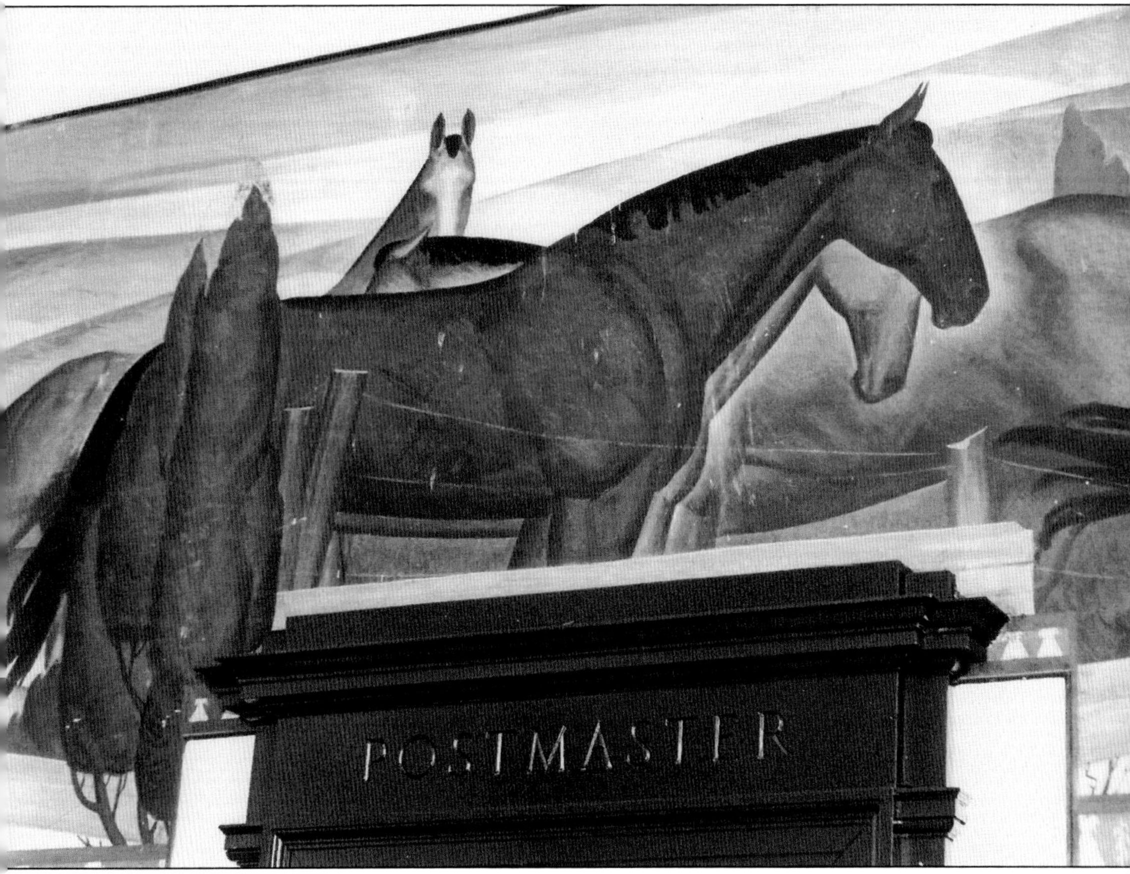

The U.S. Post Office at 4325 Gallatin Street opened in October 1935—the sixth building to serve as regional center. The Colonial Revival building was designed under the treasury's supervising architect, Louis Simon. Hyattsville resident assistant postmaster general Smith Putnam oversaw many construction details. Artist Eugene Kingman (1909–1975), nationally known for his landscapes, painted these murals of the local countryside. The $1,390 tempera on gesso commission was installed December 1937. (City of Hyattsville.)

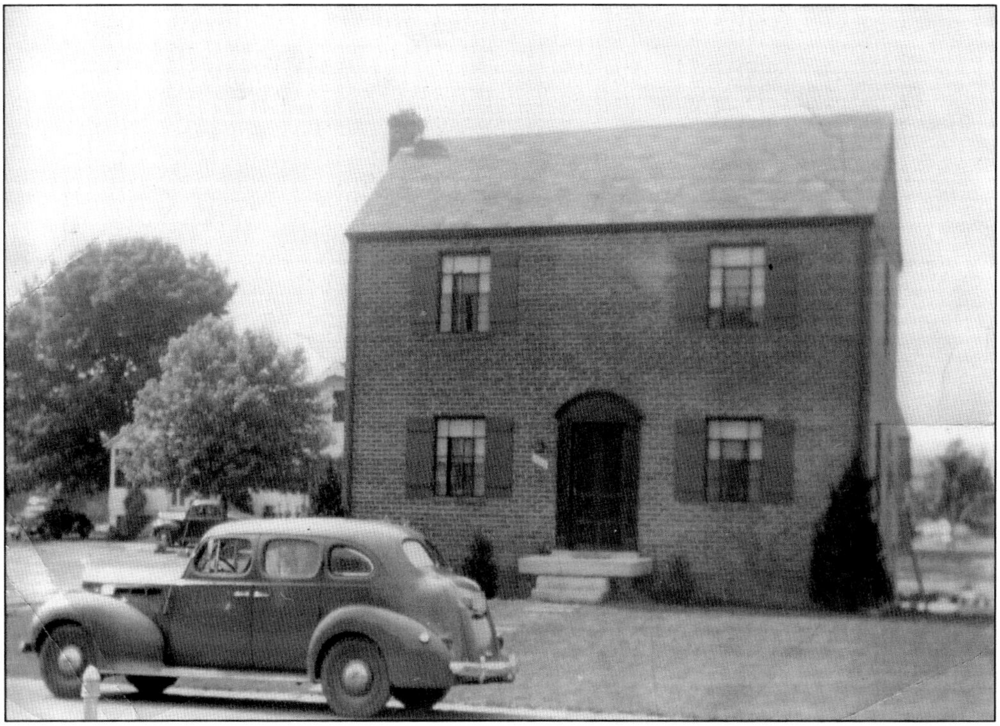

The Ager family farm and surrounds remained rural until 1935, when developers began subdividing and selling lots close to the District line. Green Meadows subdivision was platted in 1940 and built by 1942, complete with the Ager Road School. The single- or double-family attached homes were mostly brick Colonial Revival, similar to this first home in the subdivision. Green Meadows was annexed by Hyattsville in 1957. (Kathy Albertson.)

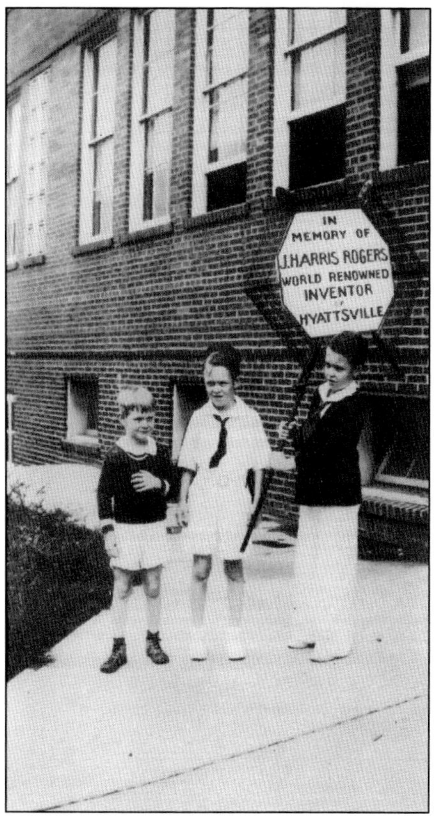

A third generation of the Rogers family celebrates their ancestor at an elementary school festival in the early 1930s. Phil (center) and Jimmy Rogers (right) and a friend bear the sign reading, "In memory of J. Harris Rogers world renowned inventor of Hyattsville." (Georgetown University Library, Special Collections.)

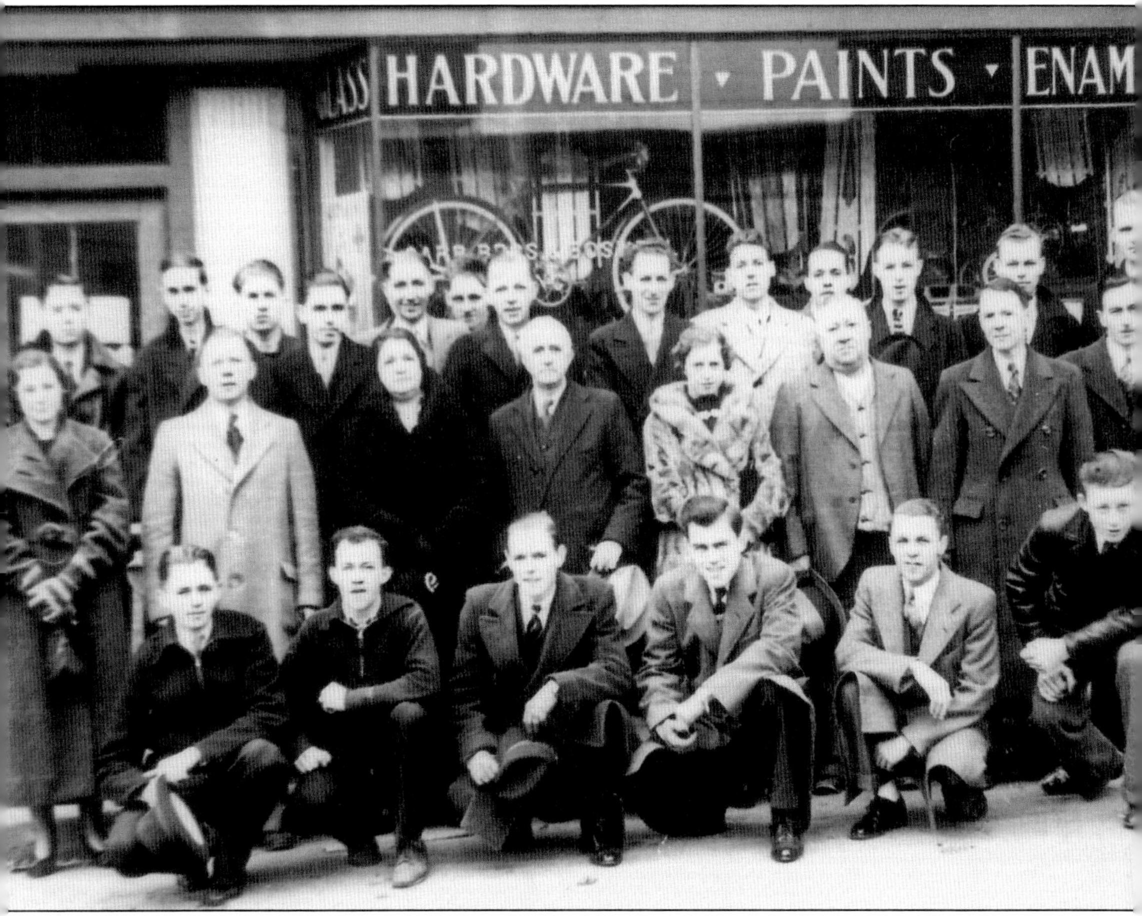

C. F. Carr and Brother opened about 1900 on Baltimore Avenue, selling meats and groceries and eventually hardware. By this October 1936 employee photograph, the business was Carr Brothers and Boswell. Brothers G. Hodges (second row, between the women) and B. Ashby managed the grocery section, and Harry A. Boswell (second row, far left) managed the general merchandise. (City of Hyattsville.)

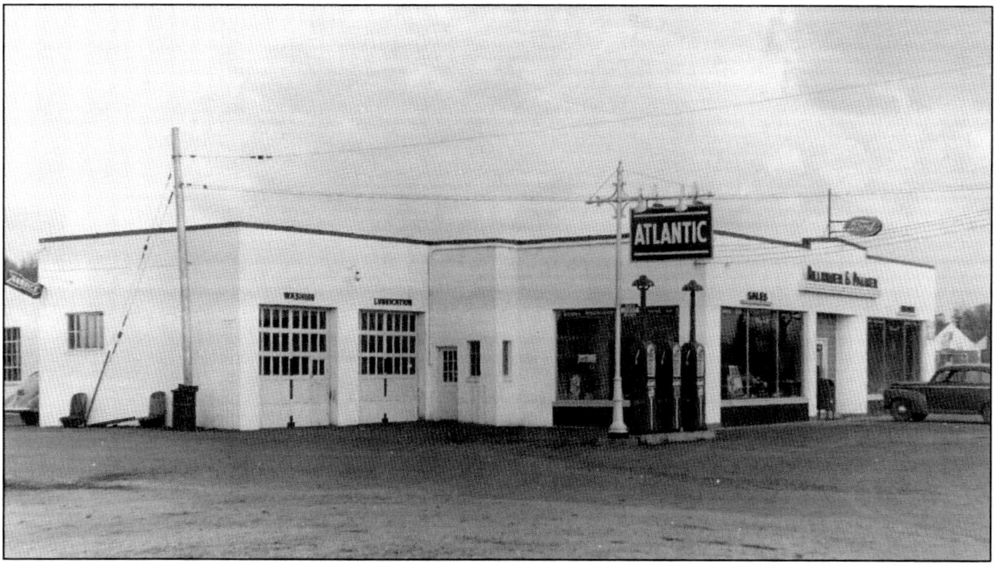

Frank Palmer moved his Spencer (Gallatin) Street Ford dealership to Columbia Road (3032 Hamilton Street) in the late 1930s. With new partners, he opened as Billhimer and Palmer Ford. The business offered sales, maintenance, gas, and car washing. (PGCHS.)

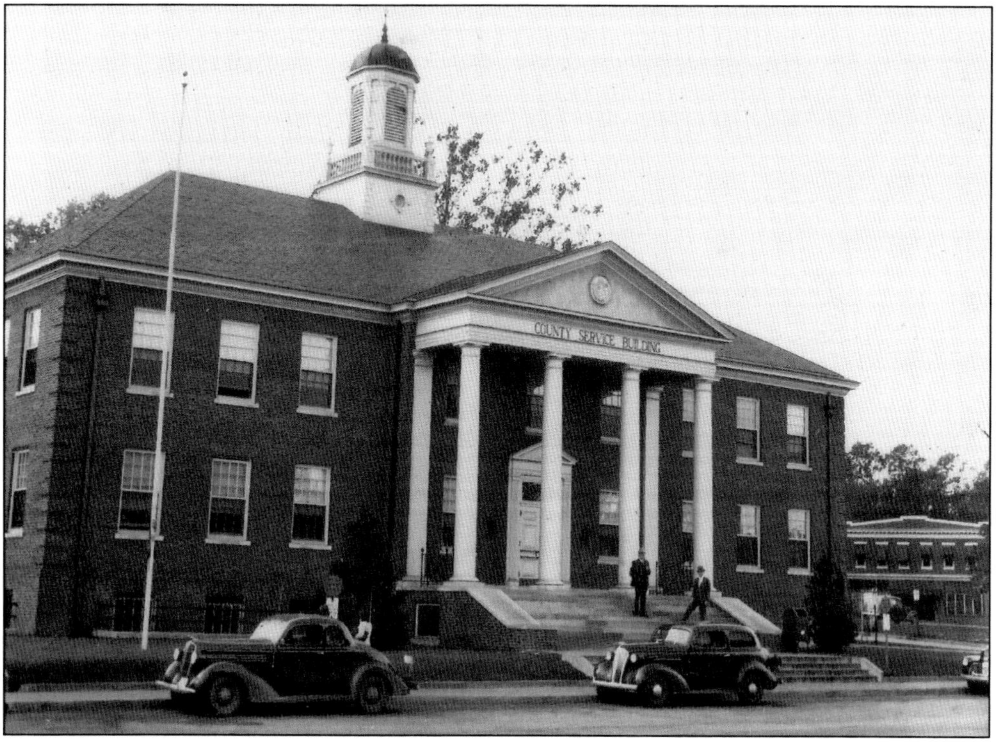

Prince George's County commissioners proposed the Baltimore Avenue site of Dr. James Rogers's home Firwood for a new county services building in 1938. With much local opposition, this and six other homes were demolished for the $125,000 Works Progress Administration building and parking lots. A large crowd gathered for the October 13, 1939, dedication with a debut performance of "Hail! Prince George's" by locals William Moore and Frederick Orton. (John Small.)

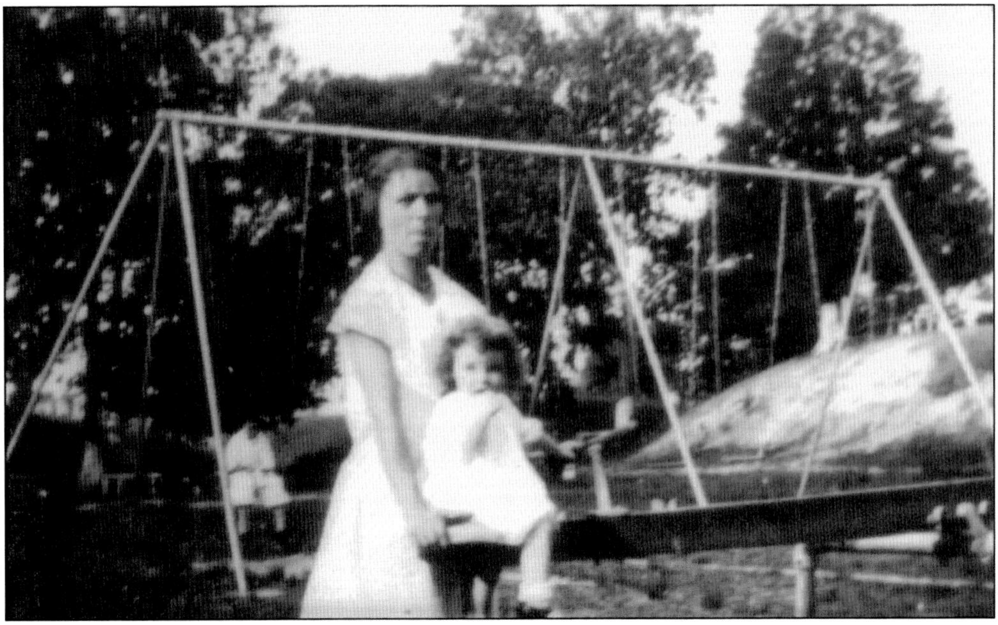

W. P. Magruder donated land for a community park after Wine's Woods was developed. The city named it William Pinkney Magruder Park, and entrance gates were dedicated on May 22, 1937. Mount Hermon Lodge officiated with a formal dedication by Worshipful Master Charles Prince. The Sons of the American Legion, Squadron No. 3, Drum and Bugle Corps led attendees to the flagpole, where Capt. Hugh McClay presented Mayor H. T. Willis a flag. Members of the Roland Read family played at the park shortly after its dedication. (Both Mildred Ford.)

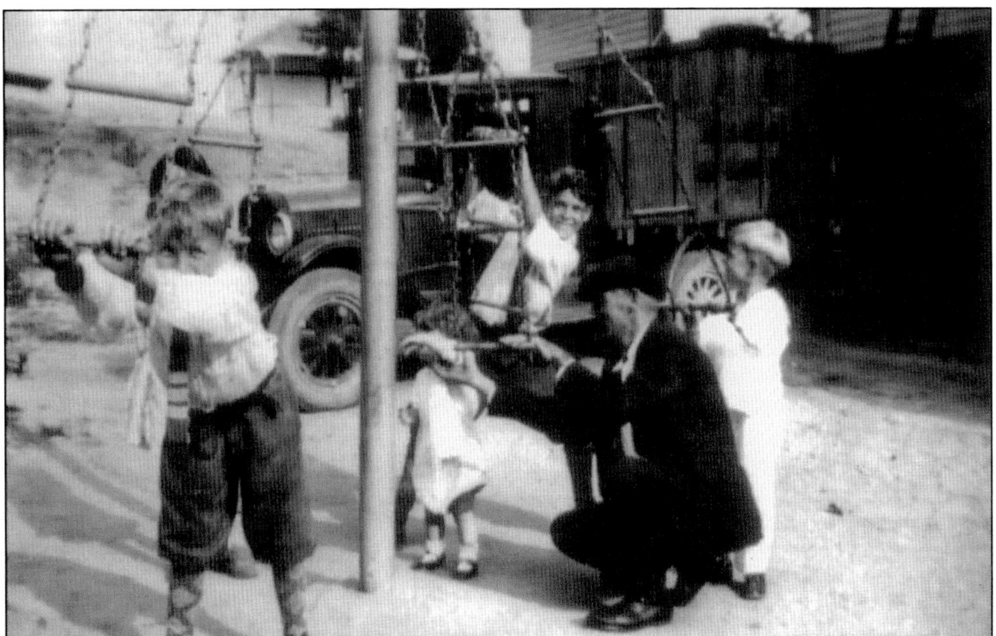

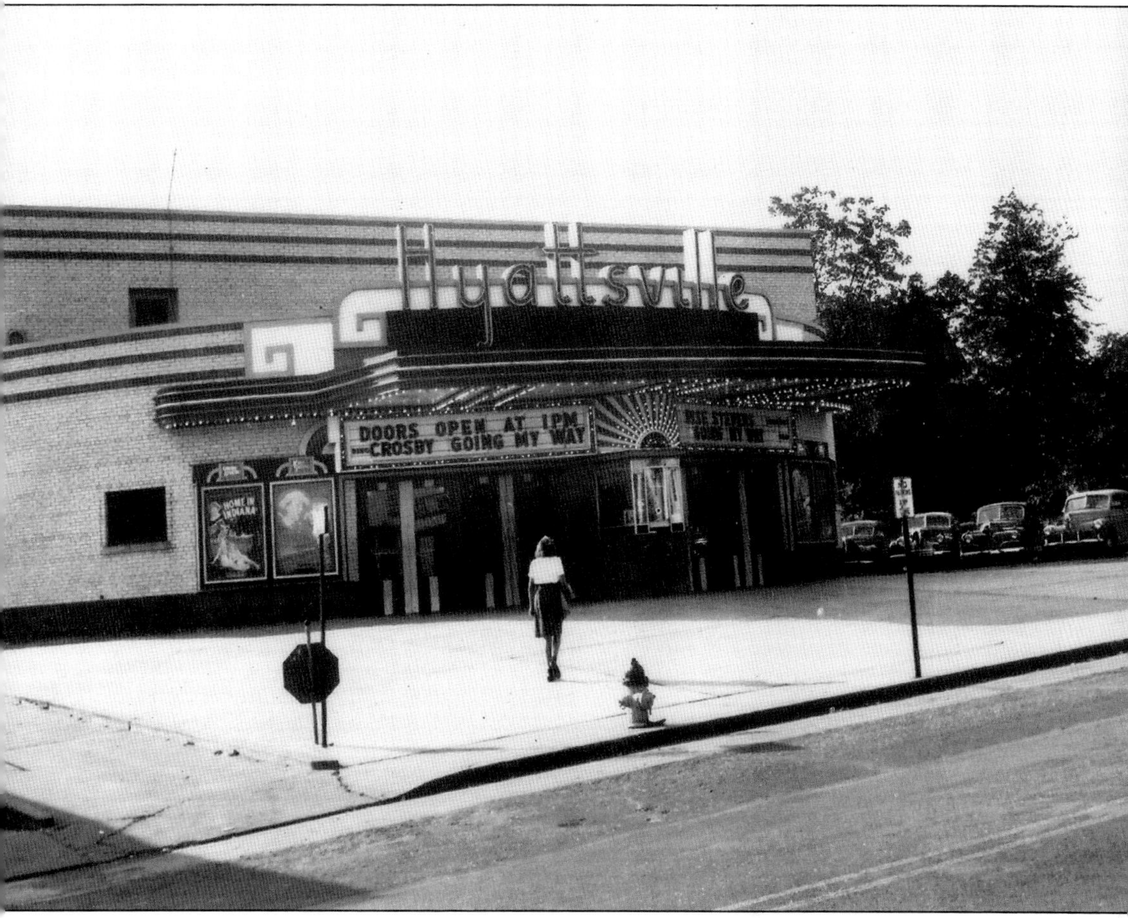

Owner Sidney Lust opened the 1,000-seat Hyattsville Theater, at 5612 Baltimore Avenue on November 21, 1939, with a gala featuring floodlights, a band, and state dignitaries. The inaugural show, *What A Life*, cost attendees 35¢. The theater, designed by internationally known architect John Eberson, had a blue and brown color scheme. Eberson was celebrated for his innovative and prolific designs. The theater was closed in 1965 and demolished the following year. (John Small.)

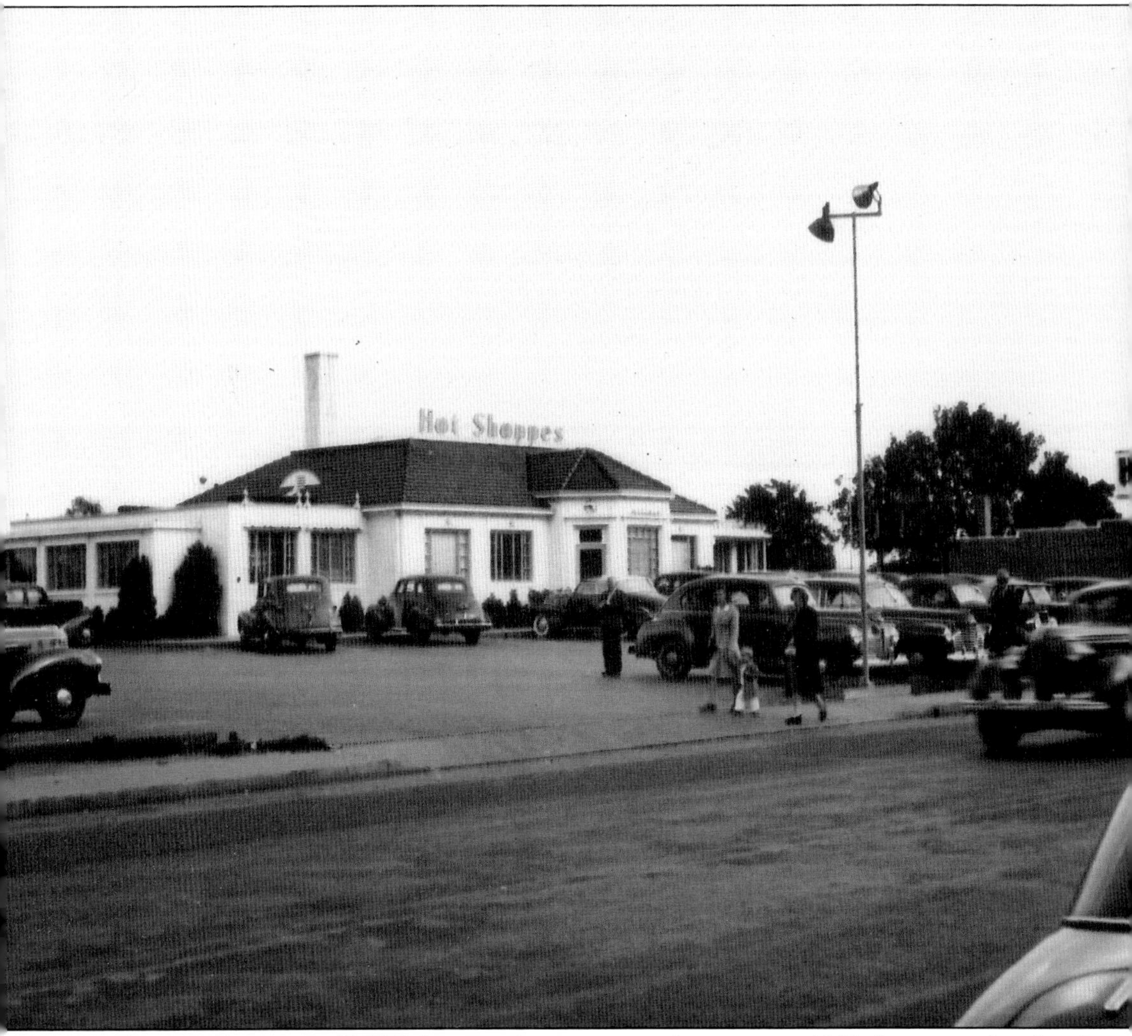

The Hot Shoppes, at 5305 Baltimore Avenue, opened in summer 1940, featuring the chain's prototypical orange-tile roof, coffee shop, drive-in carhop service, and uniformed "Running Boys." J. Willard Marriott and Hugh Colton pooled $6,000 to open a Washington, D.C., soda fountain serving Allen and Wright (A&W) root beer in May 1927. Adding tamales, chili con carne, and "Bar-B-Q," the new "hot" name was born. This location closed in 1962. (John Small.)

Owner Oscar Hiser constructed the Hyattsville Bowling Alley, at 5503 Baltimore Avenue, in 1940. With 24 lanes and a soda fountain, the alley served as a recreational and social gathering place for the region. When Hiser went bankrupt, Field's Buick purchased the property and moved its dealership showroom there in the 1950s. The property was demolished in 2006. (John Small.)

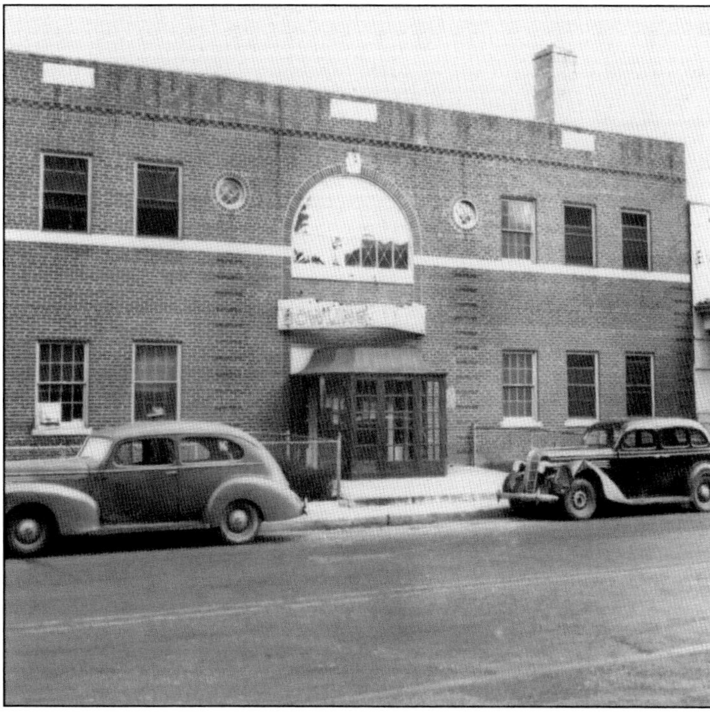

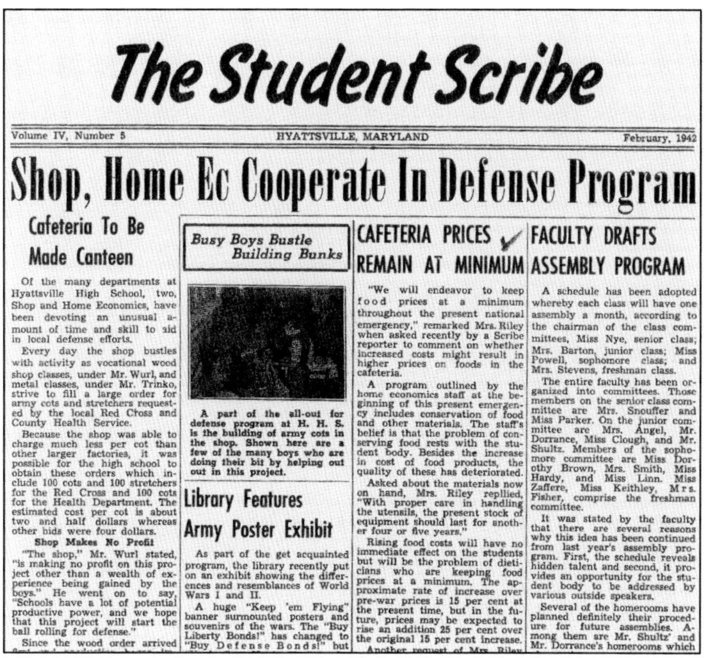

The Student Scribe

Volume IV, Number 5 — HYATTSVILLE, MARYLAND — February, 1942

Shop, Home Ec Cooperate In Defense Program

Cafeteria To Be Made Canteen

Of the many departments at Hyattsville High School, two, Shop and Home Economics, have been devoting an unusual amount of time and skill to aid in local defense efforts.

Every day the shop bustles with activity as vocational wood shop classes, under Mr. Wurl, and metal classes, under Mr. Trinko, strive to fill a large order for army cots and stretchers requested by the local Red Cross and County Health Service.

Because the shop was able to charge much less per cot than other larger factories, it was possible for the high school to obtain these orders which include 100 cots and 100 stretchers for the Red Cross and 100 cots for the Health Department. The estimated cost per cot is about two and half dollars whereas other bids were four dollars.

Shop Makes No Profit

"The shop," Mr. Wurl stated, "is making no profit on this project other than a wealth of experience being gained by the boys." He went on to say, "Schools have a lot of potential productive power, and we hope that this project will start the ball rolling for defense."

Since the wood order arrived

Busy Boys Bustle Building Bunks

A part of the all-out for defense program at H. H. S. is the building of army cots in the shop. Shown here are a few of the many boys who are doing their bit by helping out out in this project.

Library Features Army Poster Exhibit

As part of the get acquainted program, the library recently put on an exhibit showing the differences and resemblances of World Wars I and II.

A huge "Keep 'em Flying" banner surmounted posters and souvenirs of the wars. The "Buy Liberty Bonds!" has changed to "Buy Defense Bonds!" but

CAFETERIA PRICES REMAIN AT MINIMUM

"We will endeavor to keep food prices at a minimum throughout the present national emergency," remarked Mrs. Riley when asked recently by a Scribe reporter to comment on whether increased costs might result in higher prices on foods in the cafeteria.

A program outlined by the home economics staff at the beginning of this present emergency includes conservation of food and other materials. The staff's belief is that the problem of conserving food rests with the student body. Besides the increase in cost of food products, the quality of these has deteriorated.

Asked about the materials now on hand, Mrs. Riley repllied, "With proper care in handling the utensils, the present stock of equipment should last for another four or five years."

Rising food costs will have no immediate effect on the students but will be the problem of dieticians who are keeping food prices at a minimum. The approximate rate of increase over pre-war prices is 15 per cent at the present time, but in the future, prices may be expected to rise an addition 25 per cent over the original 15 per cent increase.

FACULTY DRAFTS ASSEMBLY PROGRAM

A schedule has been adopted whereby each class will have one assembly a month, according to the chairman of the class committees, Miss Nye, senior class; Mrs. Barton, junior class; Miss Powell, sophomore class; and Mrs. Stevens, freshman class.

The entire faculty has been organized into committees. Those members on the senior class committee are Mrs. Snouffer and Miss Parker. On the junior committee are Mrs. Angel, Mr. Dorrance, Miss Clough, and Mr. Shultz. Members of the sophomore committee are Miss Dorothy Brown, Mrs. Smith, Miss Hardy, and Miss Linn. Miss Zaffere, Miss Keithley, Mrs. Fisher, comprise the freshman committee.

It was stated by the faculty that there are several reasons why this idea has been continued from last year's assembly program. First, the schedule reveals hidden talent and second, it provides an opportunity for the student body to be addressed by various outside speakers.

Several of the homerooms have planned definitely their procedure for future assemblies. Among them are Mr. Shultz' and Mr. Dorrance's homerooms which

After Pearl Harbor, the country mobilized for war. Hyattsville High students obtained government contracts constructing 200 cots and 100 stretchers for the local Red Cross and county health services. By February 1942, vocational wood- and metal-shop classes built cots for $2.50 a piece, filling their orders with no profit. Home economics classes practiced first aid and food preservation. Students opened a day care for children of women entering the work force. (John Small.)

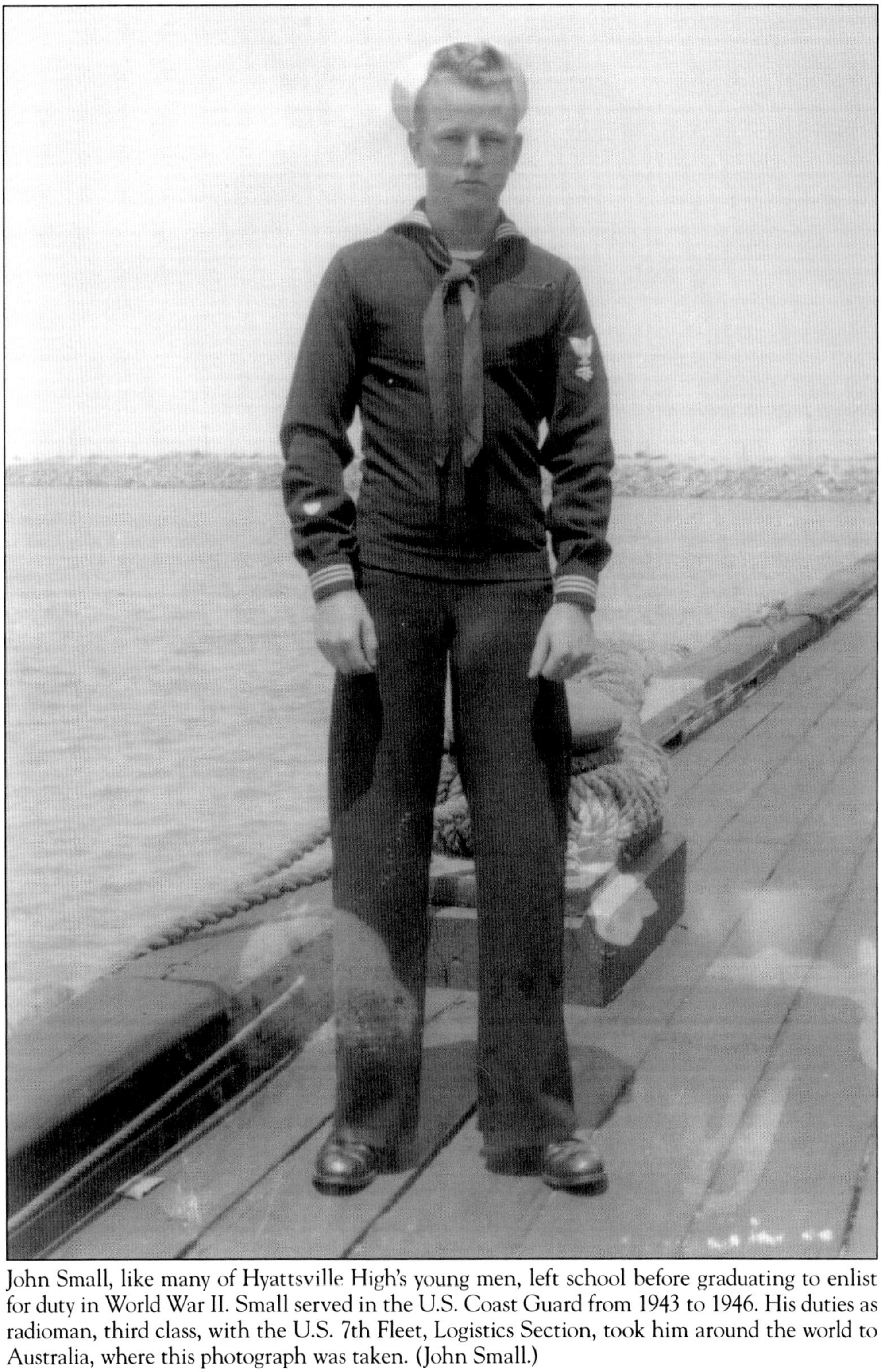

John Small, like many of Hyattsville High's young men, left school before graduating to enlist for duty in World War II. Small served in the U.S. Coast Guard from 1943 to 1946. His duties as radioman, third class, with the U.S. 7th Fleet, Logistics Section, took him around the world to Australia, where this photograph was taken. (John Small.)

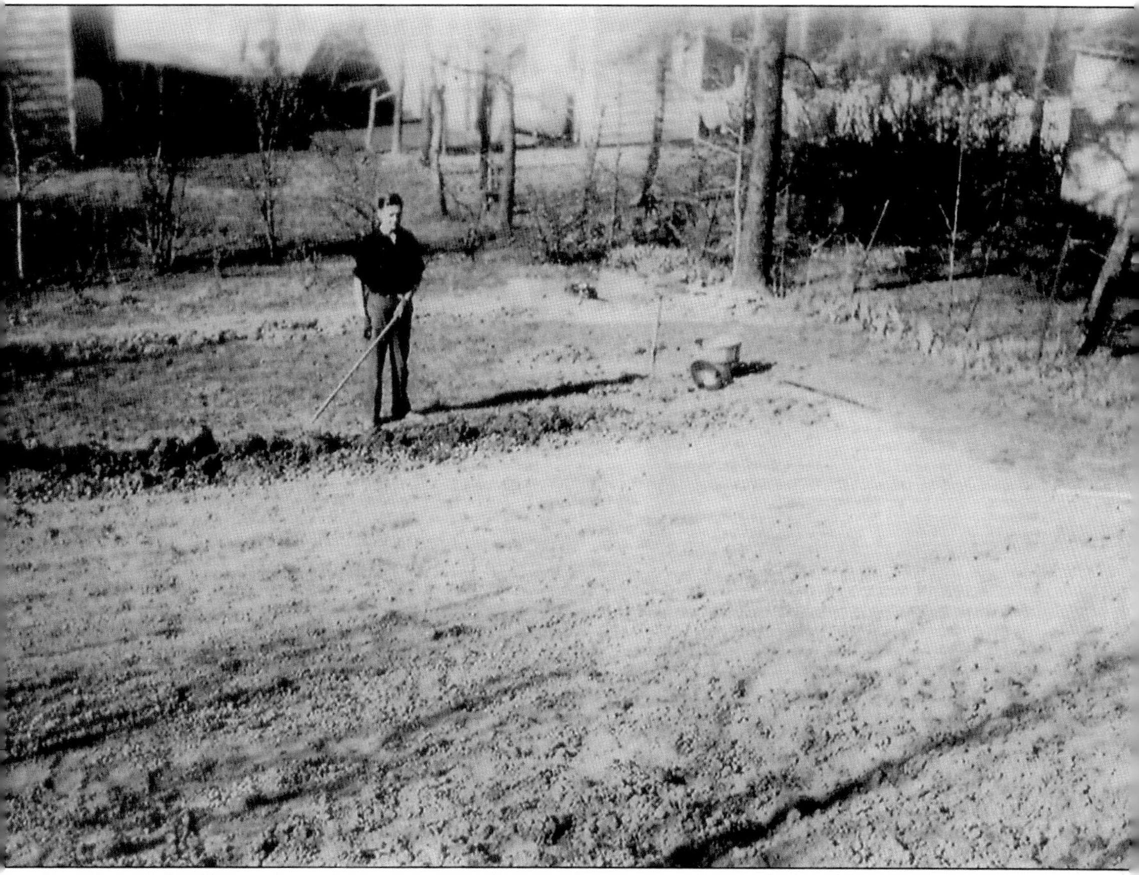

Resident John Kent plants his victory garden in the spring of 1943 behind his home at 4204 Kennedy Street. These gardens were planted to reduce pressure on the public food supply caused by the war and were found to boost the morale of those on the home front. (Doug Dudrow.)

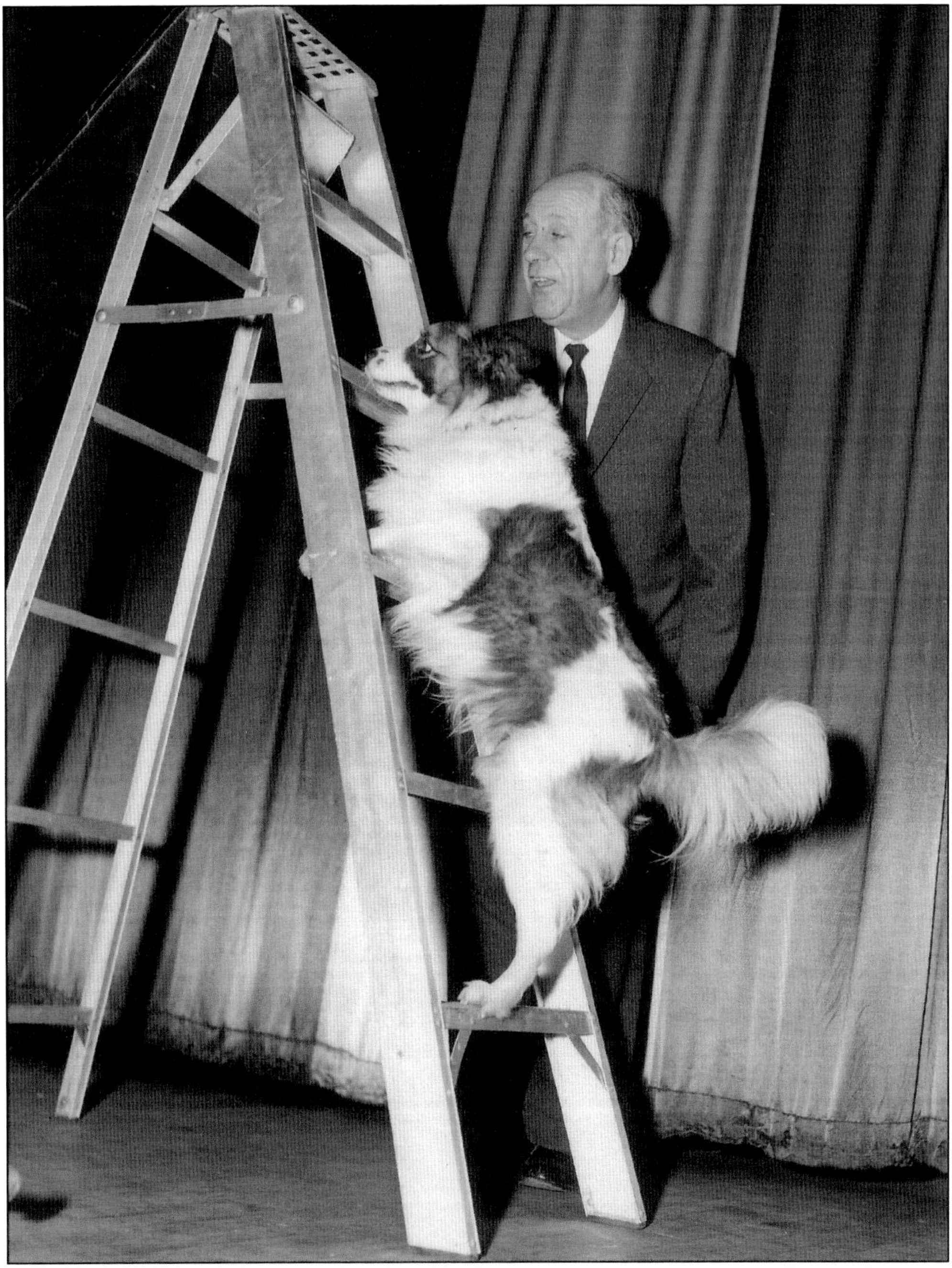

David Ginsberg (1904–1990) moved to town in the mid-1930s. Ginsberg was known by many as the annual Easter Egg Hunt master of ceremonies and as manager at both the Arcade and Hyattsville Theaters. "Uncle Dave," as he was more commonly referred to, was an admired local personality for his charity and work with area children. Dave and dog Rusty entertained at the theaters and fund-raising events throughout the area. (PGCHS.)

Four

MODERN DEVELOPMENT

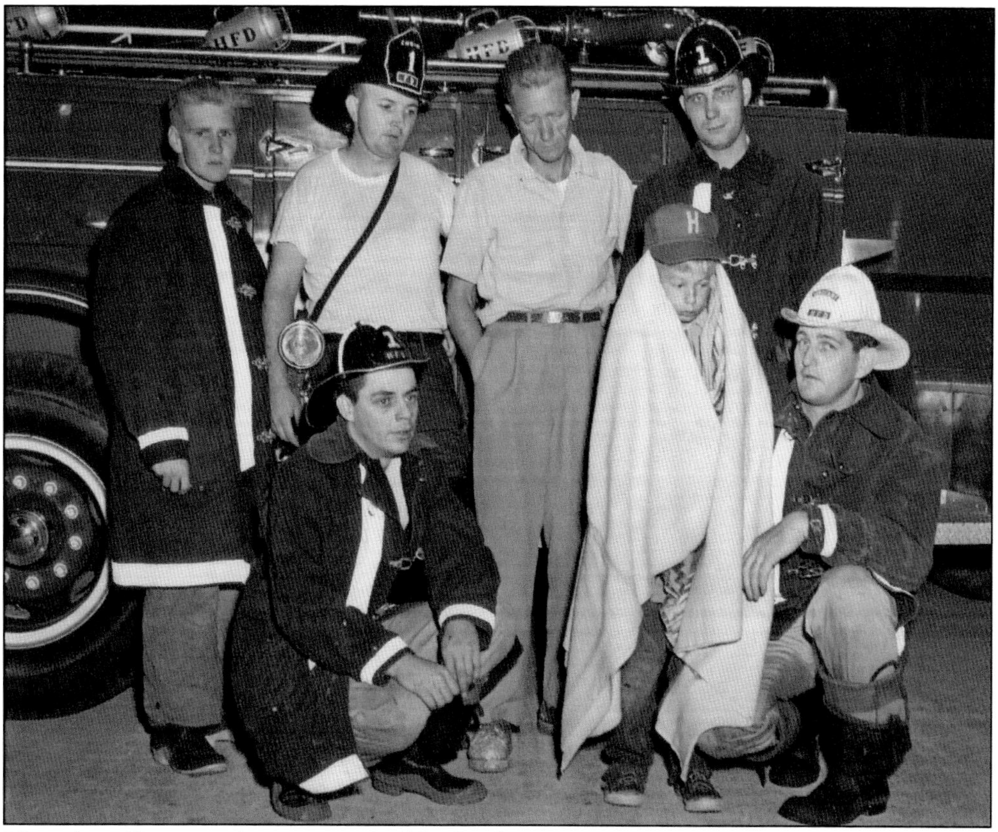

More than 60 county firemen searched for Stephen Payne, 11, of 3901 Oliver Street, on August 12, 1954. He was missing for 31 hours. A 30-minute search located him asleep in a bed of leaves behind the Forty-second Avenue Convalescent Home, camping under the stars. With a blanket and cocoa, local firemen brought him home. Pictured here from left to right are (first row) H. Murray, Stephen, and Sgt. Francis Geary; (second row) Robert Yeabower, Robert Groshon, Paul Payne, and John Grimes. (PGCHS.)

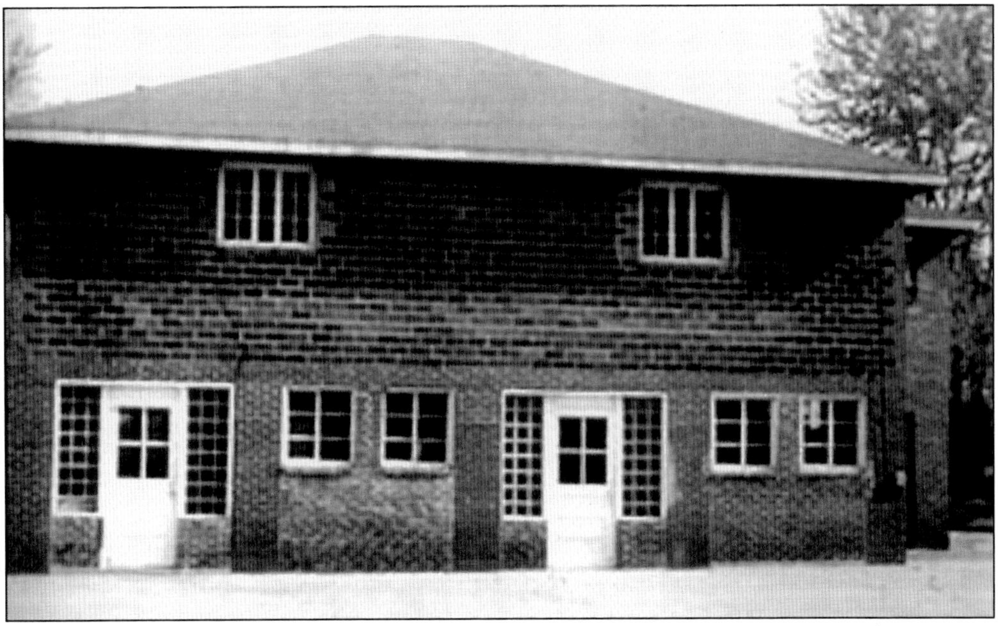

DeMatha Catholic High School opened in September 1946 under the Very Reverend F. Cyprian Nusca, Provincial, and the Very Reverend Michael Nardone, Superior. Eighteen students were educated and prepared for the Trinitarian Order in the Monastery. By 1947, eighty young men from local Catholic families requested schooling. This six-car garage, nicknamed "Fort Necessity," was quickly modified to house classrooms and offices. (DeMatha.)

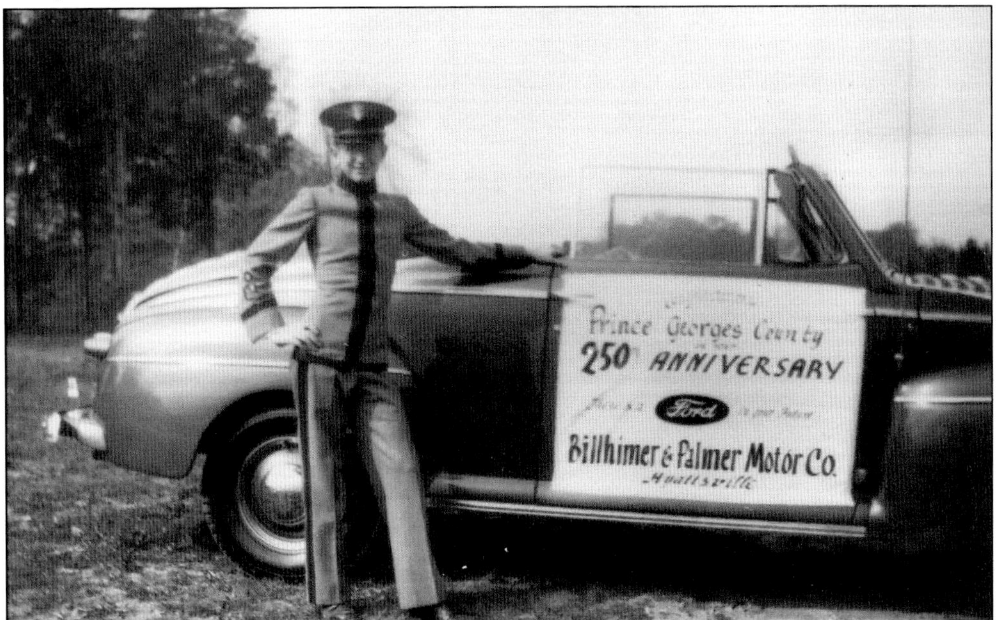

Prince George's County marked its 250th anniversary in 1946 with yearlong festivities. A parade wound its way south on Baltimore Avenue from College Park, making its way to the fairgrounds in Upper Marlboro. Frank Palmer Jr. stands next to the Billhimer and Palmer Ford entry. The day's festivities concluded with an evening dance at the armory. (PGCHS.)

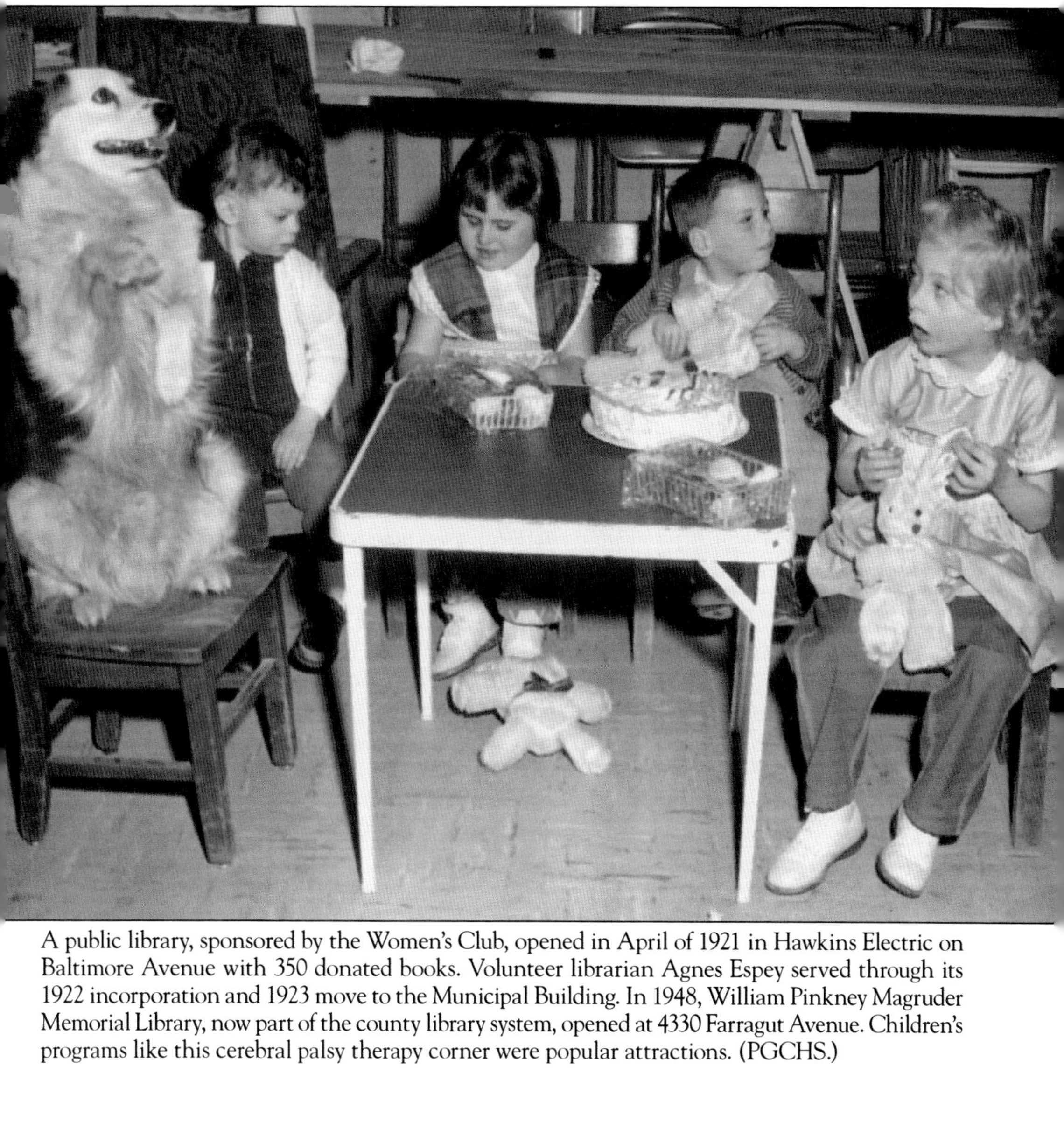

A public library, sponsored by the Women's Club, opened in April of 1921 in Hawkins Electric on Baltimore Avenue with 350 donated books. Volunteer librarian Agnes Espey served through its 1922 incorporation and 1923 move to the Municipal Building. In 1948, William Pinkney Magruder Memorial Library, now part of the county library system, opened at 4330 Farragut Avenue. Children's programs like this cerebral palsy therapy corner were popular attractions. (PGCHS.)

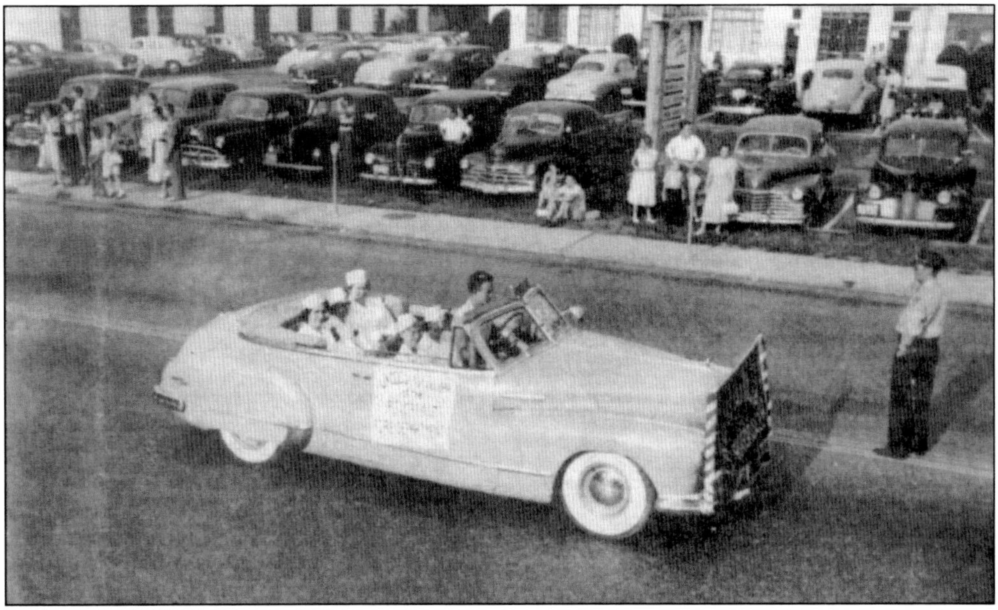

Hyattsville policeman Kenneth Moureau directed traffic in front of the Hot Shoppes during the Independence Day Parade on July 4, 1950. Moureau stands in front of the car with the Ladies Auxiliary of the Riverdale Fire Department. (Betty Moureau.)

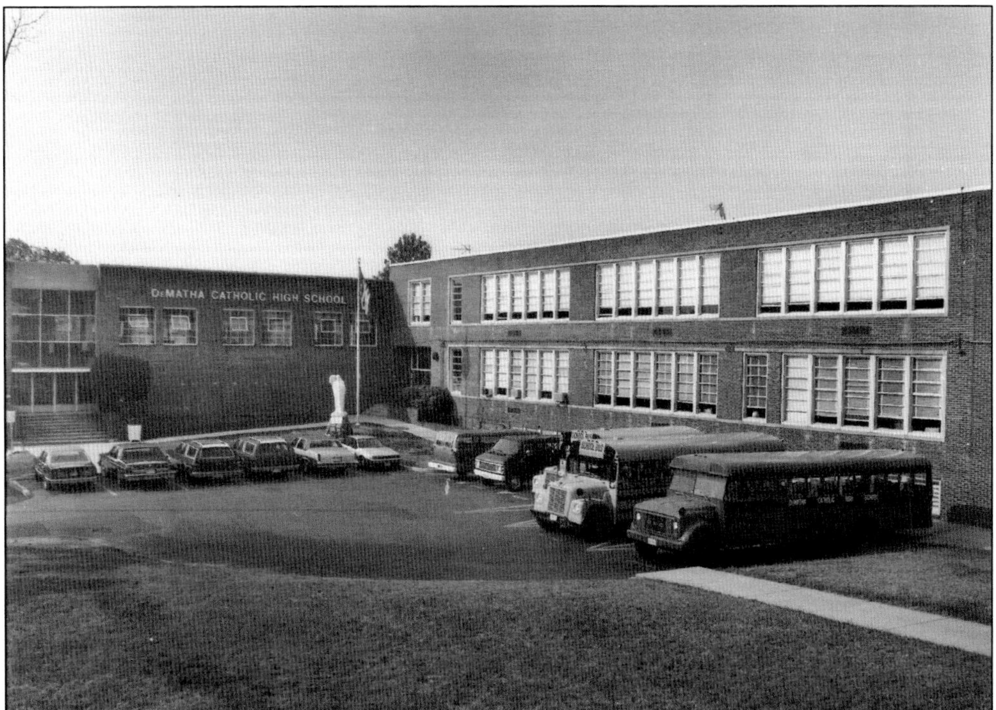

DeMatha Catholic High School's first building designed for secondary education was begun in 1949 and opened in 1950. The building contained classrooms, a library, cafeteria, chapel, laboratory, and an auditorium-gymnasium. The third floor was not completed until 1951, housing additional classrooms. Today this is known as the "old wing." (DeMatha.)

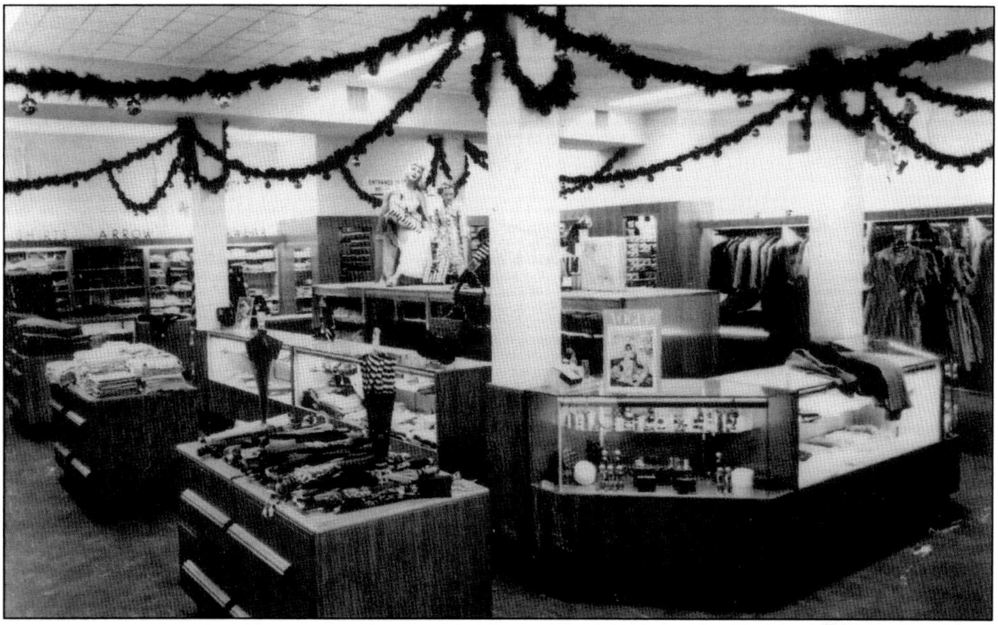

Deitz's Department Store stayed in the same location but modernized its interior displays. Keeping up with the desires of the 1950s consumer required quite a change from its establishment as a dry goods retailer. (PGCHS.)

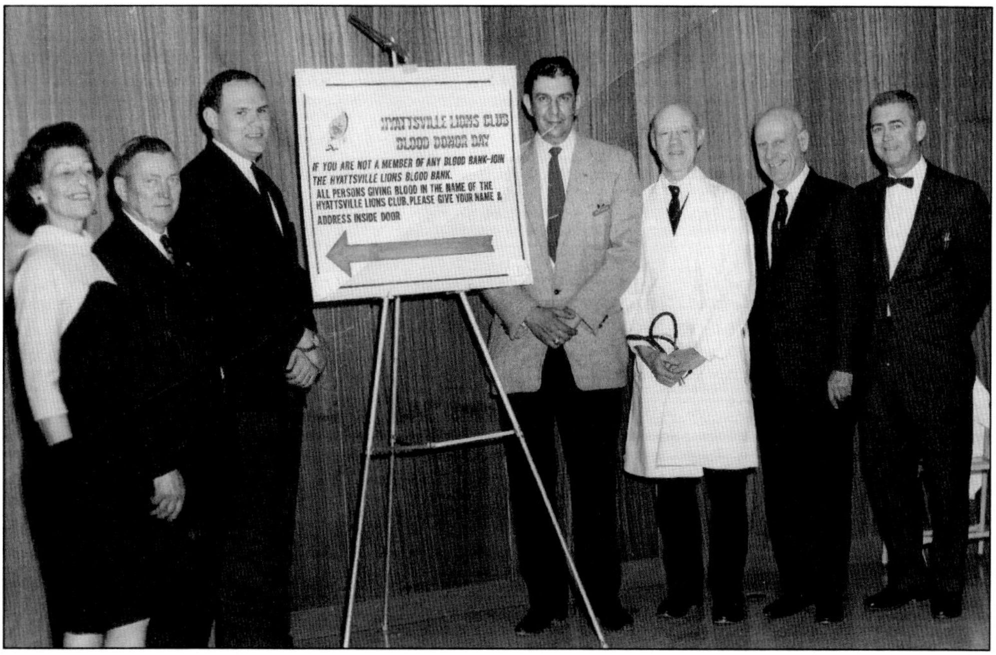

Lions International chartered their Hyattsville chapter on March 29, 1937, in a ceremony at Beaver Dam Country Club. Local members organized "to take an active interest in the civic, commercial, social, and moral welfare of the community." During its 70-year history, the chapter sponsored drug awareness programs, boys and girls clubs, educational activities, and health and welfare causes, particularly visual disabilities. These local members organized a 1950s blood drive. (Nina Faye.)

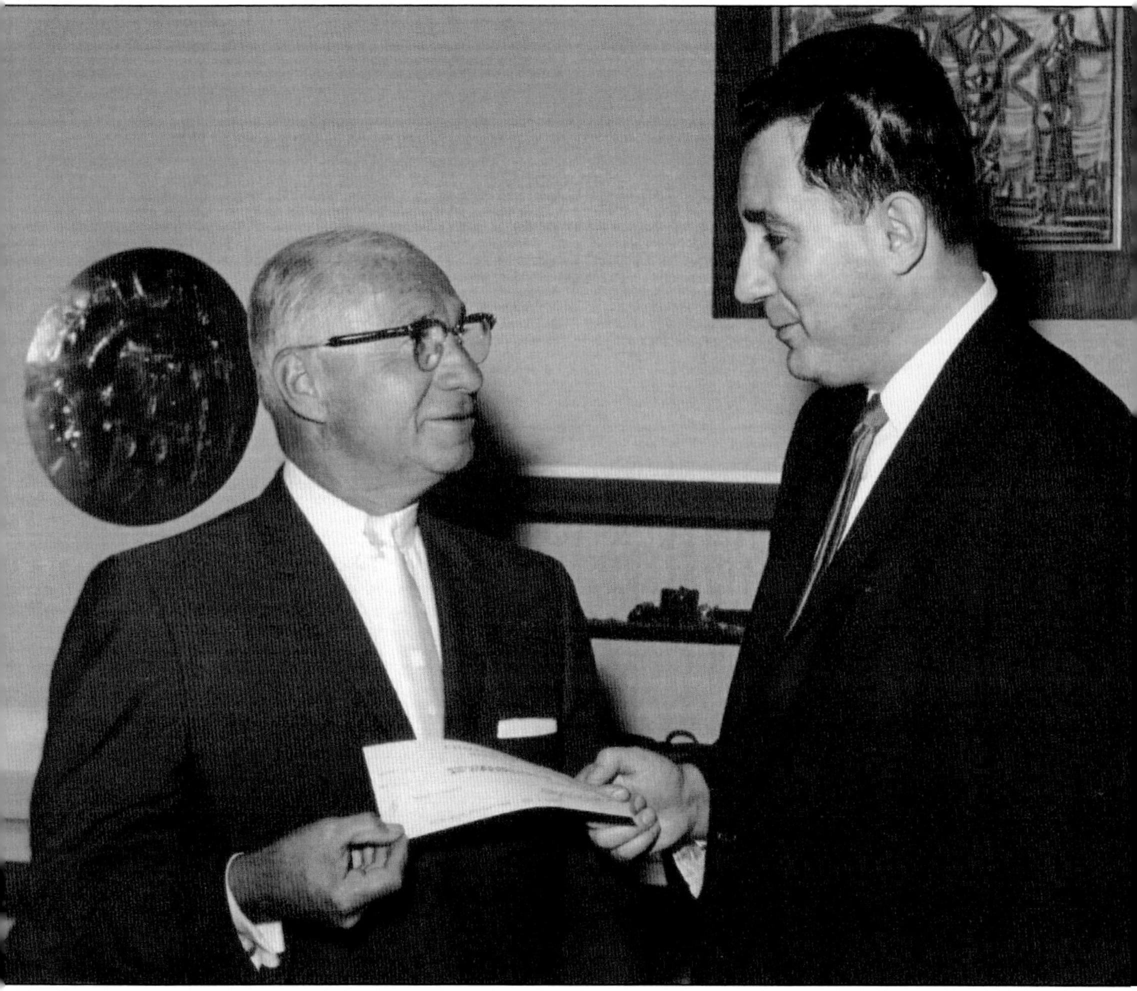

Philip Lustine, director of Citizens Bank of Maryland, purchased $50,000 in State of Israel Bonds for the bank's 1951 portfolio, along with nine other major area banks. Lustine (left) accepts the bonds from Israeli Embassy minister plenipotentiary Mordechai Gazit. Prime Minister David Ben-Gurion offered the bonds to obtain funding for immigrant absorption, to construct a national infrastructure, and to engage the Diaspora community in building the new Jewish state. (PGCHS.)

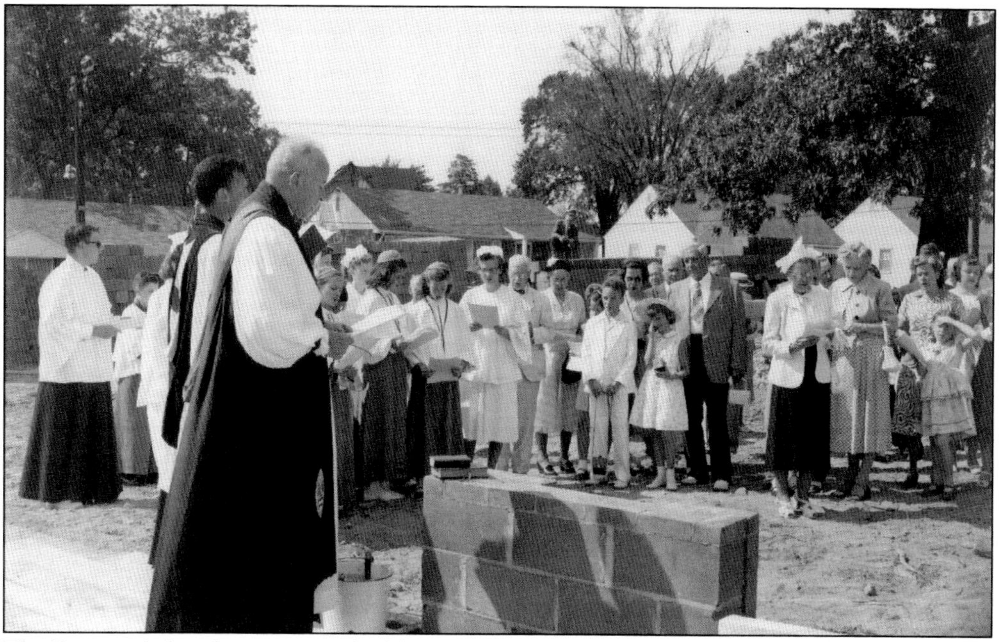

The Episcopal church outgrew its building for a second time and in 1947 purchased 5901 Thirty-sixth Avenue. St. Matthew's Parish now combined Hyattsville, University Park, University Hills, and Lewisdale. A rectory was completed on the site first in 1951. July 12, 1953, the cornerstone-laying ceremony for the $127,000 parish hall was held. The Pickney Memorial Episcopal Church on Gallatin Street was sold to another congregation. (Kathy Albertson.)

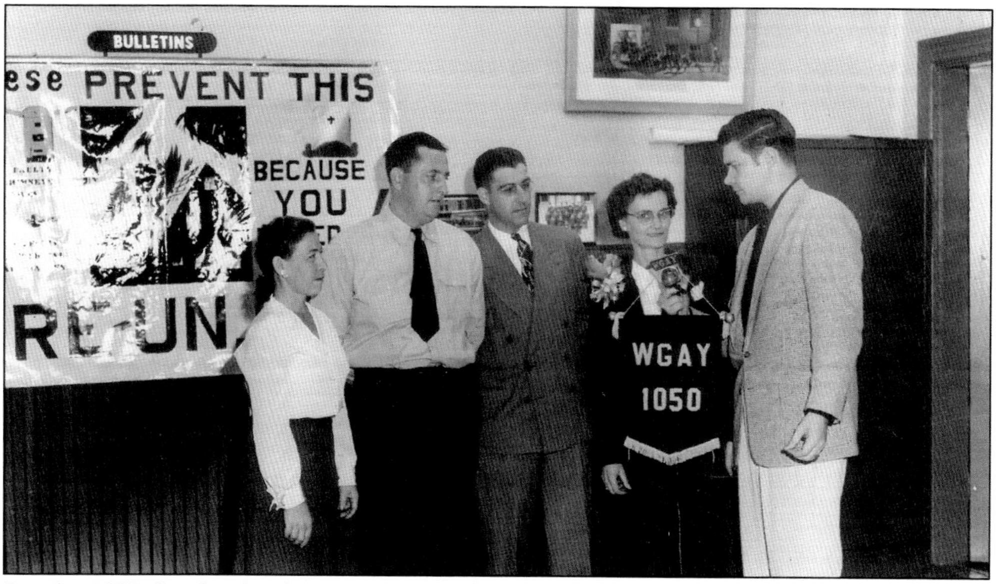

Popular 1950s local radio show *Hya Hyattsville* normally recorded with emcee Chuck Dulane (right) from neighborhood homes, but to highlight Fire Prevention Week, WGAY 1050 relocated to the fire station. From left to right, Rose DiVincenzo, local auxiliary, president; Chief Charles DiVincenzo; Councilman George Griebel, fire commissioner; and Alice Grimes, state ladies' auxiliary president are interviewed. The October 8, 1951, broadcast was recorded amid the station's alarms and bells. (PGCHS.)

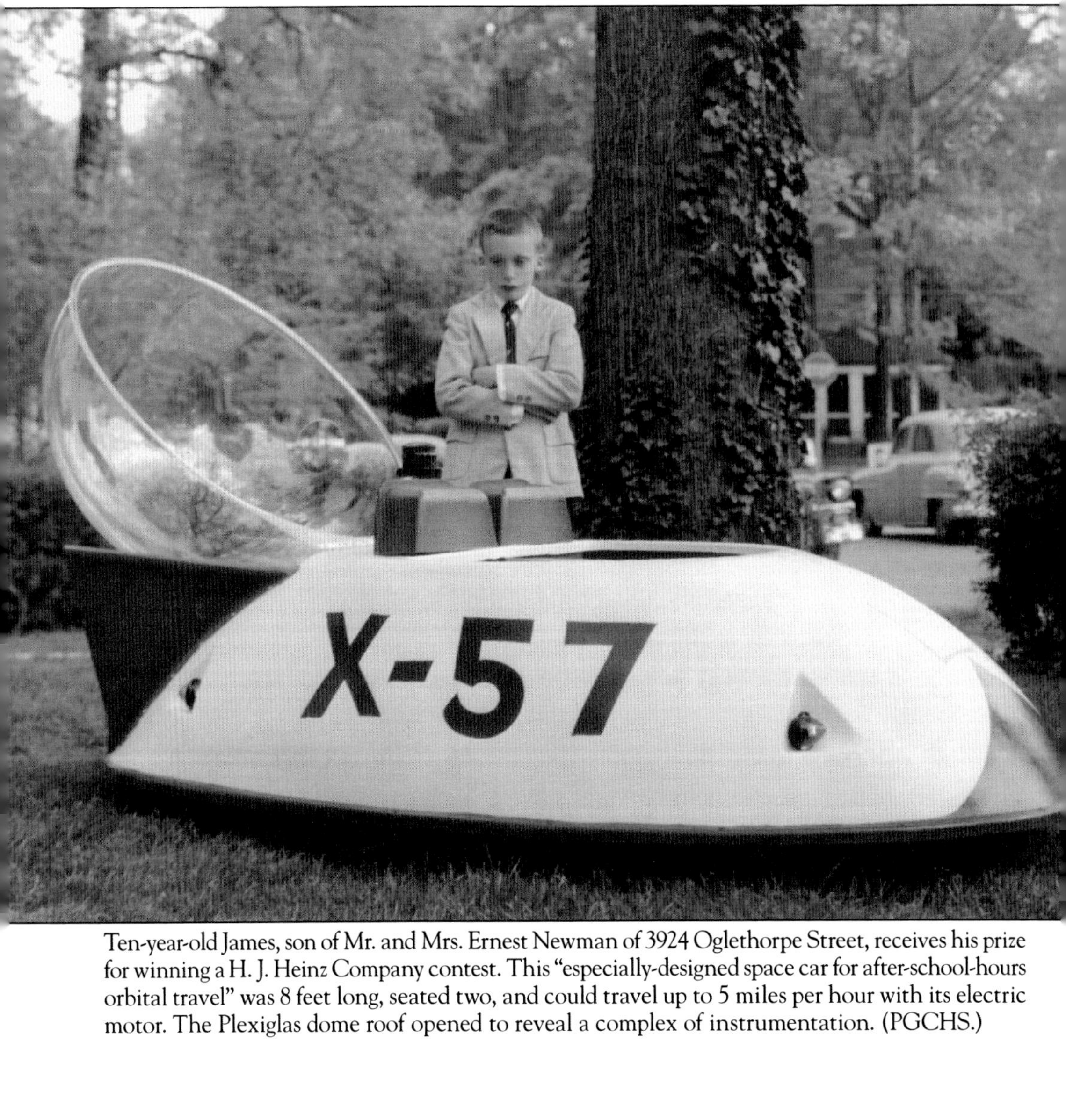

Ten-year-old James, son of Mr. and Mrs. Ernest Newman of 3924 Oglethorpe Street, receives his prize for winning a H. J. Heinz Company contest. This "especially-designed space car for after-school-hours orbital travel" was 8 feet long, seated two, and could travel up to 5 miles per hour with its electric motor. The Plexiglas dome roof opened to reveal a complex of instrumentation. (PGCHS.)

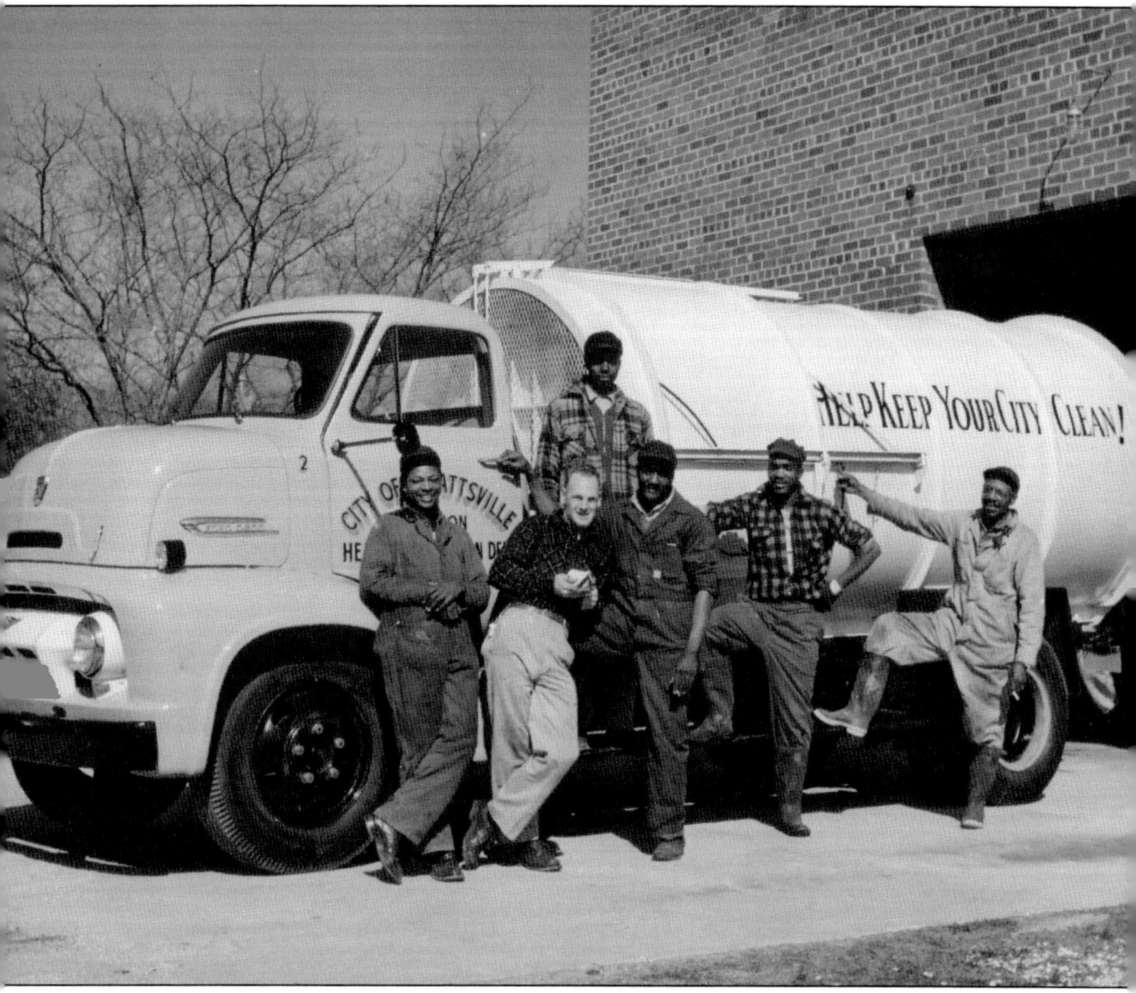

The city's first Packmores garbage and trash trucks arrived in October 1953. Maintenance crew members, from left to right, Nathan Bright, Johnny Beryman, Norwood Seales, Charles Hurt, Buster Briggs, and Land Jones display the new vehicles. (City of Hyattsville.)

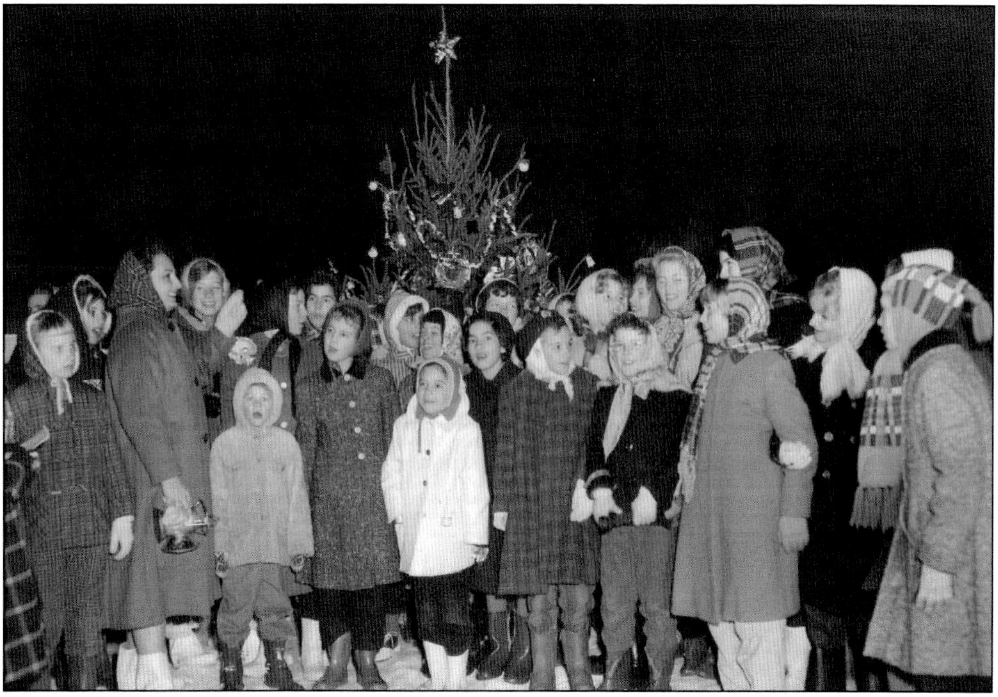

Hyattsville has long held the tradition of lighting a city Christmas tree. These 1950s carolers sang around the city tree. (PGCHS.)

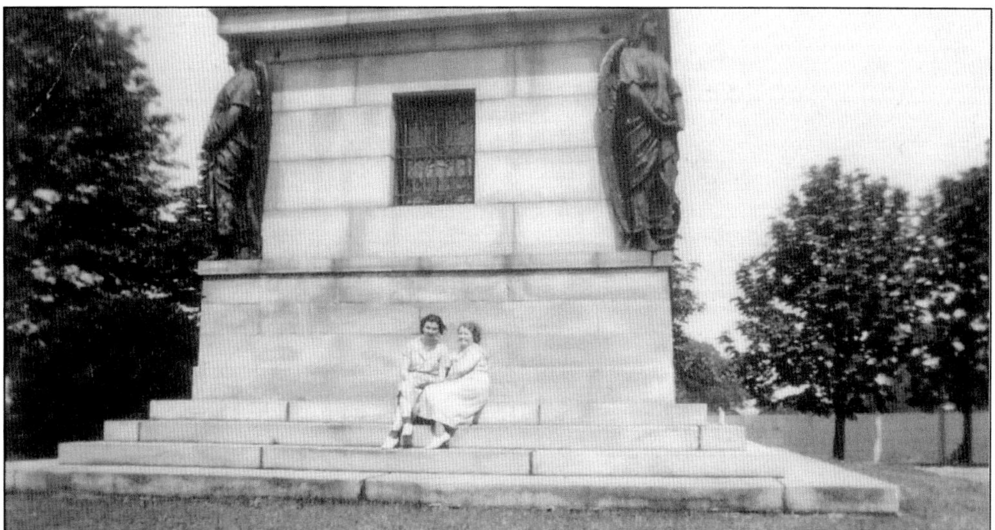

Bellevue had several fountains and a swimming pool and included the family mausoleum. The structure was designed by architect Artemis and decorated with Louis Tiffany stained-glass windows. When the farm was sold in 1955, the family moved the mausoleum to Rock Creek Cemetery. (City of Hyattsville.)

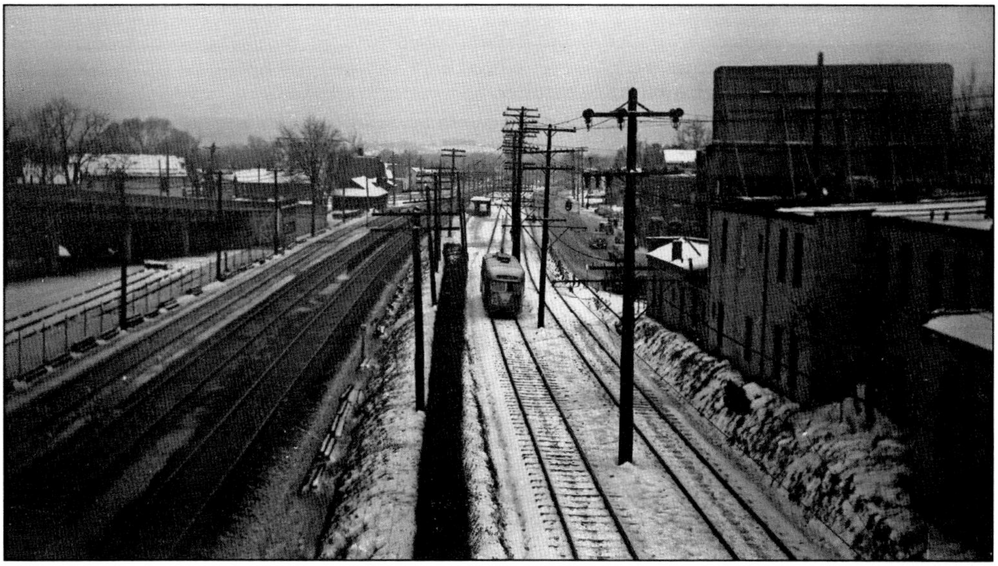

Streetcar service continued throughout the metropolitan area until 1961, first through Washington Railway and Electric Company (WRECO) in 1933 and then the Capital Transit Company in 1955. Hyattsville service on the No. 82 line ran from Washington's Potomac Park to Branchville, Maryland. (HSWDC.)

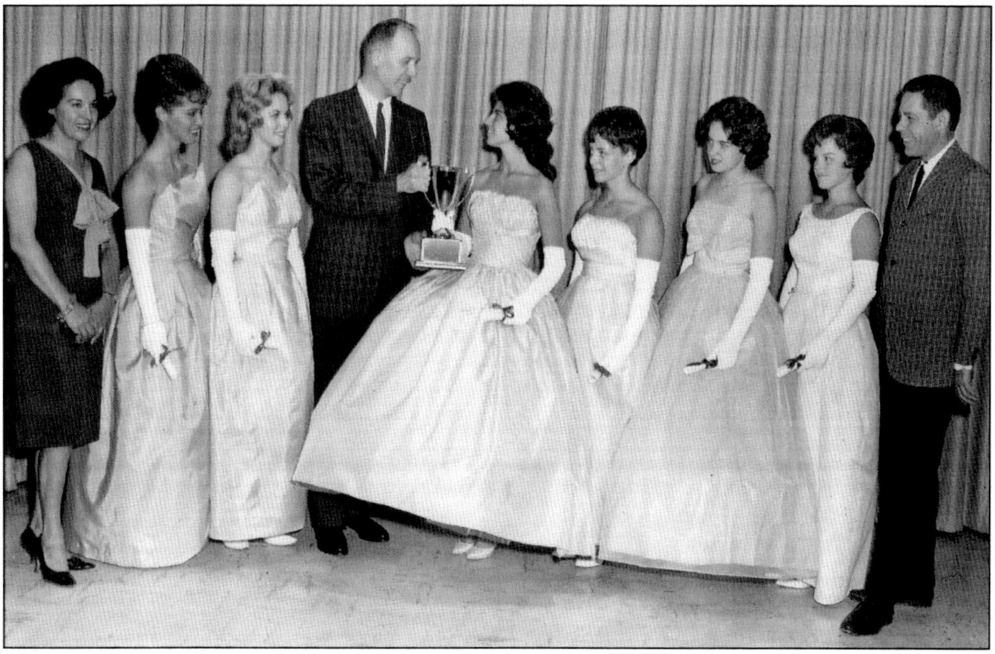

Councilman William Hendrix presented Mary Del Borrell, of 6620 Twenty-fourth Avenue, a loving cup after winning WMAL-TV's *Woman's World* Miss Independence contest. Del Borrell reigned over the Magruder Park mammoth Independence Day celebration with her five competitors as maids of honor. From left to right are WMAL-TV's personality Lorraine Flocks; Michele DeMarco, Suitland; Kathy Foster, High Point; Hendrix; Del Borrell, Northwestern; Kathleen Henry, Bladensburg; Paula Hill, Duval; Eileen Mobley, Laurel; and Pete Jamerson, *Woman's World* emcee. (PGCHS.)

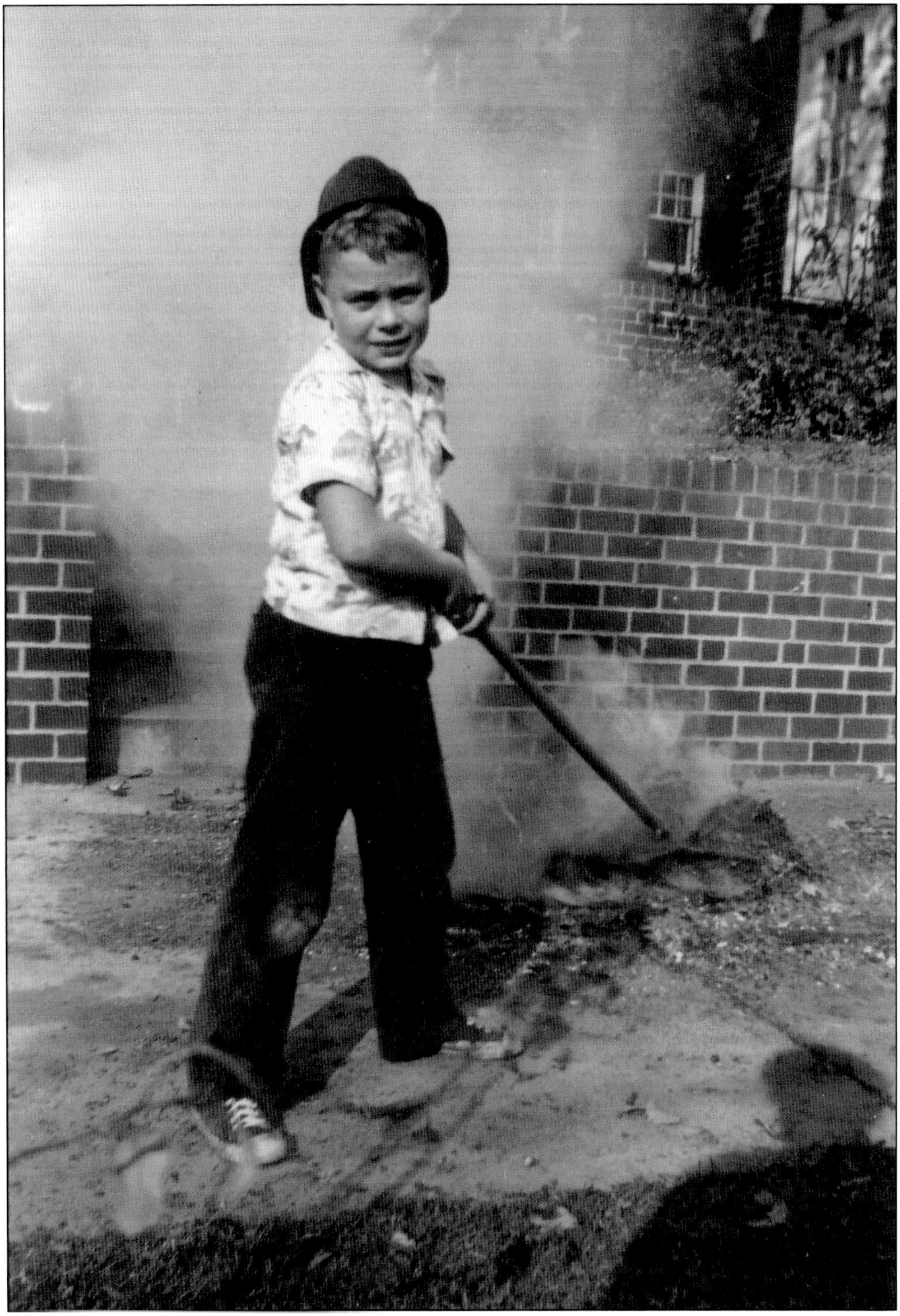

Burning fall leaves was a common occurrence around town. Frank Durgin, age eight, rakes the leaves at his 6001 Forty-first Avenue home into the driveway, where they were burned in November 1955. This was the last year it was legal. (Nina Faye.)

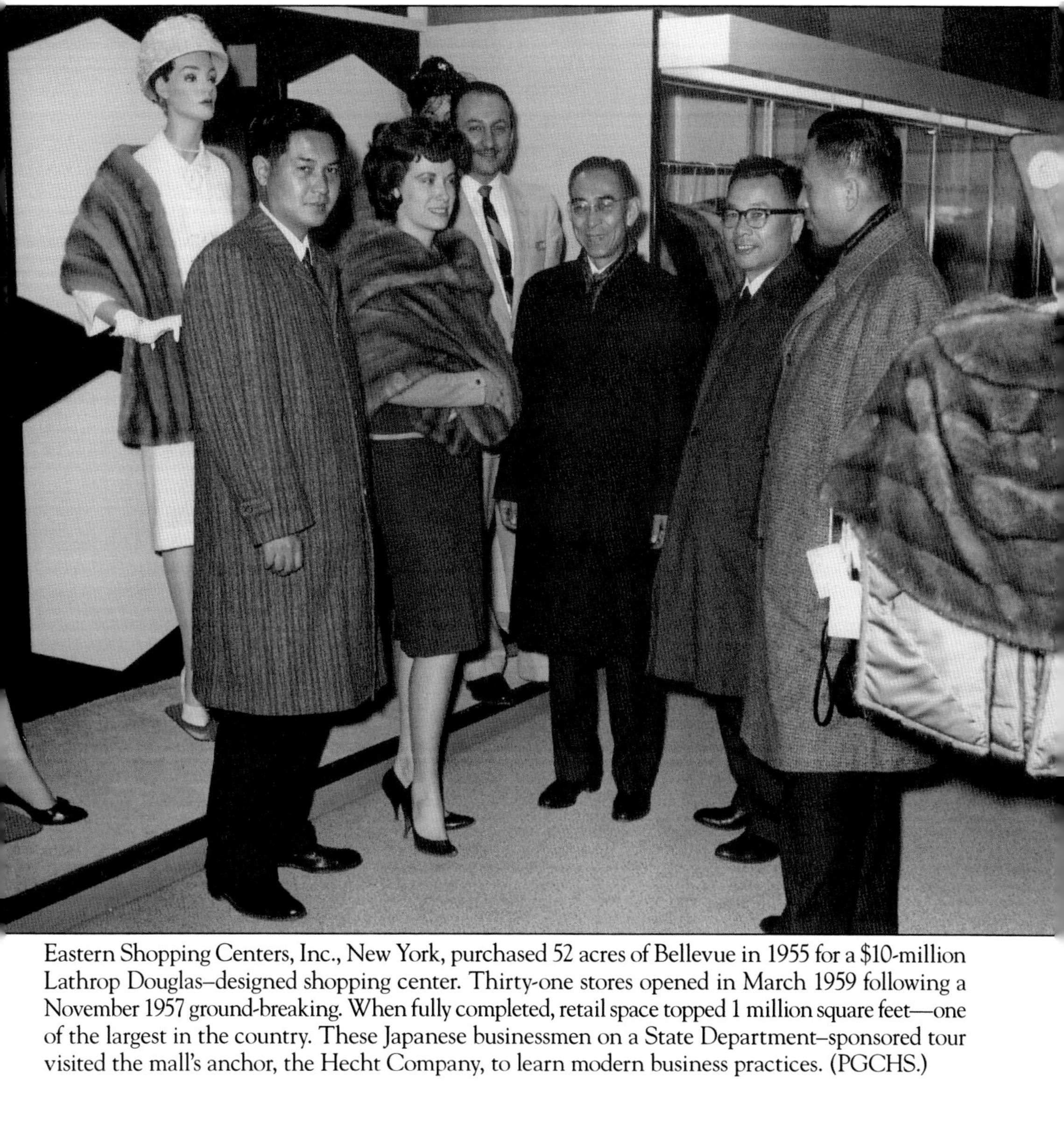

Eastern Shopping Centers, Inc., New York, purchased 52 acres of Bellevue in 1955 for a $10-million Lathrop Douglas–designed shopping center. Thirty-one stores opened in March 1959 following a November 1957 ground-breaking. When fully completed, retail space topped 1 million square feet—one of the largest in the country. These Japanese businessmen on a State Department–sponsored tour visited the mall's anchor, the Hecht Company, to learn modern business practices. (PGCHS.)

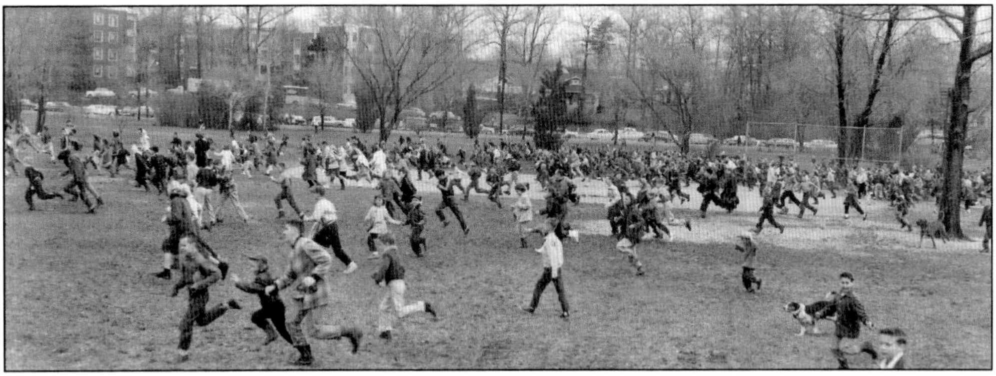

The Kiwanis Club of Prince George's County was chartered in 1934 as a group of business and professional men dedicated to community service and ethical standards in professional and personal relationships. The Kiwanis have sponsored the annual Magruder Park Easter Egg Hunt since April 1936 under Pres. John White. This 1958 event kicked off with the traditional "cackleberries" hunt hidden by the Easter Bunny's Kiwanis helpers. (PGCHS.)

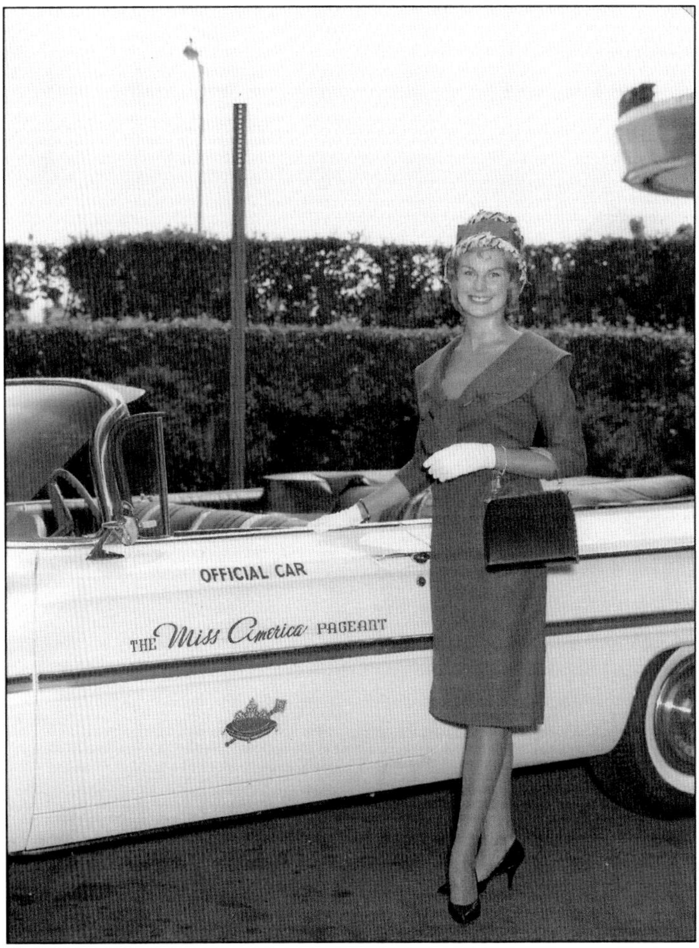

Robin Carole Davis of 4304 Emerson Street was crowned Miss Maryland 1960. This pageant was an official preliminary to the Miss America Organization. Davis went on to represent Maryland in that competition. (PGCHS.)

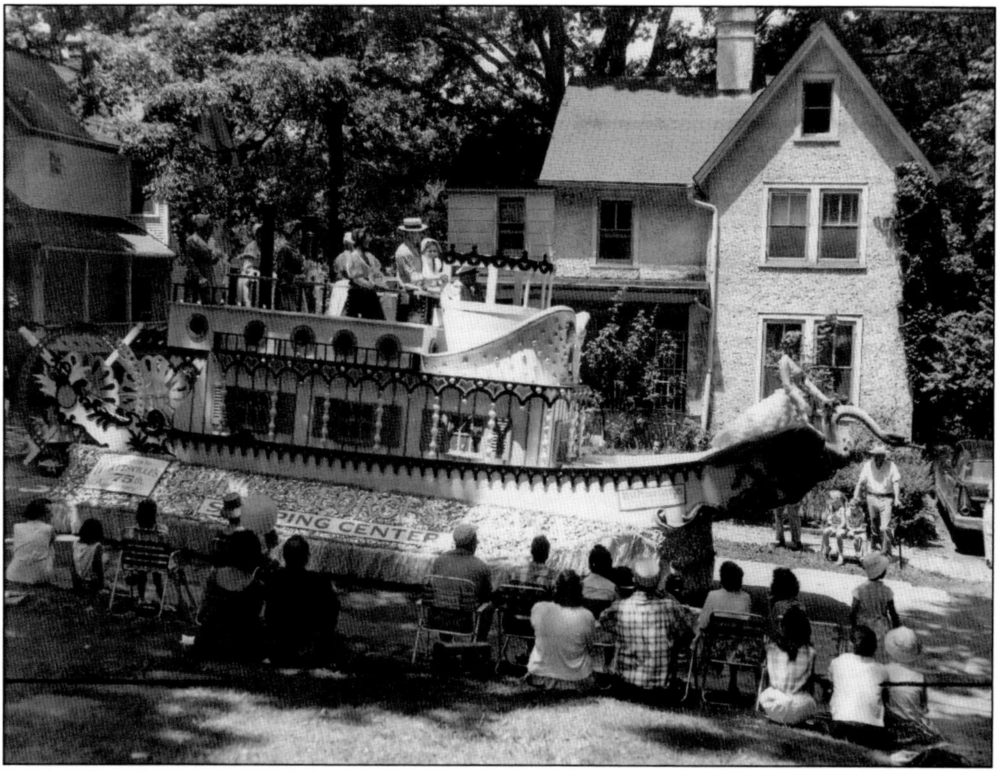

Hyattsville's 75th Diamond Jubilee Anniversary was celebrated with a daylong special commemoration on October 6, 1961. Jacob Walker was appointed general chairman overseeing the organization committees. WMAL Radio's Frank Harden and Jackson Weaver were marshals and emcees for the parade seen here. Sporting events and fireworks filled the day, capped off by the "Old Timers" dinner dance hosted by DeMatha. (PGCHS.)

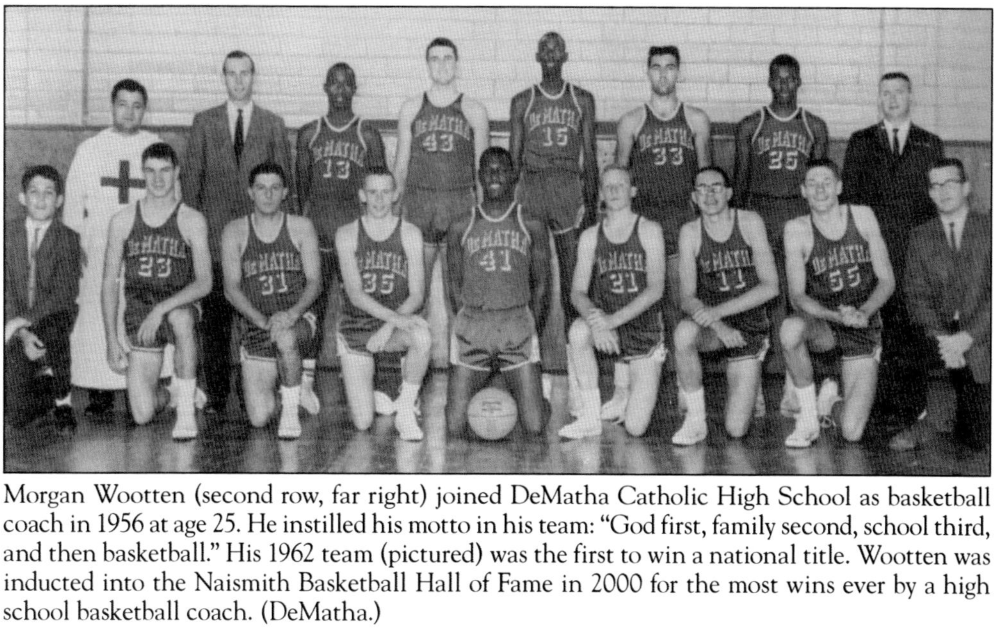

Morgan Wootten (second row, far right) joined DeMatha Catholic High School as basketball coach in 1956 at age 25. He instilled his motto in his team: "God first, family second, school third, and then basketball." His 1962 team (pictured) was the first to win a national title. Wootten was inducted into the Naismith Basketball Hall of Fame in 2000 for the most wins ever by a high school basketball coach. (DeMatha.)

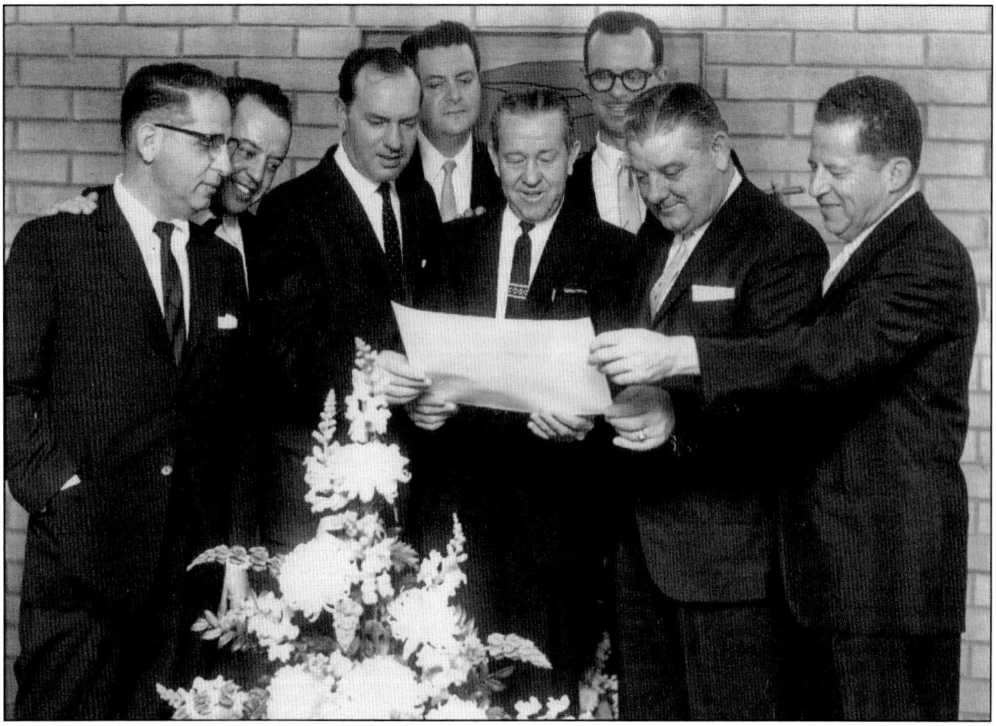

Oglethorpe House, at 4410 Oglethorpe Street, was the first high-rise in the county in 1962. The eight-story apartment building had 143 units, air-conditioning, and pool recreation area. Officials and developers celebrate its completion: (from left to right) Milton Fleisher and Louis Zuckerman, Meltzer Group; Mallon Middleton and Julius Katz, city council; Perry Wilkinson, Speaker of the House of Delegates; Louis Meltzer, president, Meltzer Group; Jesse Baggett, county commissioner; and Lynwood Satorioris, Meltzer Group. (PGCHS.)

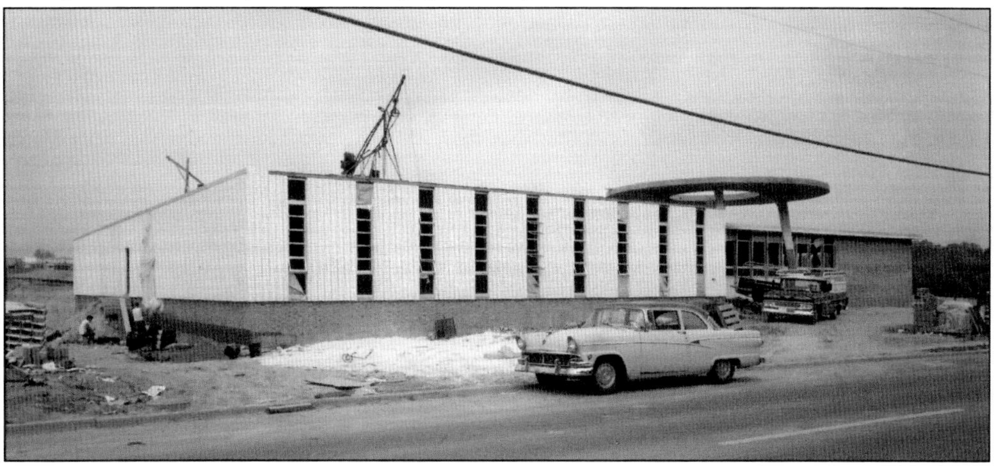

County commissioners borrowed $1 million in January 1959 for land, construction, and equipping of the first regional library. Mount Rainier architects Walton and Madden designed the 42,000-square-foot building for 6530 Adelphi Road. Bladensburg contractors Permanent Builders Company worked from the October 15, 1962, ground-breaking until January 19, 1964, when state senator Winship Wheatley of Hyattsville and Gov. Millard Tawes dedicated the library in President Kennedy's memory. (PGCMLS.)

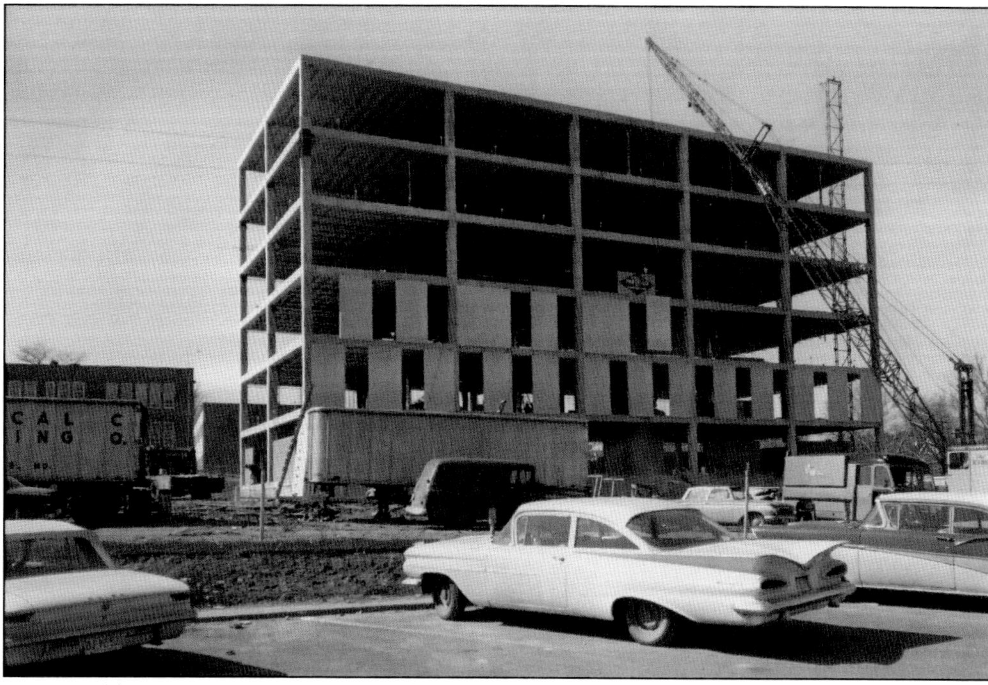

A sum of $900,000 in Municipal Building Certificates of Indebtedness was sold equally to Suburban Trust Company and Citizens Bank of Maryland in 1962 for construction of a new city office building at 4307 Jefferson Street. Architects Kea, Shaw, and Associates and general contractor James L. Partello, Inc., completed the building for its November 25, 1962, dedication. Mayor Joseph Lilly (below, center) presided over the ceremonies. The building was demolished in 2006. (Both City of Hyattsville.)

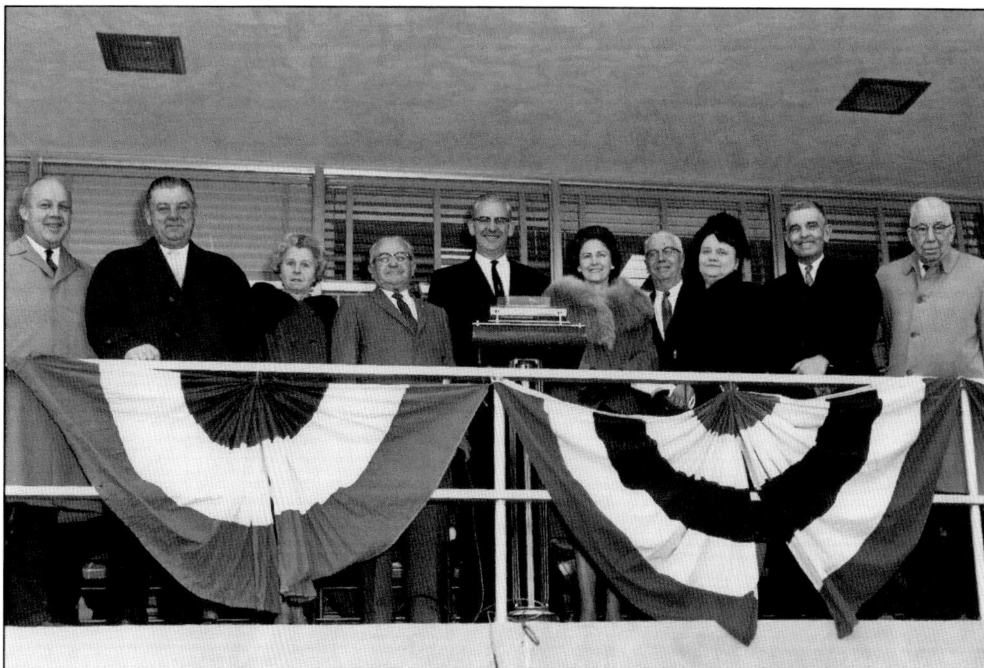

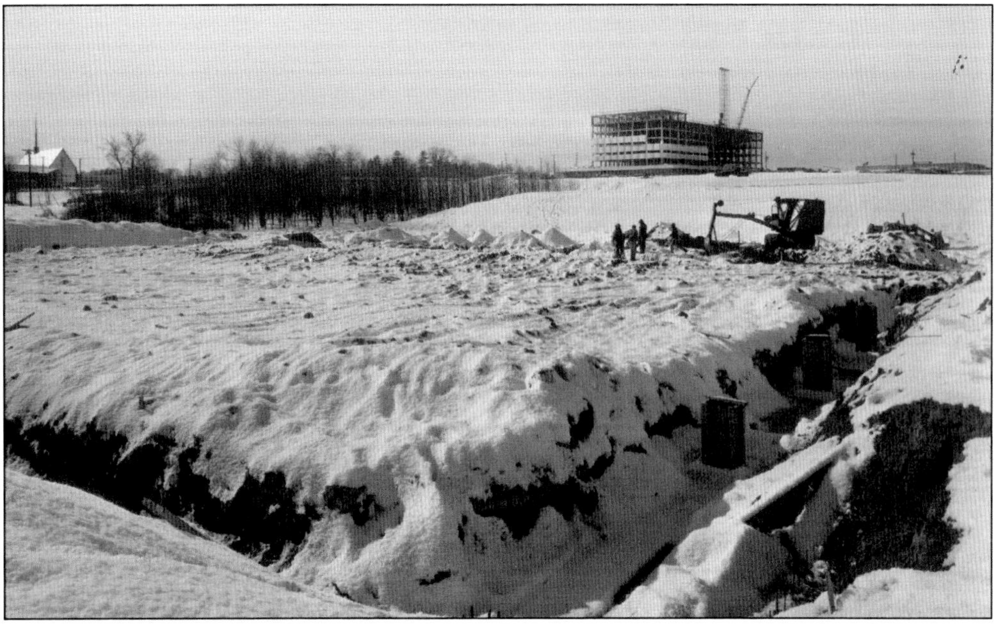

Marvin and Herschel Blumberg, Bancroft Construction Company principals, bought 140 acres of the Heurich farm in 1955. They envisioned a $78-million office/residential satellite city, "New Town Center," designed for the Year 2000 Plan for orderly suburban growth. Internationally known architect Edward Durrell Stone was selected. Stone designed the Kennedy Center and the National Geographic Society building. The Plaza Towers West is seen here under construction in January 1963. (PGCMLS.)

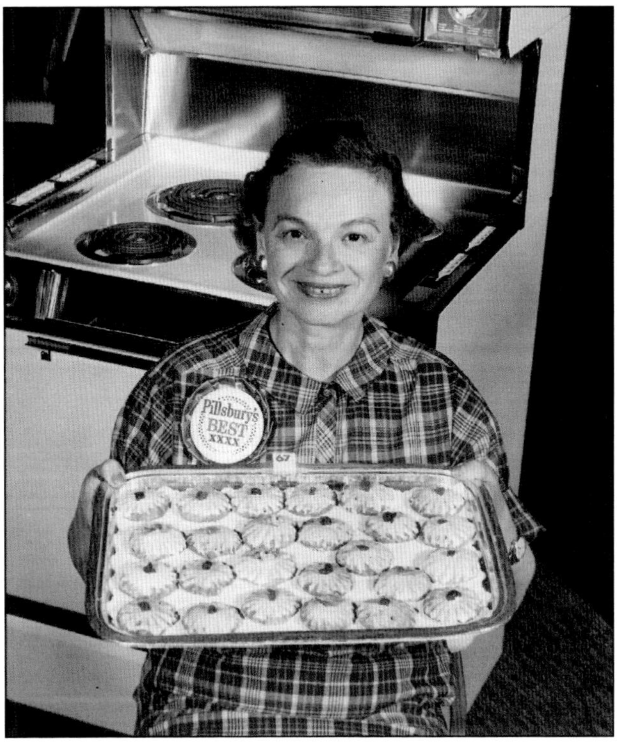

Jean C. Wahlers of 5904 Thirty-sixth Avenue displays her entry in the Pillsbury 15th Grand National Bake-Off at the Beverly Hilton Hotel, in Los Angeles, California, on September 16, 1963. Wahlers and 79 other senior entrants received an all-expense-paid trip and the General Electric range and mixer used in the competition. (PGCHS.)

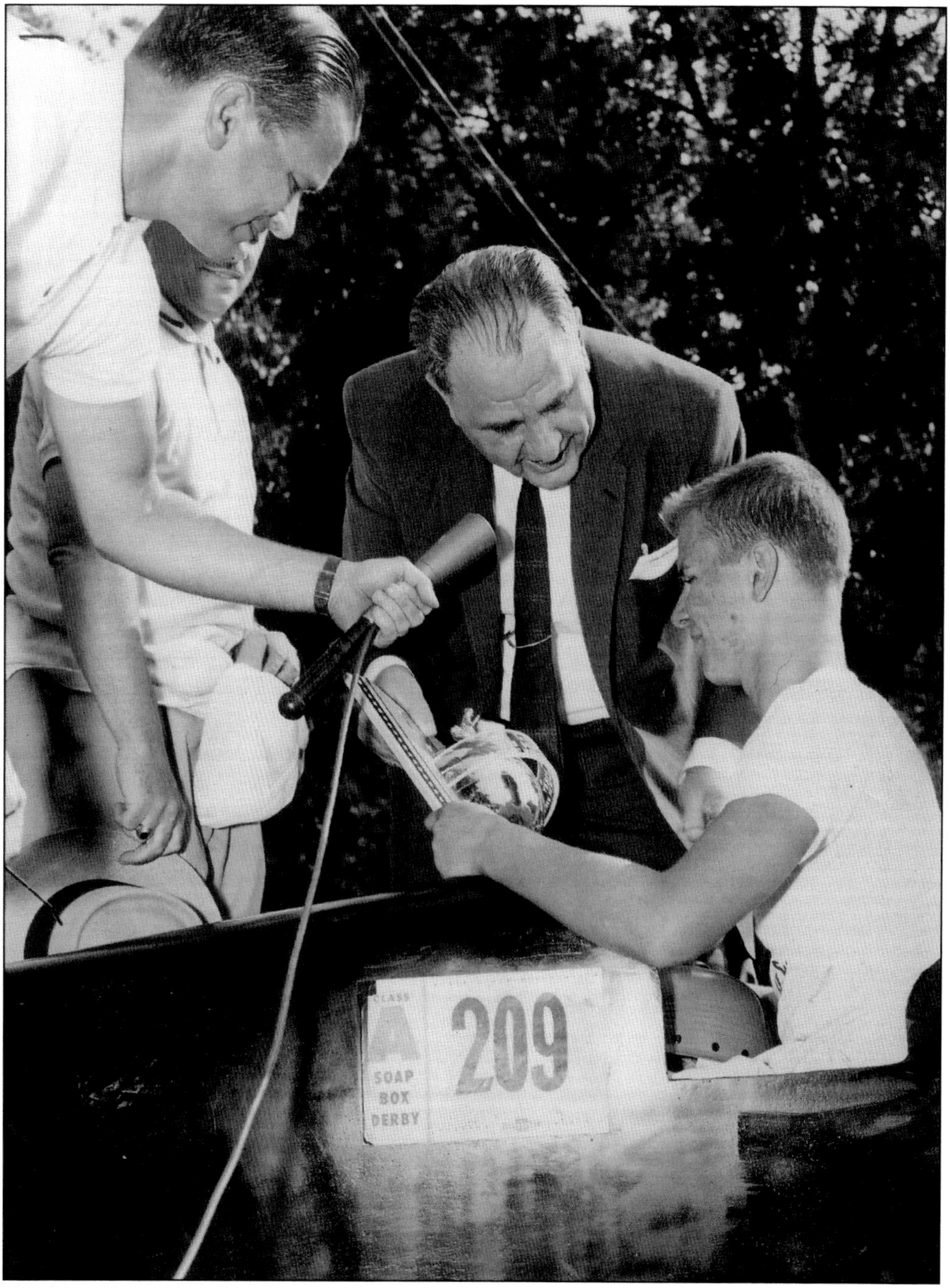

Floyd Metzler, Chevrolet Zone manager, presents the winning trophy in the 1963 Washington, D.C., soapbox derby contest to Mike Sales of Hyattsville. WRC-TV sports commentator Jim Simmons (left) and William Coyle, station sales manager, question Sales about his win. The derby was sponsored by the American Legion and Chevrolet. With his win, Sales was eligible to compete in the national championship. (PGCHS.)

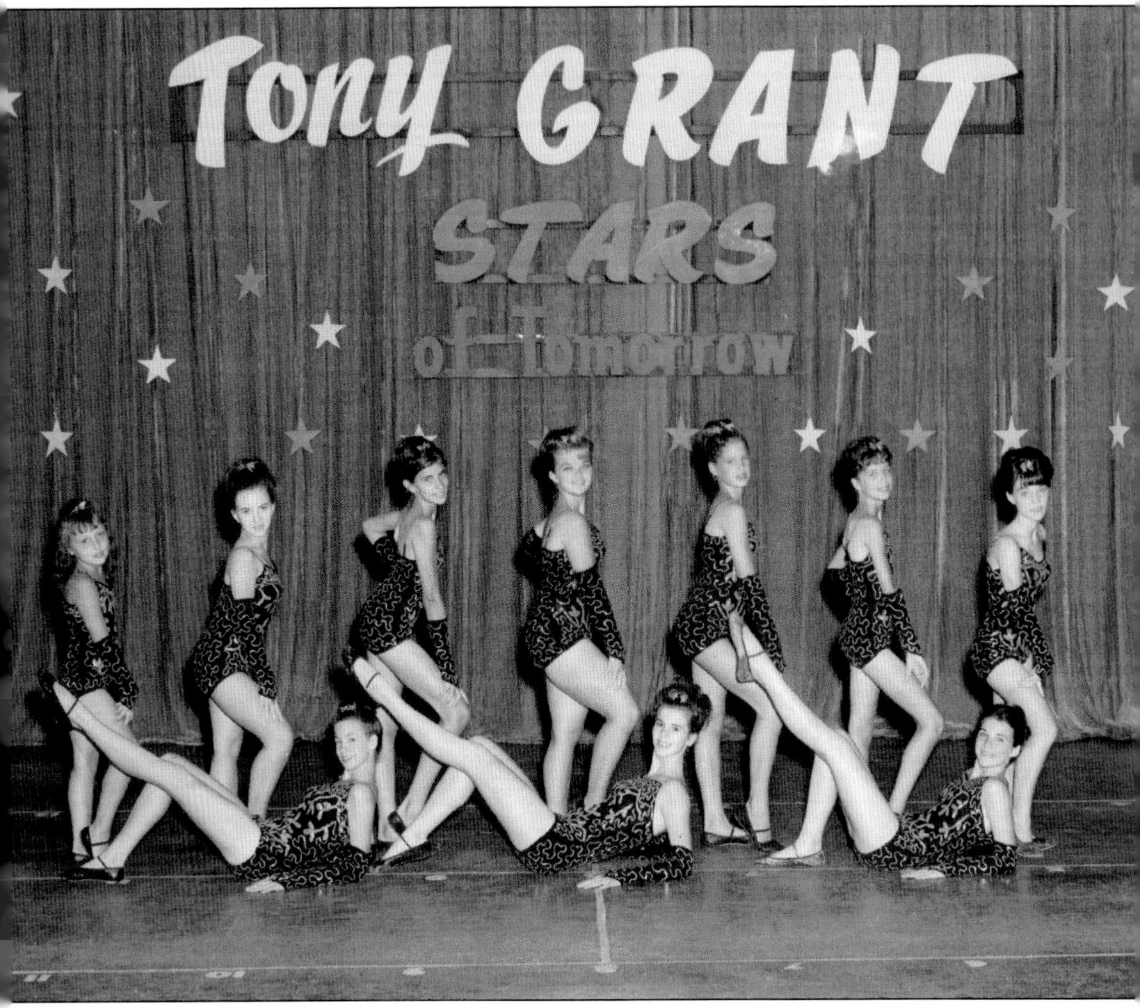

Atlantic City, New Jersey's Steel Pier stretched more than a half mile out over the ocean and was billed as "the showplace of the nation." One of its top draws was *Tony Grant's Stars of Tomorrow.* The program was a forerunner of television youth performance competition shows, featuring sensations like Frankie Avalon. Local performers the Bobbie Smith Dancers, of 3828 Hamilton Street, competed on the show. (PGCHS.)

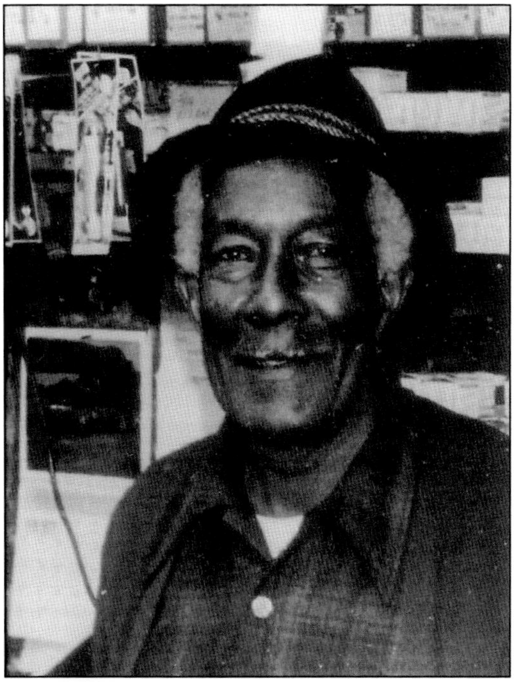

The success and longevity of Hyattsville Hardware can be attributed to its employees. Charles "Queenie" Queen (born 1911) was a well-known assistant to any shopper needing help. The store did not look much different than in its early days. A supply of just about everything was kept on hand. (Right, PGCHS; below, Historic American Building Survey.)

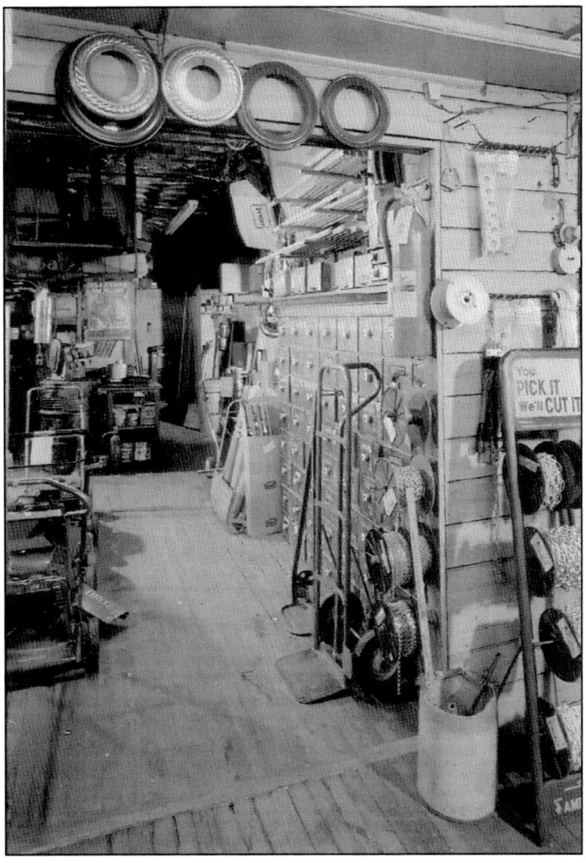

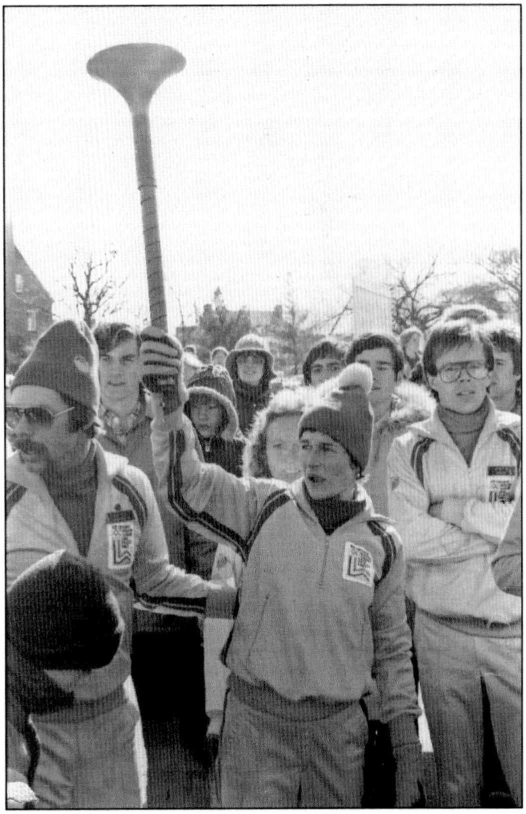

On February 1, 1980, the Olympic flame traveled north on Baltimore Avenue as part of its 1,000-mile overland journey from York, Virginia, to Lake Placid, New York, for the XIII Winter Olympic Games. Mayor Thomas Bass spoke briefly at the noon ceremony in front of the armory before speaker Morgan Wootten, DeMatha basketball coach, continued the city's theme of student athlete. (PGCHS.)

The National Guard deactivated the armory in July 1972. Washington, D.C., developer David Shikles, of David-James Builders, bought the property in 1982. Shikles proposed a 20,000-square-foot renovation with banquet hall, theater, restaurant, and retail. The project was viewed as the cornerstone of Hyattsville's Route 1 redevelopment plan. The armory was listed in the National Register of Historic Places in March 1980. "The Castle" grand opening was held April 20, 1985. (City of Hyattsville.)

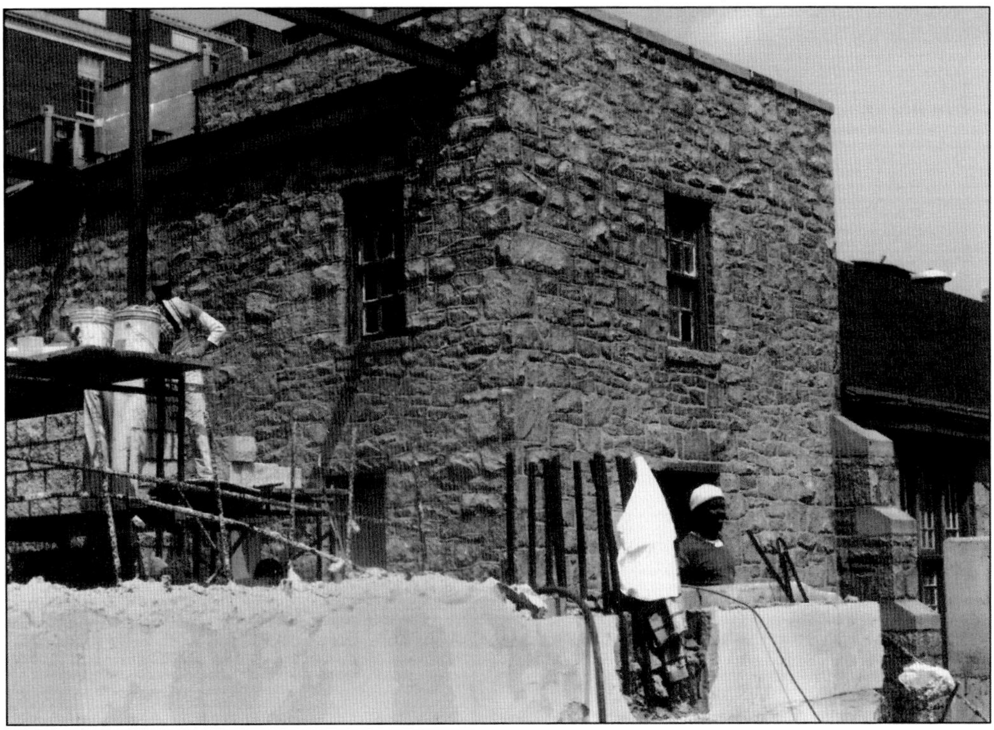

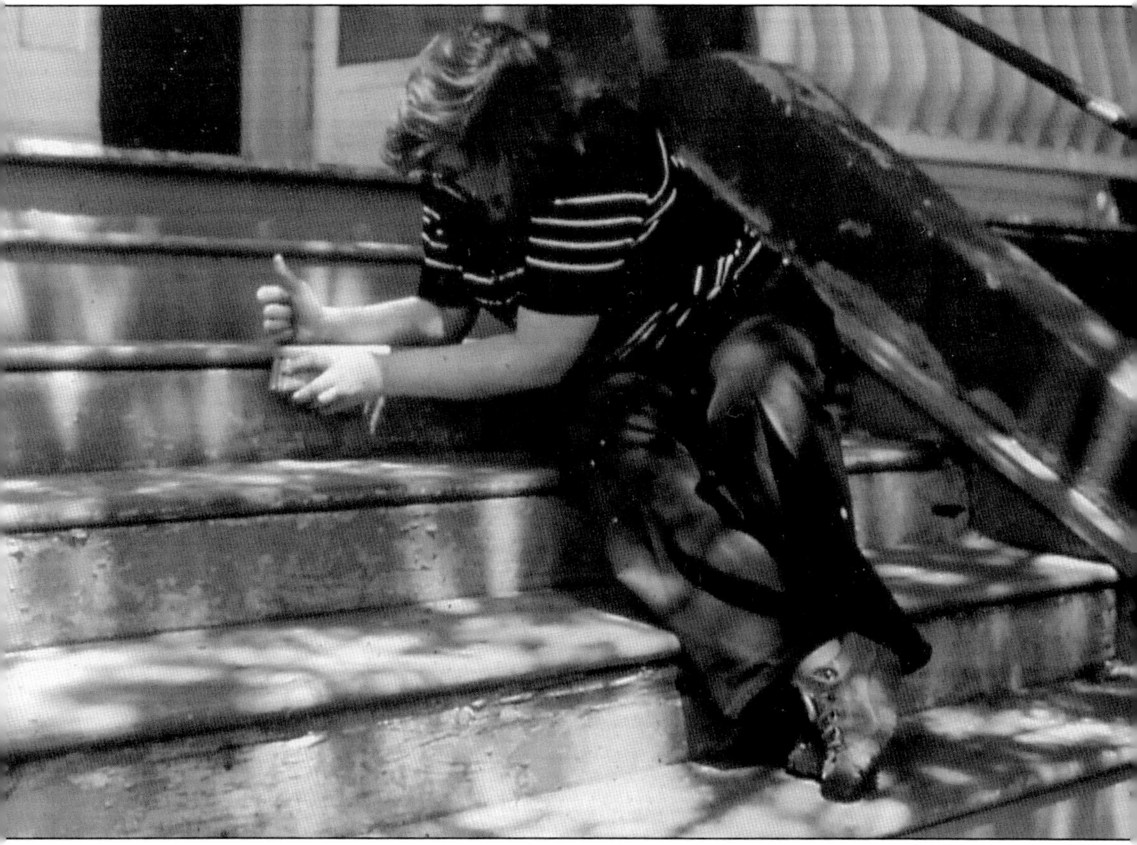

Sharon Sweeting scraped the stairs of 4112 Gallatin Street in preparation for painting. Sharon and her husband, Lester, purchased their home for its history. The 1897 Victorian pattern-book plan was built by local bookbinder Lewis Holden and his wife, Mary. With nearly a century of wear by their ownership, the home needed restoration. As original incorporators of the Hyattsville Preservation Association, the Sweetings valued the support offered its members during their endeavors. (HPA.)

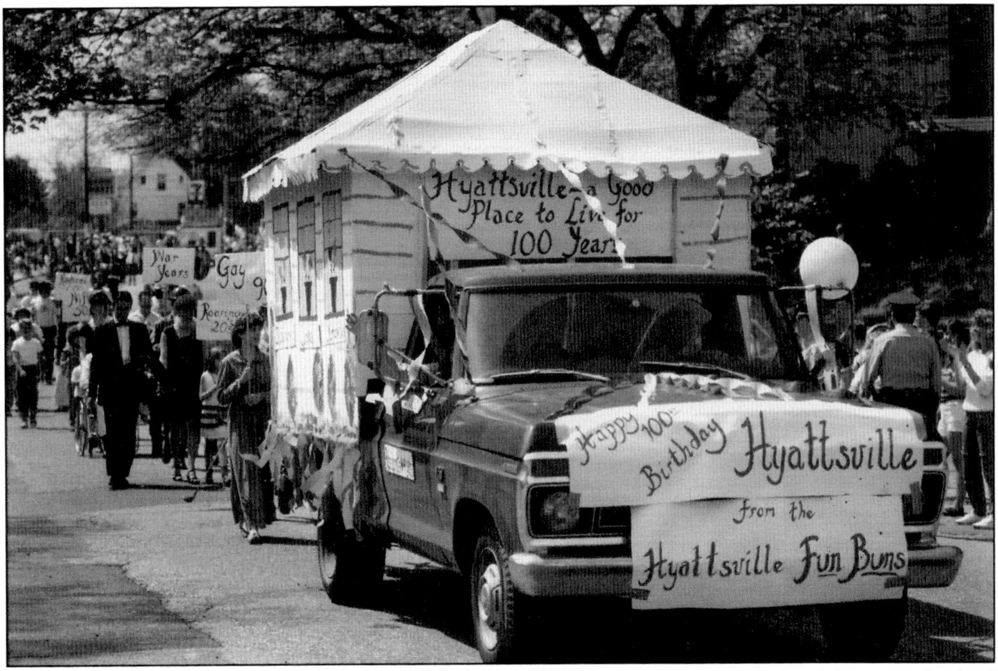

The year 1986 marked Hyattsville's 100th anniversary. Yearlong centennial celebrations kicked off with a January 18 ice-carving contest and ended December 22 with a "Light Up the Sky" holiday decoration contest. The April 26 annual parade held special significance as entrants, like the Fun Buns, saluted the city with birthday regards. (City of Hyattsville.)

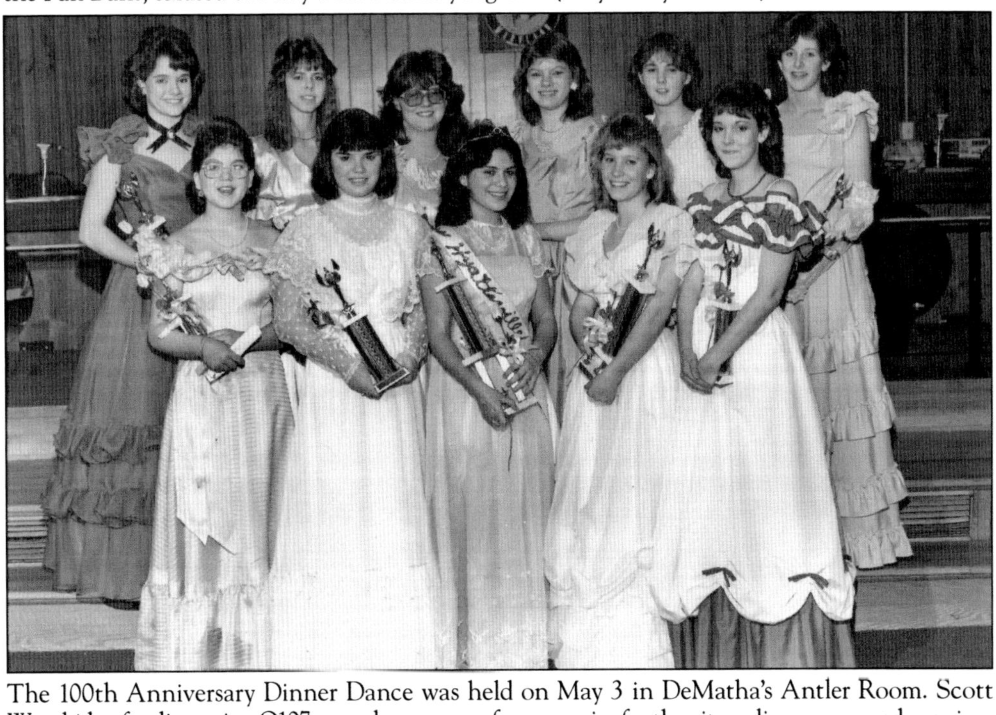

The 100th Anniversary Dinner Dance was held on May 3 in DeMatha's Antler Room. Scott Woodside of radio station Q107 served as master of ceremonies for the city police–sponsored evening. Miss Hyattsville Vicki Tripletti (center) and her court were honored. (City of Hyattsville.)

Hyattsville Preservation Association

HPA is a group of friends and homeowners preserving and promoting the excellence of American architecture and home living found in the city of Hyattsville. HPA members dedicate their personal resources and energies to the restoration of many of Hyattsville homes, commercial structures, and neighborhoods.

HPA held its inaugural meeting on February 14, 1980, in the city council chambers. The association was intended as a support group for homeowners attempting to restore and maintain some of Hyattsville's older homes.

Pairing with the city's Historic Preservation Task Force, HPA supported the designation of the Hyattsville National Register of Historic Places historic district in 1980. With a 2004 expansion, the district now includes 1,000 buildings. In addition, the city has three additional National Register listings and 14 Prince George's County Designated Sites.

HPA, Inc., is a nonprofit organization incorporated on April 15, 1982. The original incorporators were George Armstrong, Suzanne Cooper, John Lautz, Judith ("Amanda") Machen, Paul Schopf, Jane Seigler, Margaret Spurlin, Lester and Sharon Howe Sweeting, and Phil Winterfeldt.

HPA's programs are many and varied. HPA celebrates May as National Historic Preservation Month with the annual Hyattsville Historic House Tour—2009 marks its 30th anniversary. Meetings and seminars are conducted on community issues, oral histories, home design and repair, historic preservation, antique cars, and gardening. Members maintain a city garden plot in the 5100 block of Baltimore Avenue. Advocacy for preservation and responsible renovation are core principles of the organization. This book was born from HPA's digital and oral history preservation program. Hyattsville history is fast disappearing without a proactive policy.

For further information, write HPA, PO Box 375, Hyattsville, MD 20781, or visit preservehyattsville.org.

Discover Thousands of Local History Books Featuring Millions of Vintage Images

Arcadia Publishing, the leading local history publisher in the United States, is committed to making history accessible and meaningful through publishing books that celebrate and preserve the heritage of America's people and places.

Find more books like this at
www.arcadiapublishing.com

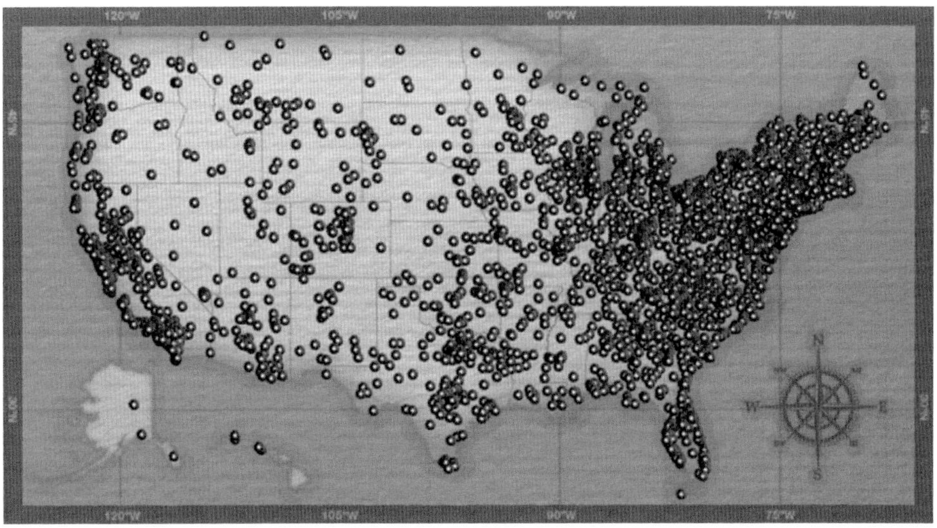

Search for your hometown history, your old stomping grounds, and even your favorite sports team.

Consistent with our mission to preserve history on a local level, this book was printed in South Carolina on American-made paper and manufactured entirely in the United States. Products carrying the accredited Forest Stewardship Council (FSC) label are printed on 100 percent FSC-certified paper.

MADE IN THE USA